THE CONSULTANT'S GUIDE TO GETTING BUSINESS ON THE INTERNET

THE CONSULTANT'S GUIDE TO GETTING BUSINESS ON THE INTERNET

HERMAN HOLTZ

JOHN WILEY & SONS, INC.
New York · Chichester · Weinheim · Brisbane · Singapore · Toronto

#37187376

11.17.98

This text is printed on acid-free paper.

Copyright © 1998 by Herman Holtz.
Published by John Wiley & Sons, Inc.

This publication is designed to provide accurate and authoritative
information in regard to the subject matter covered. It is sold with
the understanding that the publisher is not engaged in rendering legal,
accounting, or other professional services. If legal advice or other expert
assistance is required, the services of a competent professional person
should be sought.

Library of Congress Cataloging-in-Publication Data:
Holtz, Herman.
      The consultant's guide to getting business on the Internet / by
   Herman Holtz.
         p.   cm.
      Includes index.
      ISBN 0-471-14924-1 (pbk.: alk. paper)
         1. Internet marketing.   2. Marketing consultants.   3. Internet
   marketing—Computer network resources.   I. Title.
   HF5415.1265.H655   1998
   658.8'00285'4678—dc21   97-18068
                                                            CIP

Printed in the United States of America

10 9 8 7 6 5 4 3 2 1

If I had a genie with the power to bestow on me a magic wish, I would choose to name and thank here all the readers of my earlier books on consulting, with special notice to those who have been so thoughtful as to write and telephone with their comments and questions. I can think of no others to whom it would be more appropriate to dedicate this book, with the hope that it, too, will find favor with them.

CONTENTS

LIST OF EXHIBITS

THE CONSULTANT'S GUIDE TO GETTING BUSINESS ON THE INTERNET

CHAPTER 1

Consulting Is a Business

This book is not about the Internet per se. It is a book about marketing, marketing your services as an independent consultant. It is about marketing your services online, which means marketing via the Internet, for practical purposes, because the Internet dominates online activity today and has become almost synonymous with *online*. The orientation of the book is thus as a guide to using the Internet to find and win business.

Is marketing on the Internet different from marketing elsewhere, via other means and other media? Yes and no. The principles of marketing effectively do not change because you employ a new and different medium, such as the Internet, but the practices, the means by which you implement and apply those principles to use the medium well, do change. That is what this book is really about: how to implement the established marketing principles effectively in the online milieu that is the Internet. Of course, you must understand the medium to use it well, just as you must understand, in each case, the special characteristics, needs, and practices of marketing by mail, over the telephone, in print advertising, on radio and television, or by knocking on doors, literally or figuratively. (All direct marketing equates metaphorically to knocking on doors, of course, regardless of the medium.) In that connection, however, bear in mind that despite its spectacular and speedy growth, the media we know as the Internet and the Web (technically, they are separate systems) are still quite new and most uses are still tentative and experimental: We are still in an early stage of learning how to use these media most effectively.

We all launch our consulting practices with certain assumptions about marketing our services, which assumptions may or may not prove to be accurate and useful premises. When I started to offer my services as a proposal consultant, it was my premise that my best market would be the small electronics firms. That was undoubtedly because I was myself trained as an electronics engineer and had spent years working with small and large electronics firms engaged in research, research and development, and manufacturing, and in a variety of services related to those fields, including writing, lecturing, and training. I was thus more familiar with firms of this nature than with others. However, I further assumed that acquiring the major corporations as my clients would be a stretch beyond my modest reach as an independent consultant just spreading his wings, and so I thought it wise to focus on the smaller companies as my marketing targets, perhaps even as niche markets.

I soon enough found that I was wrong in more than one way. My most productive market targets proved to be firms in the business of contracting for the development of custom computer software systems and programs. I also soon learned that large corporations responded to my offers as well as small ones did. It was the benefits of what I could offer and my credentials as an expert capable of doing what I promised, not my size as a business organization, that attracted clients, I found.

One lesson to be learned here is to make your predictions and guesstimates, for you need premises on which to base your start. But understand that they are only estimates, at best, based more on bias and wishful thinking, probably, than on experience and knowledge of the hard facts. Therefore, be prepared always to find your premises in need of refinement or even grossly in error and in need of total reassessment. Thus, be ready always to adjust those estimates without hesitation to the reality of your experience, as you encounter that experience. Most important, learn how to compel yourself to be objective and ready to drop practices that do not work. That is especially important here because almost everything we do online at this time is experimental to at least some degree.

AN INTERNET OVERVIEW

It is the marketing potential of the Internet and how to exploit it most effectively that concern us here. For those objectives, we need no great depth of technical knowledge of the Internet. We need only functional knowledge of the Internet, those few basic functions that will enable us to use all the relevant online facilities. Therefore, I will provide here only the most limited discussions and explanations of the Internet technologies and offer only that which you need to understand so that you can navigate the Internet and use the online technology to win clients and contracts. That will include getting a good understanding of the communication facilities of the Internet, especially e-mail, and limited explanations of the many technologies underlying the system.

You will need, also, to understand or at least recognize the many acronyms and jargon of Internet technology, if only to understand what you read and avoid confusion. I will define and explain the most common terms, the ones that you will most certainly encounter, as we proceed. There is also a glossary for quick reference at the back of this book.

THE MAJOR ELEMENTS OF THE SYSTEM

Diverse as the Internet system is, for our purposes we need to be aware of and concerned with just three major functional elements of the system: They are e-mail, the Usenet, and the World Wide Web. But the Internet is far from a simple system. Within those three major elements are many activities, features, and subordinate functions, representing a great deal of knowledge to be mastered for effective use of the system.

E-MAIL AND E-MAIL ADDRESSES

E-mail is without question the most used capability of the Internet. When you gain access to the system, you will get an e-mail address and be able to reach everyone else in the world who has his or her own e-mail address and access to the Internet. Your own e-mail address and your link to your host or home system provide that linkage via the world's telephone circuits.

Your host is a domain and has a unique domain name. I subscribe to a service whose domain is paltech.com, and my e-mail address is thus holtz@paltech.com. I have a friend who subscribes to the clark.net service, so his e-mail address is [his name]@clark.net. Subscribers who connect through the America Online service are [name]@aol.com. CompuServe subscribers have e-mail addresses made up of their [CompuServe identification number]@compuserve.com, and they can use those addresses to communicate across the system. In most access systems, you are not required to use your personal name but may use any name or code you wish, and some subscribers prefer to be anonymous, so you find such addresses as sharpy@aol.com or 3xyz@zippy.edu.

The domain names are coded to reflect the nature of the holder. Here are six domain name suffixes you may encounter to designate the source of the Internet access:

arpa:	an ARPANET-Internet identifier
com:	a commercial company
edu:	an educational institution
gov:	a government agency or body
mil:	a military organization
net:	an access provider
org:	any other organization

These are what may now be regarded as the "traditional" domain suffixes. However, so rapidly and so extensively has the Internet grown that it has already become difficult to find enough given names or prefixes to the existing domain suffixes to satisfy the overwhelming demand for domain identities. A standards-setting committee for the Internet has therefore developed an additional set of seven domain suffixes for Internet domains. They are these:

firms:	businesses
store:	companies selling goods

4

info: organizations providing information services
web: organizations related to Web activities
arts: cultural and entertainment entities
rec: organizations relating to recreational activities
nom: individuals

Exhibit 1-1 illustrates e-mail via one of the several newsreader software systems. It reproduces a post I sent to a gentleman whom you will meet later in these pages. He was kind enough to furnish some material that will appear in this book, and it is with his permission that I use this and other material I gained from him.

The portions preceded with ">" are quotations from his post. His post ends with a three-line entry that is his *signature*. Everyone using e-mail may use such a signature, which you compose yourself. With most e-mail software, you can set it to add your signature automatically to each mes-

Exhibit 1-1
SAMPLE E-MAIL LETTER

```
Eudora - [Duncan Stickings, 06:48 AM 10/18/9, Re: WWW Page for Consultants]
 File  Edit  Mailbox  Message  Transfer  Special  Window  Help
 [Normal]    ЯH Signature    MIME                          Send
>
>I get about one lead a week now because of Big Dreams. Big Dreams is a
>newsletter I publish on personal development and small business topics.
>I am a training consultant, and I mainly offer courses locally in the
>Vancouver, BC area. I do offer several programs that can be remotely
>facilitated, and as I said I get about 1 inquiry/lead per week.
>
>Some of the things that make it work. I have my biography on line, plus
>I have been publishing for about one and a half years on the web now.
>People get to know about me before we interact and thus there is some
>rapport.
>
>If you like, you can check out my pages and/or chat with me privately.
>
>--
>Duncan Stickings <duncans@wimsey.com>      Tel: (604) 760-1631
>Alpine Training and Development            Fax: (604) 931-2135
>Big Dreams: http://www.wimsey.com/~duncans/BigDreams
>
>       Thanks for the account. It is just the kind of thing I am looking
for. May I use your name in reporting it in my book? (I do not quote or make
attribution without permission.) I will have a look at your web page, in the
meanwhile, and follow up if I have questions.
```

sage you send out, so you may use your signature in any way you please, including to deliver an advertising message. Mr. Stickings uses his signature to refer you to his Web address, where you may read his newsletter, *Big Dreams.*

THE USENET

One major area of the Internet is composed of a huge assortment of discussion groups, many thousands of them, covering what seems to be every conceivable subject, serious and frivolous. The network of computer users constituting this collection of discussion groups is referred to as the *Usenet,* a contraction of *User's Network;* the discussion groups are, collectively, *newsgroups,* although they are, in turn, subdivided into two types, moderated and unmoderated. The latter are entirely open and anyone may post a message there. The moderated groups are controlled, managed by someone who reads the messages from respondents and decides what will and will not be posted. Some of these are, indeed, devoted to presenting news, but most are on specialized subjects, some frivolous, some serious, of interest to subscribers.

I subscribe to misc.business.consulting and other newsgroups that I log on to occasionally, but these assortments of groups change continually: New groups start (sometimes inspired by a dramatic news event or to constitute a fan club of some entertainment or sports figure, such as alt.fan.elvis-presley) and existing groups drop out. I check on new groups periodically to find any that may be useful for me.

Exhibit 1-2 illustrates some of my current choices. There were only 24 messages in this group, alt.business.seminars, at the moment of this screen capture, of which I have been reading message number 4. But the traffic varies enormously, and this group may have five times that number of messages tomorrow. In fact, I have seen many groups with hundreds of messages posted. One recently listed over 2,000 messages.

I encountered a post from Wayne Lundberg on the misc.business.consulting newsgroup recently that summed up almost perfectly the central idea I had in mind in conceiving this book originally.

Lundberg is a manufacturing engineer who got into big company consulting because, he says, ". . . of my experience in change, starting it,

Exhibit 1-2
A FEW USENET GROUPS

```
┌─────────────────────────────────────────────────────────────────────┐
│ ▤             Trumpet News Reader - [News]                    ▨ ▨ │
│ ▤  File  Edit  Special  Group  Article  View  Window  Help        ▤ │
│ Seasoned Senior Exec. for Rent, by GeneStluka, 6 Oct 1995 17:37:47 -0400 │ 4 of 24 │
├─────────────────────────────────────────────────────────────────────┤
│ alt.building.jobs                    alt.journalism.moderated         │
│ alt.business                         bit.listserv.techwr-l            │
│ alt.business.home.pc                 biz.comp.services                │
│ alt.business.misc                    biz.general                      │
│ alt.business.seminars                biz.marketplace.discussion        │
│ alt.journalism.freelance             biz.marketplace.non-computer      │
├─────────────────────────────────────────────────────────────────────┤
│ Hugh Bryan              ===>>> Free Lucrative Home Based Business <<<=== │
│ us000056@interramp.com  <<<<CHECK THIS OUT>>>>                         │
│ Chris Boyd              FREE sign up - The Best Opportunity in the U.S. │
│ ►GeneStluka             Seasoned Senior Exec. for Rent                 │
│ Wally Glenn             Re: ──────>Fast Cash In A Flash<──────         │
│ make money              try me its easy$$$$$                           │
│ **PAGERS**@dial156.concom.com Dallas to New York in 30 seconds        │
│ Bernardo Brummer        Re: WANTED: Evaluators for a High Tech Turnkey Busin │
│ thbn@empnet.com         Ground Floor Opportunity in Australia          │
│ amsl@wl.net             SuccessSaver                                   │
│ Marilyn J Carter        MLM Seminar – Eugene, Oregon USA              │
├─────────────────────────────────────────────────────────────────────┤
│  │  <<  │   >>   │ View/list │ Format │ Skip all │ Post │ Follow │    │
│  │ Reply │ Archive │ Extract  │                                       │
└─────────────────────────────────────────────────────────────────────┘
```

driving it, conquering it, fighting resistance to it, etc. I'm now trying to teach/lead the sixth largest company in all of Mexico into learning how to compete against Wal-Mart, Carrefourt, and other invaders due to NAFTA." Here is part of the message he posted as part of a discussion thread on that newsgroup:

> Lester—The advice from Nick, Ray, Robert, and John in response to your request for assistance is beautiful. Here is a perfect example of the value of this new medium. People helping people—networking—and, I believe, the secret of marketing, especially in the international area which you purport to be a part of.
>
> Most of my work is in Mexico and you simply don't get in the front door without having somebody first telling your prospect about you in one form or other. As more and more net surfers from around the world get involved you will have more and more opportunities to GIVE advice over the net

leaving your PS with what you do. Get them to open the doors for you in their countries.

Usenet groups are divided into *hierarchies,* mainstream and alternative. Mainstream newsgroups are international, although not necessarily available at every access site, while alternative newsgroups tend to be local. Newsgroups have multipart names that help identify what they are about, as the few examples given previously illustrate. There is one true news hierarchy, Clarinet, and newsgroups in that hierarchy have names beginning with "clari," as in the following examples:

    clari.biz.economy.world
    clari.biz.market.report
    clari.canada.politics

It's easy enough to divine the purpose of each of these newsgroups. The newsgroups with titles beginning with "comp" are devoted to computer subjects, such as

    comp.binaries.mac
    comp.editors
    comp.graphics.research

Some newsgroup names can become rather lengthy, although they are usually descriptive of their area of interest:

    alt.rock-n-roll.metal.progressive
    rec.arts.comics.marketplace
    soc.religion.christian.bible-study

WORLD WIDE WEB

While e-mail is undoubtedly the most widely used function of the Internet, probably the greatest amount of interest and press coverage is given to the World Wide Web, referred to universally as "the Web." The Web lives up to the Internet image of huge numbers and worldwide reach. A recent report by one of the major search services puts the number of Web pages at more than 24 million. That is the area that has all those complex-looking addresses that you see increasingly being advertised in print and on TV, such as http://www.win.tue.nl/scarlatti. That particular address is the URL—Uniform Resource Locator—of the Web site of Domenico Scarlatti, advertised in the 1995 edition of the *Internet Yellow Pages,* an Osborne/McGraw-Hill publication. There, you can be tutored in some of Domenico Scarlatti's harpsichord exercises, which is a typical promotional device: The site is Domenico Scarlatti's *home page,* as such presentations are called.

Whereas Usenet newsgroups and e-mail exchanges are strictly text presentations, Web sites and home pages offer graphics—drawings and photographs—in full color. Presenters on the Web can and do also present graphics in motion and sound, and even in interactive presentations. In the latter, you, as a user, are invited to enter your name and address, ask for additional information, or make comments. Some sites invite visitors to register their names in a logbook and even to respond to questionnaires that will result in their being listed in an online directory of sorts. One large bookseller maintaining a busy site, for example, uses a program to "interview" authors and publishes the results in a directory that any visitor can call up and read. That capability for interviewing visitors can be used as a great asset to develop leads for follow-up. In fact, inasmuch as the basic idea of the Web is to present hypertext presentations (presentations that offer the user many choices to which he or she may link), Web pages are inherently interactive. Visitors do need suitable browser software, such as Netscape or Microsoft Explorer, to take full advantage of these special interactive facilities and features. In fact, as the Internet and Web develop further technologically, they offer ever more sophisticated presentations, which require later, more advanced versions of the popular browsers to take full advantage of their newer features.

Exhibit 1-3 is a black-and-white representation of the first screen of a home page of a government agency, the Small Business Administration. On screen, it appears in color, of course. This page is followed by additional pages with many links that may be invoked to branch to other presentations. Invoking the Financing Your Business link brings up a list of government programs to help small businesses gain financing. But a number of other links are provided, in addition to those visible in the figure.

Exhibit 1-3

A HOME PAGE ON THE WEB

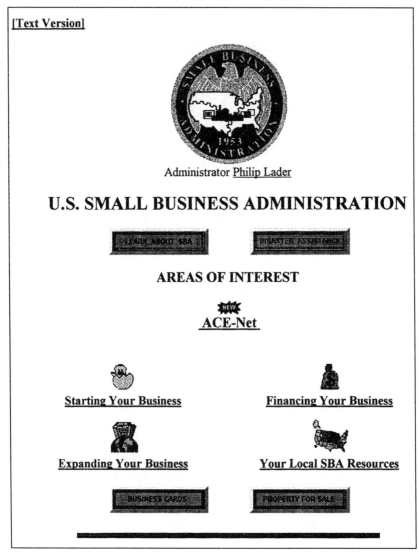

[Text Version]

Administrator Philip Lader

U.S. SMALL BUSINESS ADMINISTRATION

LEARN ABOUT SBA   DISASTER ASSISTANCE

AREAS OF INTEREST

NEW
ACE-Net

Starting Your Business   Financing Your Business

Expanding Your Business   Your Local SBA Resources

BUSINESS CARDS   PROPERTY FOR SALE

MARKETING PROTOCOL ON THE INTERNET

It is variously reported that up to 30 to 35 million people use and contribute to the Internet. But interest in access to the Internet is growing so rapidly that all estimates are almost immediately dated. The concept that 30 to 35 million users all over the world are logging on and, presumably, surfing the Internet every day is impressive, even awe-inspiring. It is not surprising, then, that many businesspeople regard the Internet as an advertising and marketing bonanza, a low-cost way to reach and sell to millions of prospects. The mouths of myriad marketers were soon watering with anticipation of turning the Internet to their use as a marketing windfall. Alas! It soon proved to be not quite the manna from heaven it had at first appeared to be, for more than one reason that we shall be discussing.

The newsgroups of the Usenet came to attention early, even before most of us were familiar with the Web. The Web required relatively sophisticated knowledge and software—browsers required to navigate the Web effectively were still relatively crude at that early time, and the newsgroups were much easier to gain access to and navigate. So it is not exactly surprising that the newsgroups were the obvious first targets for advertising, and soon such headlines as these began to appear in many of the newsgroups:

FREE INFORMATION ON MONEY-MAKING PLAN
A FOOLPROOF NEW WAY TO MAKE MONEY ONLINE
NO INVESTMENT NEEDED; MAKE $80,000/YEAR
NEW NETWORK MARKETING PLAN
GET IN ON GROUND FLOOR
COMPUTERS FOR SALE, BOTTOM PRICES
MAKE A FORTUNE IN YOUR SPARE TIME

Initially, this usage of the newsgroups met a great deal of opposition. Even if the headlines and offers flooding the newsgroups were not of this snake oil variety, they would have been offensive to most newsgroup subscribers, most of whom regarded the Internet as a place where there ought to be no commercialism at all. However, with thousands of newsgroups and the complete ease and low cost of sending out the message to them, it was and is quite easy to automate the propagation of such messages. Thus, many advertisers who either did not know or did not care that they would meet with intense opposition and reprisals soon swamped the Usenet system, making many of the newsgroups little more than billboards pasted over with myriad commercial notices, most of them of the same get-rich-quick variety. Discussion-group members were alarmed, and they reacted promptly. Volunteers took it on themselves to police their groups and lead the reprisals against transgressors. Placing a commercial notice indiscriminately in a great many newsgroups has come to be known as *spamming,* that term inspired by a TV show in which there was a restaurant that specialized in serving Spam in myriad recipes. Most groups now have a FAQ, a list of frequently asked questions and answers, including the group's own protocol. Offenders are usually referred to the group's FAQ or even sent a copy, as a first reproof, with more aggressive measures to follow if the offender persists, as some do.

A state of equilibrium followed, with some newsgroups succumbing to the wave of commercial use. There are, consequently, a great many newsgroups on the Usenet that are devoted to business, where you may post advertisements without reprisal, if the notices are relevant to the general usage of the group, because there is nothing posted in these groups that is not a commercial notice: Advertising notices are their sole content. Here are a few current such groups:

    alt.business.consulting
    alt.business.misc
    misc.forsale
    misc.forsale.computers
    misc.forsale.computers.discussion
    misc.forsale.computers.mac
    misc.forsale.computers.pc-specific.audio

Some of these are general, while others are specialized. Posting irrelevant advertising in a specialized group—for example, offering computer software in a newsgroup devoted to buying and selling antiques—will often get you a disapproving reaction, too, even though the group accepts commercial notices. Offering a service or a line of new products to a group dedicated to selling used items—a typical "for sale" group—is likely to earn rebuke, for example.

Marketing by E-mail

Many people today attempt to turn e-mail into a mail-order medium, using e-mail in the same manner that direct-mail and mail-order marketers use surface mail to send out large quantities of so-called junk mail. I have been subjected to some of this junk e-mail, and I found it somewhat offensive, whereas I am not offended or disturbed by thick envelopes of printed advertising matter arriving in my mailbox, perhaps because I usually recognize printed advertising literature for what it is before I open the envelope and so can dispose of it immediately if I choose to. But a lengthy e-mail message is not always easily recognizable as advertising. Marketers who use e-mail in this way generally understand that they are vulnerable to reprisals if respondents are sufficiently annoyed, so they usually try to soften the impact by tactful and discreet apologies for their intrusions and by offering a means for recipients to have their names and addresses removed from the mailing list or promising that they will not be solicited again unless they request more information.

There are other more subtle and more sophisticated ways in which e-mail can be used effectively and without reprisal for marketing, especially for such professionals as independent consultants. E-mail can be used in electronic versions of older methods of online marketing, such as online newsletters and mailing lists, to which recipients subscribe voluntarily. Announcements of such newsletters and mailing lists are usually made via newsgroups, home pages on the Web, and e-mail campaigns, describing the items and inviting all to subscribe. Many online newsletter publishers, however, simply send unsolicited copies announcing the award of a free subscription and including directions for unsubscribing.

Newslettering Online. There are many online newsletters in existence already, and the number is growing steadily. Some are for-profit ventures, with subscriptions available at a price. But there are also many free newsletters, usually circulated by e-mail and published as marketing promotions. The cost of distribution is quite small, and it is easy to send copies out as e-mail letters by automatic means that will be discussed later.

Exhibit 1-4, is a black-and-white reproduction of the front page of Duncan Stickings's newsletter, *Big Dreams,* which is presented on his home page at http://www.wimsey.com/~duncans/BigDreams. This is, of course, a Web URL, which takes you to his Web site, where you will be introduced to Stickings and what he does, as well as to his newsletter. Stickings distributes this newsletter electronically without charge as his own marketing promotion, and he reports that he finds this newsletter an effective lead generator. Here are his own words on the subject, explaining how his promotion works and why it does so:

> I get about one lead a week now because of Big Dreams. Big Dreams is a newsletter I publish on personal development and small business topics. I am a training consultant, and I mainly offer courses locally in the Vancouver, BC area. I do offer several programs that can be remotely facilitated, and as I said I get about 1 inquiry/lead per week. Some of the things that make it work. I have my biography on line, plus I have been publishing for about one and a half years on the Web now. People get to know about me before we interact and thus there is some rapport.

Mailing Lists.　Mailing lists are something of a compromise between newsletters and newsgroups, with elements of both: They use multiple e-mail addresses as the means for meeting and conducting group discussions. The discussions are compilations of e-mail from members of the list. One subscriber raises a provocative question or makes a pungent observation, and many others then respond with accounts of their own experiences or thoughts on the subject.

There are many such mailing lists to which you may subscribe. One well-attended one that I sponsor myself is for freelance writers, and subscribers to the list check in from all over the world with their remarks. The discussions are helpful, and they sometimes generate market opportunities directly. A post that appeared only this morning invites anyone who is interested to offer his or her own candidacy to write any of a series of booklets one subscriber describes and invites participants to write.

It is much simpler to participate in a mailing list than in a newsgroup because there is less to learn about the mechanics of use. E-mail is the

Exhibit 1-4
A SUCCESSFUL ONLINE NEWSLETTER

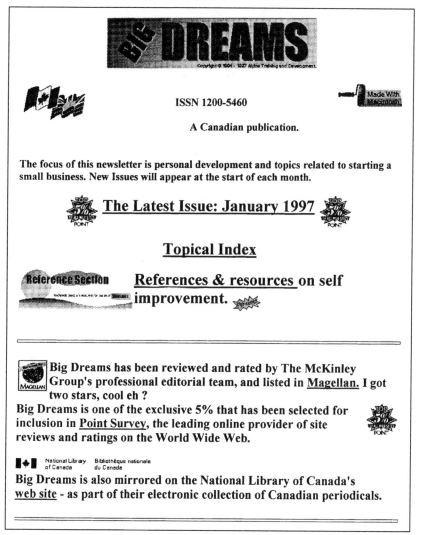

ISSN 1200-5460

A Canadian publication.

The focus of this newsletter is personal development and topics related to starting a small business. New Issues will appear at the start of each month.

The Latest Issue: January 1997

Topical Index

References & resources on self improvement.

Big Dreams has been reviewed and rated by The McKinley Group's professional editorial team, and listed in Magellan. I got two stars, cool eh ?

Big Dreams is one of the exclusive 5% that has been selected for inclusion in Point Survey, the leading online provider of site reviews and ratings on the World Wide Web.

National Library   Bibliothèque nationale
of Canada   du Canada

Big Dreams is also mirrored on the National Library of Canada's web site - as part of their electronic collection of Canadian periodicals.

simplest element of the Internet to learn, while newsgroups can be more difficult to navigate, depending on the Usenet software you use. But even the simplest newsgroup program is somewhat complex to use, compared with most e-mail software.

MARKETING ON THE WEB

Many Web pages are modeled on and made to resemble billboards, catalogs, sales letters, newsletters, demonstrations, shopping malls, and sundry other kinds of traditional marketing media and devices. Moreover, many of these presentations are used in multistep marketing—lead-generation programs—and often in conjunction with the other elements of the Internet, usually by referring the reader to a Usenet group, advertising a free newsletter, or inviting the reader to send for more information via e-mail. Many pages also have response devices, such as forms for comments, registration, and other feedback to be sent to the advertiser by e-mail directly from the Web site. The advertiser may then follow up the lead by e-mail or other means. This is the most appropriate strategy for marketing consulting services, since marketing professional services is rarely a one-call proposition, but generally requires at least two steps: developing sales leads and following up the leads to close them. In practice, while this represents two phases of marketing activity, it may require multiple follow-ups and presentations to develop the lead into a signed contract.

The influence of conventional print media is clearly apparent in most Web designs: Many Web sites are somewhat similar to a direct-mail package, with the online equivalent of a sales letter, a brochure, and a response device, the latter usually in e-mail form. Many of the presentations made on Web sites are analogous to the presentations offered in traditional magazines, with color illustrations, interesting articles, response devices, and various offers from many advertisers. Common to these and other Web site designs are the hypertext links to other sites. These links are de rigueur in Web design, as both attractions and quid pro quo exchanges with other Web sites, where all benefit from referrals to each others' sites, although some Web site owners charge fees for listing others' Web site addresses. (Another way to publicize your Web site and attract visitors is to list it with the many research facilities with Web sites; another is, of course, personally posting as many notices of your existing site as you can manage.)

Marketing on the Internet is not as simple nor as promising as many think, and certainly not as simple or surefire as many entrepreneurs who sell marketing services promise their prospects. It is, for so many, the rainbow with the promised pot of gold at the end that seems to be impossible to reach. Far too many users approach marketing on the Internet and the Web from the perspective of traditional marketing, trying to force-fit that established pattern into the Internet online milieu. That is an effort that produces mixed results, with the greatest gains made by those who sell advertising space and services to those who are so hopeful of great and immediate gains from offering their wares and services in this new medium, even before they know how to gain full access to the Internet. For those who need it, here is a primer on gaining access to the Internet.

GETTING ON THE INTERNET

To gain access to the Internet, you need an Internet account of your own or access via someone else's account. Many users gain access to the net via an employer, a college, a BBS (electronic bulletin board system), a freenet, or some other organization. In most cases, that furnishes only limited access, offering text (no graphics) and e-mail only—often e-mail only, which appears to be enough, for many.

It is possible, as a step up from this kind of access, to get a *shell account* from an Internet Service Provider. This provides a closer approach to full access, including access to newsgroups and other text-only facilities and functions. It makes use of the service provider's software and is an option generally used by those whose computers are not capable of supporting full access to the Internet and Web systems.

To get full access to the Internet and World Wide Web, you must get a full-service account with an Internet Service Provider. This is a source having direct access to the Internet, connected by high-speed lines and serving as separate and independent Internet sites. Connection via such an access provider gives you virtual direct access to the Internet. However, you must also have a computer that is adequate to the job, as well as the proper appurtenances or ancillary computer devices, as follows.

SYSTEM NEEDS

- **Operating system.** You will need Windows 3.1 or later—Windows 95 is in widespread use as the latest Windows software—or an equivalent system, such as IBM's OS2 system, to use and enjoy all aspects and elements of the system fully, especially the graphics.
- **Modem.** Anything slower than 9600 baud will be impracticably slow for the purpose. A modem with 14,400 baud is the norm today, but there is a rapid trend now to 28,800-baud modems, becoming more and more common, and with even faster ones, notably 36,600-baud modems, beginning to appear.
- **System memory.** 8MB RAM will serve for most purposes, although it is not much better than marginal for full use today, so more—16MB or more—is better. Anything less will handicap your usage.
- **Storage.** You need as large a fixed disk as you can afford, several hundred megabytes, at least. Disks rated in gigabytes (a gigabyte is 1,000MB) are commonly included in the computers being offered by retailers today.

System overall. Preferably, you should have a 486/66 or later model (one of the Pentiums, if you use a pc, or the equivalent if you use a Mac). The computer technology has advanced so rapidly that even the 486/66 system is almost an antique. The 66MHz system is now the low end of the pc computer configuration, for all practical purposes, as 100- to 200MHz systems are becoming more and more commonplace.

INTERNET SOFTWARE

Of course, you need proper software programs to use the various Internet functions and capabilities. Following are a few of the popular software programs found in widespread use with the Internet. Note that there are several *browsers,* and for some of the names there are several models. Each has a somewhat different function or set of functions and so is specialized in one way or another. Probably none is ideal for all purposes, although Netscape currently appears to be the most versatile and most popular—certifiably the most widely sold—with Microsoft's Explorer gaining ground steadily in competition with Netscape.

Eudora is the most popular and most widely used e-mail software, almost a de facto standard for e-mail, although you can use Netscape or Explorer for e-mail, and there are free e-mail systems too.

Eudora
    e-mail software
Trumpet Winsock
    provides TCP/IP capability
Winsock FTP
    file transfer utility
Mosaic World
    Web browser
Internet Explorer
    Web browser
Netscape
    Web browser
Cello
    Web browser
Winsock Gopher
    Web browser used to get files to be downloaded
Trumpet Newsreader
    one of the popular communications programs for navigating the Usenet

These and many other programs are available online, many in freeware or shareware versions. In many cases, the shareware or freeware version is a kind of bare-bones model, and the publisher offers you a more sophisticated model of the program at a reasonable price, as in the case of Eudora, for example. Usually, your access provider will make copies of some of them available to you, with recommendations for their use. (Of course, you are free to use programs of your own choosing, and new ones are appearing continually.) There are also a number of programs, such as Internet in a Box, available as complete packages of all the software you will need for full Internet access. As we proceed, you will see examples of typical screen presentations made by these programs, although they will be black-and-white versions, instead of the brilliant colors they exhibit on the screen. But let's go now to an important idea, one that is central to this book: the art of networking, one of the most important arts a consultant can master in marketing and building a prosperous practice. Networking is widely acknowledged as a most useful, perhaps necessary, approach for marketing professional services such as consulting. This is a reference to networking in the marketing sense—inspiring and promoting word-of-mouth advertising and sales leads resulting from referrals and recommendations, as the most productive and most widely used marketing method for professionals.

CHAPTER 2

Networking in the Electronic Age

Businesspeople have long belonged to associations of various kinds where they can network effectively, even if that is not their primary reason for joining the association. They belong to Rotary and Lions clubs, to the Masons, to the International Order of Odd Fellows, to local business owners' clubs, to professional societies, and to craft and trade associations of many kinds. Some of these groups organize "mixers"—social affairs and other gatherings for the express purpose of getting acquainted with each other for business reasons; others have regular meetings that are inherently mixers, although not officially recognized as such. (In fact, it is supposed to be an article of faith in some of the most prominent fraternal organizations that one does not join the organization for marketing or other business purposes, but only with loftier motivations, and so one practices such activities as indirectly and inconspicuously as possible, if at all!)

Tom Zoss was one independent consultant I encountered via a newsgroup on the Internet who had a tale to tell me about his own activities relevant to that idea: Tom early recognized the need to market his consulting services aggressively, if he was to achieve success in consulting. He is, in his own words, "an attorney and corporate marketer who became a full-time consultant in 1983, offering strategic and marketing planning to a range of customers small and large." (His firm is Zoss Communications, Inc., in South Bend, Indiana.) He said to me (via e-mail), "I realized that mass mailings didn't establish any personal 'touch' that could lead to an intimate personal relationship, a real necessity to beginning the kind of consulting work I do. In fact, most of my new business seemed to come from a referral from another advisor (accountant, lawyer, salesman, consultant)."

This is true for many, if not most consultants. The kinds of service the typical consultant provides and the working relationship between the consultant and the client are such that the typical client is reluctant to entrust his or her business to a total stranger without some special reason to have confidence in the consultant. Confidence of that nature does not result from advertising hyperbole. It results from personal recommendations and other factors—for example, a long-term awareness and favorable impression of the consultant's existence—that persuade the client to perceive and accept the consultant as an able and dependable professional. Networking is traditionally one of the most reliable and successful ways of gaining that perception and acceptance.

Zoss recognized all of this, and he took appropriate action. He did two things about it, "one old-fashioned, one newfangled," as he describes it. "The old-fashioned one was to join one of the few remaining area breakfast roundtables. This was a great networking tool, special kind of mixer, and helpful to get these key influencers in the community to learn what I do and how I help people." Zoss therefore turned also to one modern-day version of such groups: the electronic bulletin board. He created a computer bulletin board of his own for consultants, entrepreneurs, salespeople, and others and he called it the Networking BBS (Bulletin Board System).

Subscription to the Networking BBS was free. It offered a place and means for visitors to gather without leaving their desks. It had lots of files and bulletins available for callers, and the files included about 4,000 shareware programs that could be downloaded, many of them business-related and helpful in running a business. (*Shareware* is computer software that may be downloaded—copied from—a BBS or other online source, such as many locations on the Internet, free of charge and used on a trial basis. Use is on the honor system, with the user asked to pay if he or she continues to use the software.) The only cost to Zoss's BBS was for a special service that he provided for those who needed it: He offered access to Internet e-mail at a small charge. He even had a special service for people who want e-mail but don't have a computer!

At this writing, after operating the Networking BBS for more than a year, Zoss reports some changes. First, the BBS was a success in his eyes: "One referral a year more than paid for the BBS overhead (about $1,000 per year in phone line, software, and hardware). I received several referrals the first year, including three that turned into billings. (My average new-client invoice is in the $3,000 to $5,000 range.)"

But the world is changing, and Zoss has changed with it. "More and more of my clients and referral friends were getting involved with the Internet, so I had to consider getting my material available on the World Wide Web. Fewer people were calling the BBS because they had other ways of receiving e-mail and information via the Internet. The trains were not stopping at my station!

"The BBS idea is a good one and I'm sure it will work for many, but I decided there was no reason to operate my own BBS when the Internet was accessible, so I closed the BBS and moved my informational files to a Web site. The shareware I was using to attract callers is available on the Internet so I no longer needed that, and I changed my outlook to one of providing outbound information."

Creating his own BBS was a shrewd move for Tom Zoss, and today, anyone can do it and even connect a BBS to one of the many BBS networks and/or the Internet. However, although you may arrange to make your bulletin board part of a larger communications system, the BBS is essentially a local system, attracting people who are, for the most part, within the same telephone dialing area. Not surprisingly, it is also a time-consuming activity and not without some expense, although Zoss has managed to contain his BBS expenses. (In the next chapter, we'll have a brief look at Tom Zoss's Web site and hear what he has to say about his Internet experience.)

A BBS OF YOUR OWN

In the earliest days of the personal computer, almost all electronic bulletin boards were in private homes, most run as something of a hobby. Even later, as businesses, government agencies, and other organizations began to establish systems of their own, a great many, perhaps even the majority, of BBSs were in their sysop's (system operator's) homes. The nature of the BBS is such that it does not require elaborate equipment, at least not for a basic system. Almost any desktop computer can be used as a BBS, given a modem, telephone connection, and suitable software.

Your BBS can therefore be a quite simple system: You do not need to rival CompuServe or even some more modest BBS to accomplish the basic objective of having your own system for attracting prospects and developing sales leads. Setting up a small-scale BBS of your own for marketing purposes is relatively simple, with a great deal of software—BBS programs that are complete BBS packages—readily available. A simple search of one of the major Internet search services produced list after list of BBS programs of many sizes and complexities. Many were basic BBS systems, while many other listings were of BBS utilities and other ancillary programs. You can start with a simple system and add to it later, if you wish.

One of the oldest and most popular BBS programs is PCBoard, which was so old and well established that it became something of a de facto standard for the many other BBS software programs, causing their authors to write them to be compatible with PCBoard. (Most are compatible also with many other BBS systems, however.) Among other well-known and popular BBS systems are Wildcat, TBBS, Mustang, and Excalibur, to name only a few of a great number.

It is possible to set up a small system inexpensively, as Zoss did, using a simple pc and a basic BBS software package, something with features that are not a great deal more elaborate than the set of capabilities offered by a modern fax-modem board. In fact, you may not even want a full-fledged BBS package but may be satisfied to run a simple e-mail host package, a system designed to provide an electronic mail capability. Such a system provides the capability to send out correspondence, reports, and other literature for respondents to receive on their own computer screens. (In fact, despite the great multimedia capabilities of the Internet overall, by far the greatest amount of Internet activity is via e-mail, a function that pervades virtually every aspect and element of the Internet.)

The great advantage of using such a simple system is that only simple computer systems are needed on both ends, the host system (yours) and the receivers owned by your respondents or subscribers. (However, if you have a system with ample RAM and disk storage, you may be able to simply multitask your BBS on it, rather than on a dedicated pc, which means that you can continue to use your computer for other purposes, while the BBS runs in the background simultaneously.) There is also the benefit that the software is simpler and less expensive than that needed to run an elaborate BBS. You can buy such software published commercially, but there are many shareware programs that are highly suitable too and are less expensive than the commercial systems. In fact, probably the bulk of BBS software is or started life as shareware. (Some successful shareware does graduate to full commercial status.) Today, BBS software systems are available to run under both DOS and Windows.

FAX AS AN ONLINE ANCILLARY

While we are discussing the hardware of online activity, let's consider the fax as a subject of interest. The Internet, commercial systems such as CompuServe and America Online, and the BBS are the three main references we have in mind when we use the term *online*. The facsimile— that is, fax—is not an online facility in the same sense, but it is at least a second cousin in that it is used freely today for speedy correspondence and, more significantly, is the other function (and a major one) of the fax-modem board in virtually all computers today. (If your computer is not more than two or three years old, it is likely that it came with a fax-modem board already installed in it, so that you do not have to have a stand-alone fax machine to have a fax capability.)

Why is a fax capability important, if you already have a BBS and e-mail to correspond with clients and prospective clients? Here is a major reason: Sending a fax to someone is a proactive or aggressive action, whereas relying on e-mail and BBS forums is a passive one. That is, fax delivers the message a few seconds after you trigger SEND, regardless of any action by the addressee, but the other party must log on to an e-mail server or BBS forum to get the message you sent. I use e-mail extensively, but when I want to be sure the message will alert the other party immediately, I use fax.

In fact, a sophisticated fax software package can provide some BBS-like functions, such as a choice of communication protocols—Ymodem and Xmodem, for example—transmission of files, and communication with BBSs and commercial services, such as CompuServe and America Online.

To extend your reach, it is possible to turn to other resources, including many powerful online tools. Essentially, you can use online capabilities of all kinds—commercial services and the Internet with all its elements, as well as bulletin boards—to do many and perhaps even all your marketing and other business functions, although many individuals curtail and even end their activities on BBS and commercial online systems, as they have gotten more involved in Internet activity. The Internet provides much more than these other online systems, although it is a more impersonal system overall, and many people find that they cannot afford the time to maintain an online presence on more than one kind of system.

ECHO NETS

Echo nets, also referred to as *relay echoes* and *relay nets,* are a means for linking a BBS to others and sharing forums or conferences in nation-wide and even worldwide networks. There are a great many such nets. Many are small nets that spring up but do not survive long, but there are a great many hardy old-timers too. There is, for example, the now-familiar Fidonet™, which is the oldest and possibly the biggest of the echo nets, although there are many others, including the popular RIME (RelayNet International Message Exchange), which has been highly successful.

Many of these nets are specialized in one way or another. Cinema-Net, for example, is a network of bulletin boards devoted to movies and show business. Geo Info Net is dedicated to earth science discussions, BigNet to portly individuals, and BirdNet to information about exotic birds. There are online systems for photography, book retailing, book publishing, ani-mal husbandry, advertising, business opportunities, stock market and investors' forums, collectors and hobbyists of all kinds, dealers related to these, sociologists, Buddhism, communications technology, vendors gen-erally, human rights issues, and almost countless other special interests.

The existence of such specialized online networks suggests one way to gain access to the specific specialized audiences you wish to target in your marketing campaigns. Obviously, subscribers to a special-interest bulletin board system or network are individuals with interests in that specialty and so are probably among the best prospects for your services.

Joining an echo net involves some expense, although not a great one, in most cases, for additional software and maintenance, including telephone costs for relaying messages. At the time of this writing, belonging to RIME incurs a yearly membership fee of $25 and some monthly fee to defray the telephone costs. It is problematical whether belonging to such a net is of benefit to you in using your BBS to attract prospects. If you are interested in local clients only, joining an echo network is probably of no help, but if you are willing to accept assignments in distant places, or if your services are such that they can be provided to clients via some means of communication without the need to travel personally to other places, there is a possible advantage in being part of a network.

What is reported by others as effective in marketing online varies widely, as do the reasons given for successes and failures cited. Many find that networking—business networking, that is, as well as electronic or online networking—is the most productive way to use the Internet to build their consulting practices. Others rely on it for more direct selling efforts via Web sites. You will find that both opinions and reported experiences vary widely on the effectiveness of marketing sites on the Web and how to best use those sites. One thing is clear: Consulting is still not a one-call business. It involves at least two major steps or phases, on-site or otherwise: The first phase is getting leads; the second phase is following up and closing the leads. Each of these steps may, in turn, require more than one phase or cycle of activity to complete, despite occasional exceptions.

The Internet includes a number of consultant-referral services, such as that of Carl Kline of San Diego, California. Kline's consultant referral service, National Consultant Referrals, Inc., maintains a Web site at http://www.referrals.com, which provides a variety of useful services to visitors. The first page of his site is reproduced here as Exhibit 2-1. Note the underlined items on the page. Each is a link to other pages or sections of the site, as are links revealed by clicking the items in boxes on the page. One such link presents introductory information, which is reproduced in Exhibit 2-2. That page offers additional links.

Exhibit 2-1
OPENING PAGE OF NATIONAL
CONSULTANT REFERRALS SITE

National Consultant Referrals, Inc.

A Free Referral Service

Networking Clients with Consultants and Experts since 1979

Our offices overlook the beautiful San Diego Harbor.

What's New?

Download Catalog
(675kb)
Consulting Contract
Template
Free Directories
New Newsletter
Consultant Survey
News Release

Do You Need a:

Select and press GO!

Consultant? ▼

Go!

Other Information of Interest

Select and press GO!

Membership Information ▼

Go!

You are invited to join our Consultant's Discussion Group, sponsored by NCRI, and share your experiences and consulting problems.

Automatically join Consulting-tools email discussion group . . .

YES!   Subscribe me!

Forms capable browser required - Just Press the button ONCE!
You will automatically be added to the CT-LIST
You don't have to type anything or fill out a form!

Exhibit 2-2
INTRODUCTORY INFORMATION
ABOUT THE ORGANIZATION

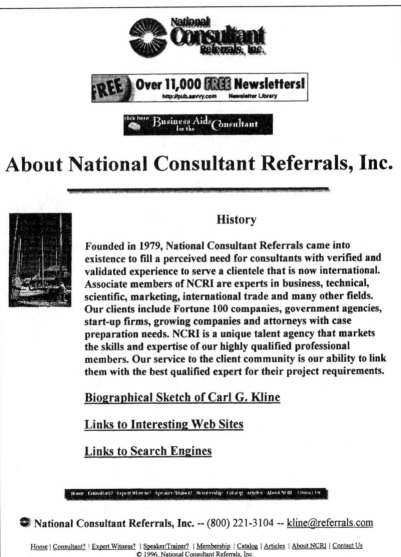

Over 11,000 FREE Newsletters!
http://pub.savvy.com   Newsletter Library

click here **Business Aids** for the **Consultant**

About National Consultant Referrals, Inc.

History

Founded in 1979, National Consultant Referrals came into existence to fill a perceived need for consultants with verified and validated experience to serve a clientele that is now international. Associate members of NCRI are experts in business, technical, scientific, marketing, international trade and many other fields. Our clients include Fortune 100 companies, government agencies, start-up firms, growing companies and attorneys with case preparation needs. NCRI is a unique talent agency that markets the skills and expertise of our highly qualified professional members. Our service to the client community is our ability to link them with the best qualified expert for their project requirements.

Biographical Sketch of Carl G. Kline

Links to Interesting Web Sites

Links to Search Engines

Home Consultant? Expert Witness? Speaker/Trainer? Membership Catalog Articles About NCRI Contact Us

National Consultant Referrals, Inc. -- (800) 221-3104 -- kline@referrals.com

Home | Consultant? | Expert Witness? | Speaker/Trainer? | Membership | Catalog | Articles | About NCRI | Contact Us
© 1996, National Consultant Referrals, Inc.

WEB SITE PRESENTATIONS VERSUS NETWORKING

Solicitations offering advertising and sales support services for Web presentations are abundant in all areas of the Internet. They are almost all based on the proposition of establishing your own site or renting space on an existing site, and the influence of older methods of advertising is evident: Web advertising sites are reminiscent of print advertising in slick-paper magazines, billboards, and direct-mail campaigns. Renting space on someone else's site is analogous to buying advertising space in a print periodical or a listing in a directory.

The similes are not exact, however, despite the many analogies possible, for Internet and Web advertising are unique in some ways. They are different from anything that has gone before, despite the tendency to design Web advertising along the lines of traditional media. One distinguishing characteristic of Web advertising—probably the most distinguishing one—is the hypertext presentation, created with HTML, Hypertext Markup Language. This provides the codes and keys for spontaneous branching to other topics and other Web sites—that is, to other files, which may be in other computers and at other locations around the globe. Connection and communication with someone on the other side of the globe are virtually as swift and easy as communication with someone down the street, given the speed with which electronic signals travel over the circuits. Physical distance between you and your prospect is of little significance when you are communicating via the Internet.

The arrangement of linkages is, in some ways, akin to being in a mall or large department store, where you may shop a wide variety of stores or departments because they are side by side or, at least, under one roof. You can thus often tour a great number of sites and view many presentations by clicking your mouse buttons wherever a link is provided. You can easily get lost in the (apparently) never-ending series of links, however, as you can get lost in some of the larger shopping malls, but most links provide a place to click your mouse for transport back to the beginning, just as large malls have exit signs. (Browser programs also have "Back" buttons that you can use to retrace your steps.)

The most prominent online marketing initiatives center on Web sites. The typical site is that of the advertising, sales, and/or promotional activities of a single organization, even of single individuals, although there is a decided trend to sharing sites as cooperative efforts or by renting space to other users. The site may thus consist of a single page or many pages. Many of the sites are in themselves business propositions, in that the owner has established it deliberately for the purpose of renting space to other advertisers, a practice not unknown in the conventional advertising industry. There are obvious advantages to both parties in renting space on an existing site. The combined efforts of everyone sharing space, each advertising and promoting that site, can create more traffic than could any single individual, for one thing. The convenience of having multiple stores in one location attracts many shoppers, which is another benefit.

As with any new medium, there is sharp controversy about the merits of marketing via Web sites. More than a few marketers have experimented with home pages and been badly disappointed with the results. One disappointed consultant remarked not long ago, "Clients don't search the Web for professional services, any more than they would hire their corporate attorney out of the Yellow Pages." Others have reported good results with direct marketing efforts via Web pages. Here is what a few have had to say about online marketing in general.

Paul Ferrara, a CompuServe sysop of a computer consultant's forum, says: "Over the years, I've gotten innumerable sales and clients via my visibility on the technical forums where I have some expertise."

Linda Abraham, author of *How to Write an OUTSTANDING Personal Statement*, says: "I think one's success depends very much on one's market. If there are bulletin boards or forums for your field and a significant number of your potential customers are connected, you can probably network effectively in cyberspace. Most of my clients are students. A high percentage of students are computer literate and connected to the Net. Therefore it is an effective way for me to make myself known."

Professor Lester Ingber, of the Virginia suburbs of Washington, D.C., is a consultant who uses the Internet effectively. He says: "The way I get clients is just by networking in the forum, exchanging messages, and so forth."

If you look closely at what those who report success in marketing via home pages on the Web have to say about their experiences, you can see that their success arises out of the strategy and philosophy of networking: It is a way of elevating your visibility and building an impressive professional image of yourself. It is gaining maximum attention for yourself as an individual professional and demonstrating what you have to deliver as a skilled and ethical specialist. The Web home page idea obviously works for a great many consultants, if not for all, when used intelligently and consistently, with an ability to be realistic about what it takes—the effort that is required—to succeed in this medium.

Teresita Dabrieo, formerly a highly successful computer consultant who now offers training and related services to high-technology consultants, makes this insightful observation about home pages: "The problem with a WWW page is that no one will see it unless you manage to somehow spread the word that the page exists and induce enough people to visit it. So you must advertise the page and do so in a manner that appeals to individuals to visit—that is, tell them what rewards await there. Of course, you must make the page rewarding with information that the visitor would find useful. It simply is not the same as an ad in a magazine that is already widely read. I believe that no single advertising or promotional effort will do you much good, unless you get lucky. Sometimes, I think we forget that it doesn't help to advertise to people who are most unlikely to ever have occasion to use our services."

THE PRINCIPAL PROBLEM OF WEB SITE MARKETING

The need to induce people to go to the trouble of seeking out your Web site presentation is perhaps the major drawback of Web site advertising: A site on the Web is not a billboard on a well-traveled highway, a notice in a widely read magazine, or a commercial during a popular TV show. These are mistaken notions that many seem to have. Visitors have to be attracted to and induced to seek out your site. As one observer remarked, marketing on the Web has the novel requirement that you must advertise your advertisement to make it work for you. The truth of that may be seen in the increasing advertising of URLs, Web site addresses, in print and on TV. However, that is really not a great deal different from advertising in general: Radio and TV programs are offered as inducements to attract listeners and viewers to listen to and watch commercials. Magazines offer stories and articles to attract readers who will read the advertisements from which the publisher actually draws income. So perhaps the principle of marketing on the airwaves is not really very different in essence from marketing successfully on the Internet after all, although the scale is much different. There may be millions of computers displaying what is on the Internet at any instant, but no site has more than the merest fraction of those computer screens displaying what is on his or her site at any given time.

E-MAIL-BASED METHODS

As noted, e-mail is by far the most popular and most used—perhaps even the most useful—of all online facilities, and it is part of or at least a readily available adjunct to all other elements of the Internet. The major use of e-mail generally is for the direct exchange of messages, but e-mail is also part of or ancillary to other areas of the Internet. Usenet groups, Web sites generally, online newsletters, and mailing lists all rely on e-mail as a major element of implementation.

Online Publications

The newsletter has long been an excellent marketing tool. Large corporations often produce elaborate and costly periodicals for their customers and prospective customers. However, today's office equipment enables even the smallest businesses to turn out simple but effective newsletters at modest costs. Here is a short list of online newsletters of interest that appear on my own screen regularly. The titles suggest what they are about:

> WEB MARKETING TODAY, A Free Tri-Weekly E-Mail Newsletter; Dr. Ralph F. Wilson, Editor <rfwilson@wilsonweb.com> To subscribe send message SUBSCRIBE WEB-MARKETING to majordomo@wilsonweb.com
>
> ZDNet Update is a weekly, e-mail alert service about the features, downloads, and events on ZDNet, a Web site. To subscribe to ZDNet Update, please send mail to: zdnet_update-on@lists.zdnet.com
>
> Consulting-Tools Discussion List, Supported by: National Consultant Referrals, Inc. List moderator: Carl Kline. To subscribe, send an e-mail request to kline@referrals.com

Web Digest For Marketers, Larry Chase/Chase Online Marketing Strategies, January 28, 1997. Free subscription at http://wdfm.com
THE BIZWEB E-GAZETTE!, JDD Publishing<Gazette@JDD-Publishing.com> Free subscription on request.

The electronic newsletter is a special form of online communication, easier to produce and even easier to write, in some ways, than the paper-and-ink version because it is usually more informal than the paper-and-ink newsletter, and it is all text—no graphics at all—when distributed via e-mail. Moreover, the text is something quite simple, of necessity, using a fixed-space font, which also encourages informality. Of course, a newsletter can be produced as a Web site or part of a Web site and can thus simulate the paper-and-ink newsletter with illustrations, color, and even sound. There is the important difference, however, of distribution. No effort is required by the subscriber to receive the e-mail newsletter: It simply appears on the scheduled date when the subscriber calls for mail. To read a Web site newsletter, on the other hand, the subscriber must make a deliberate effort, that of logging on to the Web and visiting the site. Given the great competition for the Web visitor's attention, an e-mail newsletter will probably reach a great many more readers than a Web site newsletter. In addition to that, it requires much more effort and in most cases is much more costly to develop and deliver a newsletter via a Web page than via e-mail connections. The work in producing a newsletter for presentation on a Web site is more akin to that of producing a conventional printed newsletter, with lay-out and makeup requirements, all the usual problems attendant to producing any formatted publication, and then translating it all into HTML codes. Add to that the problems of devising a format suitable to the Web, where jumping to another page entails much more than a page number (it entails a link and the HTML code to make it work), and in some ways the job may be even more onerous than that of producing the printed newsletter. You must therefore consider the trade-offs between the two approaches. It is easy to see why the e-mail newsletter is by far the more popular one.

Overall, online communications are in many ways ideally suited for newsletter and many other kinds of publishing. In fact, online publishing, also referred to as *electronic publishing* and *paperless publishing* (and even as *digital ink*) has become a field in itself, a field of increasing inter-

est, as more and more electronic newsletters and "zines" (electronic magazines) appear online, along with electronic versions of well-known print
periodicals, such as *The New York Times, U.S. News & World Report,*
and *Publishers Weekly.*

Overall, despite a few special problems in preparing a publication for
presentation on a Web site, such as those described, publishing electronically is much easier than print publishing in virtually all aspects. Those
include gathering information; assembling, editing, and formatting the content; and, especially, distributing the newsletter to subscribers. In the electronic publishing mode, using e-mail as the medium, all these functions can
be wholly or partially automated easily. Using the Internet as a medium to
distribute an electronic newsletter facilitates automation via devices that
generate the mailings to a list of subscribers. Not only is the newsletter an
advantageous method to promote your presence and professional image
online, but it is much more affordable to distribute an electronic newsletter
free of charge than to undertake the cost of a free print newsletter as a marketing promotion. It costs you your time, of course, and you will need a service to e-mail copies to a long list of subscribers. However, if you are just
starting the newsletter and mailing to a relatively short list of subscribers,
perhaps on the order of 50 names and e-mail addresses, you can do this
yourself, using your e-mail software, addressing your newsletter to the first
name and address on your list, and sending copies to the rest of the list.
You post the rest of your list "Cc:" or "Bcc:" copies. A list posted as Cc:
copies will appear at the head of the message each addressee receives, but
you can suppress the appearance of the list, with most e-mail software, by
sending the copies out as Bcc: copies. See Exhibit 2-3 as an example. It is
how I distribute an occasional article to a list of online newsletters, Web
sites, and other locations that welcome such submittals and will provide a
resource box ("about the author") or other limited advertising space for the
author. A number of consultants and other specialists use this method to
maintain their visibility and image on the Internet. I have found the results
to be well worth the effort required to do this.

The Mailing List

A very popular method for distributing information online and promoting
your presence and image in the process is the mailing list. Essentially, the

Exhibit 2-3
USING REGULAR E-MAIL FOR LIMITED DISTRIBUTION

_To: gary@stretcher.com
From: Herman Holtz (holtz@paltech.com>
Subject: Article for publication
Cc:
Bcc: gapserv@aol.com, Hehlers@juno.com, henderso@ix.netcom.com,
Hhmkt@aol.com, Holly@profitsonline.com,
HomeBased@infoback.net, homebiz@nemaine.com, ibc@sar-net.com,
JanetAC1@aol.com, JDD9@ix.netcom.com, jdpearson@wr.net,
IncomeEd@aol.com, joycepub@ns1.sccoast.net, MAILSOURC@aol.com,
MLMCentral@aol.com, mmm1@ais.net, MurphWorks@aol.com,
MyBizCoach@aol.com, myers@NS1.Content.Net (Paul Myers),
noboss@noboss.com (Dan Schwartz), mmm1@ais.net, nsi@coastalnet.com,
PageOne@aol.com, pataspra@fia.net, paulm@virtualbusiness.net,
payday@pulsar.net, phoenix5000@naxs.com, pizazz@ultimate.org,
Richard Soos<soos@soos.com>, rrr@vh.net, shilling@pobox.com,
sprtime@execpc.com, submissions@mma-network.com,
submissions@JDD-Publishing.com, submit@demc.com, TJTPUB@aol.com,
tom@usadvertiser.com, Webmaster@worldprofit.com, 5551@pipeline.com,

mailing list is a means for inspiring and leading or joining and participating in a discussion group via e-mail messages. In fact, it is a list of e-mail names and addresses of individuals who subscribe to the list and all of whom receive copies of whatever messages are posted by others on the list. They may post their own observations or respond to those already posted. However, anyone can address another on the list directly, rather than by posting the message publicly on the list. Subscribed to such a list, you may get several such batches of messages each day, one batch a day, or only one batch a week. If the traffic becomes excessive, it is often possible to get the mail as a digest, easing the burden. In the case of one list I found too burdensome, I discovered that the messages were also available in a newsgroup on the Usenet, and I then unsubscribed myself from the mailing list and subscribed to the Usenet group. That solved the problem for me: I now read the messages on the Usenet only, when I have the time and wish to, and I read only those messages that interest me at the moment. One advantage of the newsgroup over the mailing list is that I can go back to read older messages on the Usenet group without having burdened my own system by downloading and maintaining the store of all older messages, as I must do to save old messages on a mailing list. Another advantage is that my message will usually remain available to those subscribing to the Usenet group much longer than it would remain available to those subscribing to the mailing list, which is in my interest in maintaining my visibility.

You can use the mailing list in two ways. One, you can start and run one or more mailing lists of your own. Two, you can subscribe to mailing lists others conduct. I started a mailing list for freelance writers only because I could not find one that I thought to be right for the purpose, and the response has reinforced that view: The list is flourishing. But I subscribe to several mailing lists, as well as to newsletters and newsgroups. (I have trained myself to scan all of these rapidly so that I can sort out anything of interest and still find time to review all.)

Free Reports

An attractive alternative to the newsletter and mailing list is the free report. You may find it helpful to think of the free report as somewhat like a one-issue newsletter or, if you plan to issue free reports periodically when the mood strikes you or time is available, as a newsletter on an occasional schedule. (Some free newsletters are produced on that casual basis.) Philosophically, the free report is also like a calendar, report, novelty, or other attraction offered in inquiry advertising designed to elicit requests for copies. That produces a list of names and addresses that represents a mailing list of sales prospects.

Such a report may be of any length you choose. My own free reports tended to 1,000 to 5,000 words when I wrote them for print media, but now that I write them for electronic publication I keep them down to not more than about 1,000 words so that they will fit into an e-mail post. Most e-mail software will balk at sending lengthy messages. You could, of course, compress the report and send it as an attached file. The problem with that is that it is a method of spreading computer viruses, and so alert computer users are most reluctant to open any attached file and many will simply refuse to do so. (I am one who is reluctant to open an attached file.) So the safest course is to keep the messages short enough for e-mail posts, and most recipients are not looking for a lengthy tome, in any case.

There is no schedule and therefore no due date for such reports, and thus no pressure to produce it at any given time. You may write it—or compile it—at your leisure and publish it whenever it is convenient to do so. You may then circulate it to a prepared list of subscribers you have signed up in advance to receive each of your reports as you write them, or you may simply offer it to anyone who wants it and fill individual requests spontaneously, as I do. Currently, I offer two free reports, one on free-lance writing and another on marketing. I advertise them and invite readers to request them by posting notices in a modest Web site I maintain, in my signature, and in articles I contribute to others' Web sites and periodicals. I maintain these reports, too, by revising and freshening them occasionally with new ideas and new language. Of course, if you circulate your occasional reports to a prepared list, you will be producing and sending out a new report each time. You may then invite others to add their names to the subscription list and get copies of your free report. (You may, of course, soon find that you have a newsletter with no fixed schedule, whether or not you intended to publish a newsletter! However, since you never committed yourself to a schedule, that should be no problem.)

The free report should, of course, be on some subject of interest to those who are most likely prospects for your services: It should offer relevant information to anyone who wishes it (along with your advertising notice, of course), and you invite prospects, by whatever means you find convenient, to send a request for the report to your e-mail address. If requests become numerous enough to be difficult to handle manually, you can automate responses with a *mailbot,* a mail robot that will automatically respond to each request by e-mailing a copy of the report without need for any intervention by you. You can buy this as a service at a small monthly fee.

There are a great many opportunities to contribute to others' electronic publications. The list I use currently (Exhibit 2-3) is by no means an exhaustive one; there are many more places I could address. This is a service to those other publishers, as well as to their readers. You make the contribution in return for the advertising or promotional value you derive from it as a result of the *resource box* you are granted. That is similar to the signature you may attach to your e-mail posts. It is typically an allowance of perhaps 100 words or so that you may use to describe who you are and post something to advertise your service and develop sales leads. I use my resource box to make my credentials clear, in brief summary, and—much more important—to invite readers to send for one of my free reports. That then gives me the opportunity to develop the lead.

THE SIGNATURE FILE

There is one more marketing device that is an integral part of e-mail. It is the *signature,* a blurb that you create and install so that it is automatically appended to your message after you sign off. Here is a typical signature file, a quite modest one:

Joseph Smith <jsmith@north.com> Smith Computer Group.
Custom software development/tech writing services
Skyline Bldg, Suite 7121, Chrysalis City, Oregon

A signature file is usually three to five lines, although it may be much larger, and it may include a brief advertising message, a URL, an e-mail address, telephone numbers, and whatever else you think to be important. Actually, the e-mail address is usually unnecessary because it appears in the head data of your message, but you may have more than one e-mail address—many people do—and want inquiries made to the second address. You can also post here the e-mail address of an autoresponder that will send your reports out to anyone requesting them. I used that method for a short while, but found out it was not really necessary in my case, since I could handle the traffic myself quite easily.

KEEP YOUR EYE ON THE BALL

Keep a clear view of your objectives at all times. Your ultimate objective is sales, and so you are in quest of sales leads. Your immediate objective is to bring you the traffic from which you can winnow promising sales leads, by making yourself as well known as possible and establishing a highly prestigious image.

Achieving that first objective of developing a maximum number of prospects requires that you maximize your exposure, both directly and indirectly, as a result of being quoted and otherwise recognized by as many others as possible. The free report should be on some subject that is of interest to those who are likely prospects for your services: It should offer relevant information to anyone who wishes it (along with your advertising notice or promotional copy, of course), and you invite them, by whatever means you find convenient, to send a request for the report to your e-mail address. If requests become great enough to be difficult to handle manually, you can automate responses with a *mailbot* or *autoresponder,* a mail robot that will automatically respond to each request by e-mailing a copy of the report without need for any intervention by you.

Your objective can be served in a number of ways, but information is largely what the Internet is about, and a great deal of the daily traffic on the Net is that of individuals seeking information. If you become a supplier of useful information, you will be aligned with Internet visitors' goals generally and be in a right position to gain attention and, ultimately, prominence as a highly knowledgeable individual.

That element of the Internet system that gains the greatest amount of attention and is where those now well-advertised URLs—for example, http://www.something.com—will take you is the World Wide Web (that is the "www"), abbreviated generally as "the Web." Let's have a better look at it now.

CHAPTER 3

The World Wide Web

THE FALLACY OF TRADITIONAL MARKETING PREMISES

Many Internet marketers try to apply to this new medium the traditional marketing tactics and methods of old: the sidewalk pitch, direct mail, print spreads, and broadcast radio and video, while ignoring the special characteristics of the cyberspace medium. (Or perhaps the term ought to be the "plural media," because the Internet is actually a catchall term for cyberspace, and it offers more than one medium for commercial promotion.) There are similarities between its characteristics and possibilities and the characteristics and possibilities of the traditional media, but despite those similarities, there are a number of substantial differences. It makes sense to study the differences, as well as the similarities, and try to develop approaches to this new phenomenon that are appropriate to it. The HTML coding and linkages, for example, are one of the unique characteristics, and probably the most prominent feature of Web site presentations, as well as the most distinguishing one.

THE OUTSTANDING WEB SITE CHARACTERISTIC

In the previous chapter you were introduced to a typical home page. What you saw in Exhibit 2-1 was actually only the first of several pages containing underlined items, each of which represents links to which the viewer can switch by placing the on-screen pointer over an underlined item and clicking the mouse. In the succeeding pages of that Web site presentation, there are many other links to a wide variety of options. Moreover, many of those links themselves contain additional links, just as a printed index may have keywords at several levels of reference. The analogy is not really a close one, however, for the logical connection between and among the links of a Web site is not necessarily one of levels of reference or even of direct relevance, but is more in the nature of a chain, in which each link may be of equal importance and may refer you to a subject only generally related to the site where the link is offered.

Theoretically, there is no limit to the number of levels of branching and reference that may be linked in this manner in the chain, other than the total of information-storage areas available. (Since the links are often to other computers, which may be anywhere else in the world, the total storage is virtually infinite, in theory.) Thus, any presentation on a Web site may contain and/or refer a visitor to an almost unlimited amount of information. The branches may lead to material located at the same site—in the same computer, that is—or they may be to other, contemporary sites and sources (computers) throughout the Internet (throughout the world, that is), as parallel, rather than subordinate, branches.

THE ONLINE SEMINARS IDEA

Exhibit 3-1, at http://expert-market.com/seminar/, is an opening page of The Expert Marketplace Web site. The Expert Marketplace is a service for independent consultants and directed especially to clients seeking consultants, although it offers individual consultants opportunities to appear and be listed here. Note that there are numerous underlined items here, and many more appear in additional pages. Each of the boxes here offers one or more seminars on some aspect or specialty of consulting, which lends the presenter of that seminar his or her own opportunity to

Exhibit 3-1

ONLINE SEMINARS PRESENTED ON THE WEB

Online Seminars   **Expert** marketplace

Information to Help You Improve Your Business!

Marketing & Sales

Strategic Marketing: Building Critical Mass Establish the right positioning for the current phase of your company's market growth.

How to Avoid Marginal Sales Which LOSE Your Company Money Are your sales people effective or do their leads produce marginally profitable business, at best?

Management & Human Resources

You Be The Panel An overview of Peer Review, an internal dispute resolution system which utilizes a panel of two managers and three peers to resolve disputes.

Credo for Managing Change Guidelines a leader can use in managing change that will keep the troops aimed in the right direction.

Quality & Team Building

The Eight Lies of Teamwork In the evolution of teamwork, a number of popular myths, misconceptions, and poor practices have been advocated by consultants and executives.

Why Implementing Teams is Tough! Teams can help you grow and prosper, but it takes hard work.

Fundamentals of Total Quality Management (TQM) Using statistical process control to obtain the knowledge you need for TQM.

Manufacturing & Inventory

12 Key Factors That Determine World Class Just in Time Operations Find out if your company stands up to the best in the world.

Work Smarter - Not Harder, Using Time Study & Work Measurement Using time studies to increase your company's competitiveness.

Using Consultants

Query Best Sell Author Herman Holtz About Using Consultants Read responses to others' questions and send him a question yourself.

Insurance Issues to Consider When Contracting With Consultants Should you require consultants you hire to be insured?

Guidelines for Entering Into Service Agreements With Consultants How much "contract" do you need?

Information Technology

De-mystifying the ATM Architecture If the words ATM have you totally confused then read this unbiased mini-tutorial.

Environment, Safety, & Industrial

Major Changes to OSHA's Asbestos Regulations Some of the more significant changes that will affect your facilities.

Learn How To Have Your Firm's Article Appear Here

Clients Resource Center | Consultants Resource Center | Expert Marketplace Home | Search the Database | Online Seminars gain some publicity and useful exposure, addressing prospective clients. The last item on the page following (not shown here) is an underlined Comments and Questions, which, when clicked with the mouse, produces an e-mail form to use. The form is addressed to ask@expert-market.com, and will reach the site's sponsor and through him or her, the appropriate expert. As one of the presenters (actually, I was the original presenter) on that site, I can verify that presentations here do bring queries from visitors, and these queries represent sales leads, not always from interested prospects, but always contributing to your visibility and professional image.

Exhibit 3-2 is reached by clicking one of the boxes appearing at the bottom of the previous figure. It is an explanation of what is required to gain a free membership and, again, offers a Comments and Questions link to provide the visitor an e-mail form for response with a query or comment. Note how the designer of the site has again maximized the ease of interactivity—a dialogue between the advertiser and the visitor.

PROMPTING THE PROSPECT'S NEXT ACTION

On the Web, as in any other sales and marketing situation—perhaps especially on the Web, considering the special marketing problems there—it is a cardinal principle that you make it as easy as possible for the prospect to place an order or follow up in some other manner, even guiding the prospect's hand, in effect. Come as close to guiding the prospect's hand to the order form and writing the order yourself as you can. Even the most sophisticated and decisive prospects need to be encouraged, stimulated, and guided to the buying action, or they will hesitate and procrastinate the final decision. The truth is that if you do not get the necessary action *now,* it is likely that you will never get the order. And almost certainly, if you allow the end of your presentation to dangle idly and inconclusively, you will not get a follow-up by the prospect. If you rely on the prospect's initiative to take a next step, you will usually be disappointed. The more you help the prospect do what has to be done to place the order or take some other necessary next step, the more likely it is that the prospect will do so.

Exhibit 3-2
INVITATION TO MEMBERSHIP
IN THE EXPERT MARKETPLACE

Free Membership
Is Required to Enter **The Expert Marketplace**

If you forgot your password...
Send an e-mail to password@expert-market.com with your Username as the subject.

If you forgot BOTH your Username and Password...
Send an e-mail to password@expert-market.com with the subject of the message as "name: firstname lastname" where firstname=Your first name and lastname=Your last name.

NOTE: Usernames and Passwords **are** case sensitive (UPPER/lower)!

Get Your Free Membership
Enjoy all the benefits and services of The Expert Marketplace.

Members Enter Here
Try Entry Again

Tour the Expert Marketplace
View an outline of the services available here at The Expert Marketplace.

Comments and Questions

LINKS TO OTHER SITES AND RESOURCES

HTML (Hypertext Markup Language) and the free-form linkages it implements are the most distinguishing and most dominant characteristics of the Web. There is good reason for the widespread use of this feature: Obviously, the more links you establish with other sites, the more hits—visits—your site will experience. Links to other sites serve the purpose of attracting visitors in two ways: They enable you to offer visitors interesting and useful material from various sources you find, and they increase the probability of visitors or hits resulting from referrals by or from other site owners with whom you trade referrals and links.

The first consideration, offering visitors something interesting and useful to attract them, is important and no less important than the second reason. With such a vast and still growing array of sites tempting Internet surfers to visit, visitors need some compelling reason to seek out your site and spend time there with your presentation. The more interesting or useful your visitors find your offering, the more they will tend to note your Web site address (probably listing it in their "bookmark" or "favorites" file for convenient future access to your site). The more, too, that they will recommend your site to others. It helps also to provide visitors some reason to return for additional visits. Successful Web owners see to it that they have new information to offer visitors periodically, on a regular schedule, if possible. A newsletter, a new report—for example, a question and answer of the week—or other such timely and fresh material can be presented at your site for that purpose.

THE INTERNET IS NOT A MASS MEDIUM

HTML, with its linkages capability and the other features it provides to Web site presentations, is a key feature, an attractive one, of the Web. Still, in at least one way it is as much a drawback as an advantage. The *need* for linkages and other devices to attract traffic to your site points out the major drawback of a Web site: Unlike advertising placed in any of the established print and broadcast media, there is no guarantee at all that even one prospect will view your presentation. When you advertise via print, radio, or TV, you address prospects in existing audiences numbering in the thousands, in the hundreds of thousands, and even in the millions. And in conventional print and broadcast media, you may be reasonably sure that the majority of those audiences are exposed to your message. That is not so on the Internet. Look at the visitor registers posted at many Web sites, and you discover that the prospects here tend to number in the very low thousands, even hundreds, each month. Probably the average Web site is visited by only 10 to 30 visitors a day. One site advertises, for example, that it has received nearly 5,000 visits since April of this year and claims that as a symbol of success! That works out to only slightly more than 700 visits per month or fewer than 25 per day. In marketing terms, that is a pitifully small number that would not sustain even the most modest direct-mail sales campaign, nor support even the smallest business relying on direct mail as its major marketing effort. In fact, it would not even support a retail sale or almost any other kind of marketing campaign. A site I happened across this morning boasts of 65,000 visits in the past 60 days, but that means it would take an entire year to reach 365,000 prospects. Direct mailers reach many more prospects than that in a single mail drop and on a regular basis, relying on a typical response rate of from 0.5 to 2 or 3 percent!

Obviously, then, you need much better statistics than those or you must have entirely different marketing premises on which to base the marketing of your services successfully on the Web. You must base your strategy on a different set of operating principles from those based on mass media, with its premise of a tiny percentage of success in addressing a huge number of prospects. Despite the claims of many millions of users crowding that portion of cyberspace known as the Internet, the Web and Internet in general are not true mass media in any traditional marketing sense. Instead of trying to reach the world at large—the general public—with hopes of reaching the relative few most likely to be interested in your offer, you must work at reaching a highly targeted audience, visitors who appear well qualified as likely prospects for what you sell, as true sales leads. That achieved, you should be able to reverse the conventional direct marketing formula and find a large percentage of success with a relatively small number of possibilities.

This explains why the average large corporation is not setting the world on fire, in a marketing sense, in its advertising and selling on the Internet, even given the larger effort the large corporation makes on a

Web site. In direct mail, a major mail drop is in at least the hundreds of thousands of pieces and often in the millions of pieces mailed in a single campaign. Print advertising for mass marketing means advertising in periodicals that reach millions of subscribers. And the same order of magnitude, millions of listeners and viewers, is required for mass marketing on radio and TV. To date, no one has discovered a practical means of reaching these numbers of viewers on a Web site. The relatively small volume of sales that normally results from a Web site presentation is obviously not a significant factor in the total sales figures of any business for which sales success depends on selling a great and continuing volume. Thus, when a large corporation invests many thousands of dollars in Web site presentations, it is with something other than immediate sales results in mind. Such efforts are much more in the nature of *institutional advertising,* establishing a presence for anticipated future growth or for other such indirect benefits.

In a sense, this institutional advertising activity of the large business organizations is not different in its philosophy from the philosophy you and I employ in networking: As you and I do, the large corporation is also seeking to support a good image and a high level of visibility. The corporate managers also wish to keep the public reminded of the corporation's existence and what it does, even if it does not sell consumer products. That is why Boeing, General Dynamics, Dun & Bradstreet, Hughes Aircraft, and many other major corporations that do not make or sell consumer products advertise in consumer magazines and sponsor television programs: They are seeking image and visibility here—name recognition, that is—rather than sales.

A MARKETING PREMISE OF YOUR OWN

Despite the philosophical resemblance between networking and institutional advertising, the decisive factors of online marketing are far different for you as an independent consultant than they are for the large corporation. If you are a typical independent consultant, you do not require a large number of sales to be successful. A handful of sales a month, perhaps even a handful of sales per year (depending on your specialty), is probably enough for you as an average consultant, depend-

ing on the nature of the work you do and the average size of your projects. As a proposal consultant, an average of only one project per month
was enough to keep me busy and enable me to conduct my business successfully. This is no doubt true for a great many other independent consultants. The important consideration here is that an Internet marketing
goal of this kind is an entirely reasonable one for you as an independent
consultant. Unless you are somehow very much different from most consultants, you do not need a high volume of sales to have a successful
practice.

THE MARKET(S) TO SEEK

To reach that modest goal of perhaps only a few sales each month, you
need only a tiny piece of the market overall. However, you have an alternative that you ought to consider: Because of that relatively small number
of sales you need for overall marketing success, finding a niche market or
two may be a highly viable overall marketing program for you, where a
large organization would find most small niche markets too small to be
worth an effort to sell to them or perhaps even to do some marketing
research to investigate them. In fact, it usually does not pay the large
organization to invest in the marketing research to uncover the niche
markets, or so they tend to believe. For you, however, the very smallness
of the niche may be a marketing asset because you won't be competing
with the large organizations for sales in that niche, so that sometimes a
niche becomes almost a captive market. It is fortunate, too, that the Internet happens to be an excellent facility to use in marketing research. You
can use it to survey sites in a search for niche markets that are right for
you as marketing targets. You can actually conduct a great deal of your
marketing research from your office chair via the Internet.

There are other upsides to some of the problems of marketing on the
Internet. There is the advantage of much greater flexibility to tailor your
presentation and target your prospects than in traditional mass media
advertising and promotion. It's rather easy to change the copy on a Web
site. That makes testing and experimenting with your copy and
approaches much easier and even more practicable in Web advertising
than it is in direct mail.

TESTING AND EXPERIMENTING

Testing is an important concept in all marketing, but especially in direct-response marketing. Where you are dependent on that difficult-to-gauge public reaction to an offer, the investment in mailing lists, printing, and postage, or the purchase of advertising space in large-circulation print media, is a high-risk proposition. It makes good sense to do whatever you can to reduce that risk. For that reason, it is a common practice to run small test mailings or advertisements to test public reaction to the price, the product, and the presentation. That takes time and costs money. For direct mail, you must spend a great deal of time and money for new printings, mailings, and assessments of results. In print advertising it can be even worse, since you must schedule print advertisements many months ahead for most major periodicals. And even for broadcast media, time is required to prepare and schedule new commercials. These factors severely limit the number of tests you can run, although you would normally prefer to run many more. Because the reaction of the public is so unpredictable, there isn't much scientific method to testing; it is really an empirical process, experimenting with your copy, your offer, your prices, your targets, and all the other variables of marketing. So limiting the number of tests you can run is actually limiting the number of experiments you can make and the amount of useful data you can collect. Even with some costly shortcuts to overcome the unacceptable time required to run consecutive tests and experiments, such as split runs in print advertising and simultaneous test mailings, the number of tests and experiments possible is limited.

The Internet Web offers a great opportunity to overcome all this and enable you to greatly expand the amount of experimenting and testing you can do, due to the ease and speed with which Web site copy can be changed and presented, and results assessed. You can make as many changes to test as many facets of your offer as frequently as you wish. And make no mistake about how important even a small change can be: Often, a simple change will make a great difference in response because the public is so unpredictable. Lowering a price, for example, may have the reverse effect of that desired: The public may see the lowered price as evidence of low quality, especially if your price appears to be much lower than that of your competitors. For that reason, raising the price may help sales a great deal, as many have reported, with clients assigning you a higher level of quality than they assign to your competitors. Too much emphasis on a guarantee may turn clients away, alarmed by the suggestion of the guarantee as the most important consideration. A single word in your copy may be upsetting to many of your prospects and may cause them to turn away. The prospects you address may not be the right ones for you, even if your logical analysis suggests to you that they should be the best prospects. Again, it is only in conducting experiments and tests that you can know the truth with any certainty, under the "whatever works is right" principle.

Thus, you want to find and establish links to and preferably in exchange with sites likely to be of interest to the individuals and organizations you think to be your best prospects—to focused targets, that is— but you want also to validate your choices. (A section later in this chapter will furnish guidance in first steps of setting up a few links and publicizing your new site.) Necessarily, you start with your best estimates, which may be little more than intelligent guesses. Of course, some of the logic is obvious: If you sell computer services of some kind, for example, it probably won't help you much to link with a site devoted to lapidary or entertainment interests, unless they use computers extensively and buy computer services to run their businesses. But even if your choices make what appears to be good sense, without testing you can't be sure your choices are the best ones because no matter how sound your logic is, you base it upon certain premises, and those may or may not be the most valid ones for your purposes. My logic in pursuing small electronics firms as my first targets was based on my knowledge that many of these firms depend on government business. However, the relevant logic proved to be that most of the small electronics firms were well established and had sound marketing programs in place. But many of the small computer software developers were newly in business and badly in need of help, and so they proved more receptive to my appeals.

One way to approach the problem of finding your best niches is to first aim at a broad market, but define it as a number of distinct segments. Then test it, segment by segment, and narrow it gradually to the most productive segments as you gain experience and learn which are most productive and what works best. That is a kind of informal or ad hoc testing, but it is a practicable approach in many cases because of the very flexibility of the Web site and the ease with which your appeals can be changed to meet perceived needs.

Carl Kline's National Consultant Referrals site (http://www.referrals .com) provides good examples of reaching out to a rather broad group of prospects. Among the material this site offers to attract and interest visitors are articles that give readers tips on starting mailing lists and online newsletters, ideas on electronic marketing, and other useful tips. In fact, his site includes an online newsletter with a flowing stream of information. Exhibit 3-3 offers the first page of that free newsletter.

Of course, you want to keep visitors coming back, and they are not likely to return to read the same material, unless it is reference material, to which they might need to turn periodically. So you must update your site with new material regularly, such as a monthly article, a Web newsletter, new links, or other items that not only attract new visitors but provide motivation for old visitors to return to your site regularly. Treat your site as a periodical of some sort or actually make it a periodical. Encourage visitors to return for the new delights that await them. You can also encourage them to ask questions that you will answer on the site, or you can publish letters from readers, as magazines often do.

HTML: HYPERTEXT MARKUP LANGUAGE

HTML, the Hypertext Markup Language that makes the linkages and random jumps possible on the Web, is a set of codes and protocols used to write hypertext scripts for presentations on Web sites and provide the links. The codes direct the computer to carry out the various commands called for. Exhibit 3-4 shows the first frame of my own home page of my own Freelance Writing Tips, and Exhibit 3-5 shows the first page of the HTML coding for that home page. The HTML manuscript is an ASCII document containing the codes or commands, each describing an *element* of the presentation. The commands direct and specify five basic functions:

- The size and format of the text
- The integration of any graphics used by summoning the file
- The creation of the links with other elements or sites

Exhibit 3-3
FIRST PAGE OF NATIONAL CONSULTANT NEWSLETTER

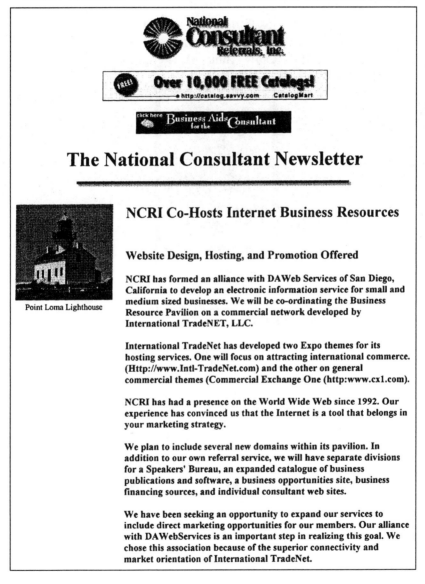

National Consultant Referrals, Inc.

Over 10,000 FREE Catalogs!
http://catalog.savvy.com   CatalogMart

click here   Business Aids for the Consultant

The National Consultant Newsletter

NCRI Co-Hosts Internet Business Resources

Website Design, Hosting, and Promotion Offered

NCRI has formed an alliance with DAWeb Services of San Diego, California to develop an electronic information service for small and medium sized businesses. We will be co-ordinating the Business Resource Pavilion on a commercial network developed by International TradeNET, LLC.

Point Loma Lighthouse

International TradeNet has developed two Expo themes for its hosting services. One will focus on attracting international commerce. (Http://www.Intl-TradeNet.com) and the other on general commercial themes (Commercial Exchange One (http:www.cx1.com).

NCRI has had a presence on the World Wide Web since 1992. Our experience has convinced us that the Internet is a tool that belongs in your marketing strategy.

We plan to include several new domains within its pavilion. In addition to our own referral service, we will have separate divisions for a Speakers' Bureau, an expanded catalogue of business publications and software, a business opportunities site, business financing sources, and individual consultant web sites.

We have been seeking an opportunity to expand our services to include direct marketing opportunities for our members. Our alliance with DAWebServices is an important step in realizing this goal. We chose this association because of the superior connectivity and market orientation of International TradeNet.

Exhibit 3-4
HOME PAGE OF FREELANCE WRITING TIPS

A Few Tips on Marketing
And Writing Marketing Materials
What You Ought to Know About Marketing Successfully from

Marketing Consultant/Writer
Author of the best-selling
How to Succeed as an Independent Consultant
and more than 60 other books on business

A specialist in marketing and writing help of all kinds--proposals, brochures sales letters, direct-mail, newsletters, ghost writing, and general writing services--by the best-selling author of more than 60 books and hundreds of marketing presentations that have won more than $360 million in sales for both small and large companies.

New! **scribe-list** New!
An email-based discussion group.
For writers, by writers.

Exhibit 3-5
HTML CODING FOR FREELANCE
WRITING TIPS HOME PAGE

```
        <!DOCTYPE HTML PUBLIC"-//IETF//DTD HTML 3.0//EN" "html.dtd">
<HTML>
<HEAD><BASE HREF="http://www.bellicose.com/freelance/">
<TITLE>Tips on Marketing and Writing Marketing Materials</TITLE>
</HEAD>
<BODY BGCOLOR="#FFFFEA" TEXT="#000000" LINK="#006868" VLINK="#000090"
ALINK="#B90000">
<B><CENTER><FONT face="Arial, Helvetica" size=4>
A Few Tips on Marketing<BR>
And Writing Marketing Materials</font><BR>
<FONT size=+1>What You Ought to Know About Marketing Successfully<BR>
from</FONT><BR>
<IMG SRC="name.gif" ALT="Herman Holtz">
<BR>
Marketing Consultant/Writer<BR>
Author of the best-selling<BR>
<I>How to Succeed as an Independent Consultant</I><BR>
and more than 60 other books on business</B></font></P>
<P>A specialist in marketing and writing help of all kinds—proposals,<BR>
brochures sales letters, direct-mail, newsletters, ghost writing, and<BR>
general writing services—by the best-selling author of more than 60<BR>
books and hundreds of marketing presentations that have won more<BR>
than $360 million in sales for both small and large companies.</P>
<P><A HREF="list/index.html"><IMG SRC="list/sl_intro.gif" ALT="New! Scribe-list,
an email list for writers!" WIDTH=362 HEIGHT=113 BORDER=0></A></P>
<TABLE BORDER=0 WIDTH=90%>
<TR>
<TD>
<P><CENTER><FONT face="Arial, Helvetica" size=4 color=blue>
YOU NEED TO STRIKE A NERVE</FONT></CENTER>
When I first advertised my services as a proposal writer, I
```

(Continued)

Exhibit 3-5
CONTINUED

---

got a few responses. But when I changed my copy, offering to <EM>help
my clients win contracts</EM>, instead of offering to help them write proposals,
I got many times the number of responses. Why?
<P>"Why" is no great mystery: The image of writing proposals did not start the
adrenaline, but the image of winning contracts struck a nerve. It got the prospect
excited with anticipation, the ultimate motivator.</P>
<P><CENTER><FONT face="Arial, Helvetica" size=4 color=blue>
THE BENEFIT, OR "REWARD," FOR BUYING</FONT></CENTER>
The principle is simple: Customers do not buy things; they buy what things do for
them. My first message focused on me and what I wanted to do: write proposals for
clients. My revised message focused on the client and what the client wanted—
contracts. It described what I would do for my clients, the benefit of using my
services.</P>
<P>That is all there is to selling. It is simple-enough, and yet a complex proposition.
The simplicity is misleading, but applying it is enormously varied and complex. That
is why you benefit from the help of a professional specialist in motivation, Unique
Selling Propositions, proposal principles, and the many other factors that go into
creating successful sell copy.</P>
<P><A HREF="sellcopy.html" TARGET="main">Writing Sell Copy</A>.
</FONT>
</TD>
</TR>
</TABLE>
</BODY>
</HTML>

- The integration of sound (audio) and external graphics
- The creation of interactive forms, if the design requires

Each HTML element appears in the manuscript between the chevron symbols "<" and ">." <IMG>, for example, denotes an image.

Note that the HTML manuscript may or may not include within it the actual text that is to be presented. If the text exists as a separate file, the

HTML manuscript can invoke (summon) a separate text file as it does a separate graphic file. The graphic of Exhibit 3-4, a surprinted photograph, is called up from another file by the HTML code when the URL is addressed, for example. The same is true for presenting links to other sites. There are HTML elements that invoke the transfer to a designated other site when the underlined word or phrase is selected. The HTML text that creates the on-screen image of Exhibit 3-4 may be seen in Exhibit 3-5.

That is all really not nearly as cryptic as it may seem at first glance. The various codes dictate fonts, colors, spacing, and other details. You may wish to create your own Web page, although there are many consultants who specialize in creating Web pages for clients. Mastering the codes is not especially difficult, if you wish to develop your own Web pages, although there is some artistry involved in the process, and the site developed for you by a specialist may be much more striking and attractive than the site you design yourself. If you do wish to develop your own site, there are many aids—HTML editors—you can get to simplify the task. Some of the leading ones are HTML Assistant, HoTMetaL, and Hot Dog, the latter reputed to be one of the easiest ones to use. Later aids to HTML programming are reported to be even easier to use, since the programs do some of the conversion of straight text to HTML codes automatically.

I find that I can infer just two logical and significant conclusions from all experience reported by Internet marketers and what I have been able to observe myself from my own experiences in marketing via the Internet:

- The market, by its nature, favors small businesses of such a nature that a relative handful of sales represents a significant market.
- The appeal must be targeted and focused as sharply as possible to address visitors with directly related interests. It should use the "Hey! You! See?" method or an equivalent approach to do this.

A popular—but hackneyed and shamefully contrived, in my opinion— way of explaining the basic advertising/sales-appeal idea is with an acronym, AIDA, which is used to present this presumed set of necessities in advertising/sales copy by force-fitting the acronym as follows:

A: get **A**ttention
I: arouse **I**nterest

    D: generate **D**esire (to buy, that is)

    A: ask for **A**ction (ask for the order)

I find logical faults in that analogy, although it does cover key points of sales and marketing. There is another explanation of classic thinking in advertising and sales promotion, expressed in terms that are somewhat more dramatic and make the idea easier to grasp. An explanation follows.

HEY! YOU! SEE?

The following is a more dramatic, simpler, and more effective way of getting the message across. This device explains the advertising/sales concept in three simple monosyllables:

- **Hey!** The opener. An attention-getter. "Look at me!"
- **You!** Yeah, *you*. This is for you . . . *about* you.
- **See?** Here is what I mean. Pay attention while I explain this.

The approach overall is the same, with the same objectives, but it explains *how* to do what AIDA says one ought to do. It says get attention, hook the reader by linking your message to the reader's interests, and present the explanation/proof that what you are presenting is in the reader's interest. If you wish to sell your consulting services, focus your appeal to apply to those who are likely to be interested in subjects relevant to your services—for example, winning clients for accounting services, getting along with the IRS, reducing telephone costs, selling editorial support, or whatever it is you do to help your clients solve their problems and satisfy their needs, for this is what motivates people to become interested and to buy.

To market anywhere effectively, but especially in a medium where your largest possible audience is far from being a mass market, and your services are likely to require a fairly substantial investment by the client, you must target with special care. In terms of running a Web site and attracting visitors who are likely to be good prospects as future clients, you need to first have a good understanding of whom you wish to attract to your site (qualified prospects), what it will take to attract them for an initial visit, and what will be required to bring them back again and again. And that brings up another consideration about programming your Web site presentation: What is your direct objective?

Of course, your overall goal is to win clients and contracts for your services. But since consulting is not normally a one-call business, the immediate and direct objective of your initial presentation is not a sale, but a step that is a precursor to a sale. Consulting contracts normally result from a multistep sales effort, including more than one presentation and, in many cases, a formal proposal and even a "dog and pony show" presentation. An effort to close a sale at the initial contact is not only unlikely to succeed, but will often alienate a prospect who sees the effort as high-pressure selling. If that happens, you will probably never be able to make that sale, so the effort is probably a strategic error in marketing.

There are lots of opinions on how to create an effective Web site. One problem with too many Web sites is the delays in loading lavish graphic presentations, which can take several minutes to be painted on the screen, whereas straight text or simple illustrations are presented rapidly. Many visitors become impatient and abandon their visits when they realize that they are going to have to wait a while for the page to appear.

The realization of that problem is beginning to dawn on online advertisers, and there is today some tendency to simpler graphics, with text advising the visitor that the graphics content has been kept low deliberately. Some sites now even offer a choice of full graphics or low graphics content. Independent consultant Tom Zoss's new Web site is an example of a site with low graphics content (Exhibit 3-6), as is my own site (Exhibit 3-4).

In the previous chapter, we reported Zoss's experience with his own BBS (electronic bulletin board system), which he ran to develop leads for consulting projects. After about a year's successful experience with it, he decided that he had to change and keep up with the times. He says, "The BBS idea is a good one and I'm sure it will work for many, but I decided there was no reason to operate my own BBS when the Internet was accessible, so I closed the BBS and moved my informational files to a Web site."

Zoss goes on to explain his marketing strategy, which obviously works for him: "I now have a Web site (http://www.zoss.com) and use information about my practice and clients, opinions, white papers, an electronic newsletter, and personal information about myself to help people get to know me. I even posted a family picture! I believe a consulting rela-

Exhibit 3-6
THE ZOSS WEB SITE VERSION

Introducing Thomas Zoss
President of Zoss Communications, Inc.

Quality consulting work requires establishing a relationship between an outside expert and an organization. The following information will help you to get acquainted with Tom Zoss and how he might be able to help you.

Thomas Zoss brings a unique mixture of marketing and company management acumen to his consulting and agency practice, which does business as Zoss Communications, Inc. He combines a blend of strong writing and planning skills with broad experience in a wide range of business environments to offer high quality advice and service to his clients.

Educated at Georgetown University in Washington, D.C., and Indiana University in both South Bend and Bloomington, he holds a B.S. degree in Management and Administration and a J.D. from the I.U. School of Law. He recently earned an M.A. in Communication Arts from the University of Notre Dame. As an adjunct faculty member, he has taught Principles of Management at the University of Notre Dame, Arts Law, Public Speaking, Public Relations, Business Law and Writing for Indiana University South Bend, and Team Management Techniques for Southwestern Michigan College. He is a past president of the Michiana Chapter of the American Marketing Association, and a regular speaker on strategic planning, marketing, and managing successful businesses.

He has helped manage or been president of companies with markets as diverse as industrial rubber goods, musical instruments and consumer electronics. In addition, he has worked as director of corporate communications and advertising, heading large creative teams and international marketing efforts in several industries. His years in full time law practice add additional expertise when working with clients in regulated industries, and when assisting in corporate acquisitions and sales.

As vice-president and creative director of a planning and marketing agency he served as a key strategist for planning proposals. He managed the creative team and headed the public relations department. Agency clients included firms in such markets as automobiles, banking, papermaking and healthcare.

A former newspaper owner and publisher, magazine editor, and television news editor and director, he has experience at all levels of press relations and publicity. He is a published author of newspaper feature stories, consumer and trade magazine feature articles and specialty market books.

tionship involves someone who decides that they will treat you like a trusted friend rather than a stranger. I try to help them move into that relationship with lots of information about me."

Zoss's opinions about the most effective look and feel of a Web site can be seen in Exhibit 3-6. "I think there is a lot of effort wasted trying to make a Web site look 'hot' and far too little time spent on the strategy, the content," he says. "I believe that the 'Keep it Simple' approach works best. A simple, clean, well-written site that any Web browser can view predictably is the best. Good writing and careful attention to your message and how you position yourself is paramount. Too much glitz ends up looking like hype, and that undermines the credibility of your message."

He reports good results. "Hundreds of visits to my site show that people are visiting, and counters on several different pages show me that many go from the initial index page to read every linked page. I have one international project to credit to the Web site, and many of my ongoing clients use the site to learn about me before things get one-on-one. Remember that the person living down the road can use the Internet, too, not just someone around the world."

I can personally confirm the international nature of the business contacts you make. My own site has brought me orders from several European, Middle East, and Asian countries. If what you do is of a nature that you can provide your services without face-to-face contact with your clients, you can count on an effective marketing program bringing you international sales leads and trade.

COSTS IN GENERAL

There is, of course, expense attached to creating and running a Web site, as there is to conduct any business activity. For that matter, there is cost attached to most of the things you may want to do to market online. Unless you are in a position to do everything yourself, you will need to buy services to set up your site and keep it running, to make regular changes to your site, to send out literature automatically, to make large-scale mailings, and to otherwise attend to all the details of running a site successfully and getting the results you want from it. There is a lot more to it than the one-time cost of creating the site and setting it up. There are maintenance functions you must attend to, and you should know all this before you get deeply involved and find that a small initial investment has only made you "pregnant," in a business sense, and now requires that you spend more money than you anticipated to protect your initial investment.

That is not, or should not be, bad news. The good news is that most of the services you will want to use online to support your Web site are not—or should not be—expensive. They require only rather simple systems and are largely automatic so that the supplier has little cost in running them. However, one supplier I spoke with when I decided to put up a modest Web site of my own told me that he was not interested in servicing any Web site for less than $200 a month. (Servicing means keeping it stored in his system, always available for anyone to log on to. It also means making the changes you want to make when you want to make them, although your vendor will probably charge you a separate fee for that unless you have made other arrangements.)

I soon found that there are many high-priced suppliers who are, to a large extent, taking advantage of those of us who know little of their technology and are somewhat in awe of the technology and those who are the masters of it. But there are many others who will provide the services you need for very modest prices. You must therefore shop around. The entire business of the Internet and everything connected with it is so new that there are virtually no standards as yet, not even de facto ones. If you undertake to do business with established, large organizations, you will find them insisting on doing business according to their own standards developed in their traditional activities, and those standards may or may not fit the cyberspace situation well. Thus, if you want to be in a position to negotiate the terms of a working agreement, you do well to seek out the smaller, more recently established suppliers, as I was able to do. They are of necessity more pliable and more accommodating, for the most part, despite occasional exceptions. In fact, it is not at all unusual for ISPs—Internet Service Providers, the folks who furnish you access to the Internet—to permit subscribers a little free storage space to set up and maintain a modest Web site at no cost beyond their regular subscription. If you have not yet signed with any ISP or wish to contemplate changing your source of access, you will find it a good idea to inquire as to the ISP's policy with regard to some free Web space. There is a good chance, at this time, that you will be able to work something out along those lines.

SPONSORSHIP AND ADVERTISING REVENUES

The word *sponsorship* is used frequently in discussions of advertising costs and revenues connected with Web sites. In a sense, it is a simple euphemism for advertising fees. Someone with a Web site that draws a relatively large number of visitors every day is in a position to rent advertising space to others. Yahoo!, for example, probably the most well-known and possibly the most popular search engine since its founding in April 1994 (pioneer days, in Internet terms!), furnishes its search service free of charge to all, as all the general search engines on the Web do. Yahoo! earns revenue by renting space for advertising banners, as others do, calling this sponsorship. Sponsorship rates vary by category, and the Yahoo! rate sheet lists such categories as "Business," "Computers," and "Recreation." An advertising banner is actually a link to that advertiser's own Web site. Thus the advertising value of a banner is more than the appearance of the advertiser's name and message; it is also a key to attracting visitors to the advertiser's own site, and for many that is the chief reason for sponsoring another's site.

Thus, the furnishing of information and related services without charge to the user is a business that depends on advertising revenues, as broadcasting and periodical publishing do. As most people probably know, the cover price of a magazine or newspaper does not defray the cost of producing and distributing the issue. The rest of the production and distribution costs, and all profits, result entirely from the advertising revenues. Without that, the periodical would soon cease to exist. The Expert Marketplace was started by an individual, for whom I furnished the first online seminar and the idea of creating that as an attraction. Industry Innovations, Inc., owner of The Expert Marketplace Web site today, has the site sponsored by Dun and Bradstreet, which displays a D&B banner on each page of the site. Advertising banners appear on my own site, under a somewhat different arrangement. The banners have nothing to do with my activities, but they are there in an exchange program, in which the other sites for which the banners provide a link fly banners that promote my site. In other cases, such a banner may produce revenue, as described, reducing the cost of running the site.

The Netscape sponsorship/advertising contract form supplies definitions for terms used in selling space on their servers. The terms defined there are "Advertising Space," Advertisement," "Link," "Slot," "Start Date," "Finish Date," "Netscape Server," and "Usage Statistics." These definitions are provided for legal reasons, but they are generally acceptable ones that are self-defining. Should you wish to have a Web site of your own, you may be able to defray its cost entirely in this way and perhaps even turn a profit.

Sponsorship of someone's site, then, consists of advertising your own Web site by "sponsoring" or renting space on well-attended sites where you can not only advertise your name and product or service, but you can advertise and provide a link to your own site. That is a relatively expensive way to advertise your site and place links to it, if you buy banner space on a site with a large attendance. It is probably too expensive for most of us as independent consultants. But there are other ways to publicize your site, ways that do not impose rental fees on you. One way is, of course, finding other site owners who are interested in exchanging links with you. Another is including notice of your site and its address in your signature file, so that you advertise it with every e-mail message you write. Yet another is to list your site address as part of every article you write for publication anywhere. And still another way is listing your site with as many of the search services as possible. (Most search services will list your site when you request it, and many have a prescribed procedure and forms for listing your site.)

In that connection, you can take advantage of Submit It!, a service that promises to list your site with a number of the popular search engines free of charge. There are many service providers who will list your site with Submit It! for you without charge, but who offer to list your site with a much larger list of search engines and directories for a fee. Or register your site with Submit It! yourself at http://www.submit-It!com.default .shtml. There are also the directories existing as Web sites and paper-and-ink directories, such as the Internet Yellow Pages published by Osborne/ McGraw-Hill.

All of this is general, laying the groundwork for developing sales leads. There are also opportunities for making direct contacts online, a subject for the next chapter.

CHAPTER 4

Finding Direct Online Opportunities

Who would not like to reach 35 million prospects, where even a response rate of 0.001 percent would be highly rewarding? It is a marketer's dream. While millions of individuals all over the world appear on and are using Internet facilities, that does not translate directly into millions of prospects for whatever is offered for sale. Even the number of "suspects" for what you offer is limited to those who view and are interested enough to read your presentation—in fact, to those who are both *able* to view and read your presentation and who can be induced to go to the trouble to do so. And the number of prospects, *true* prospects, is limited further to those who have reason to be interested seriously in what you offer and are capable of buying it—can pay for it, which often means having the authority to buy it. Those are the two factors that make a "suspect" a prospect—that *qualify* a prospect, in accepted sales jargon. Those who show an active interest in buying what you offer should be considered to be sales leads that should be actively followed up, but it is not always easy to distinguish between idle curiosity and true interest. To avoid wasting much of your time and money pursuing prospects who are not really serious sales leads, you must so qualify those you regard as prospects.

There is a logical hierarchy of development in all sales activity, including that conducted on the Internet: It is largely a screening activity, based on the recognition that only a tiny portion of all those millions of visitors to the Internet qualify as true prospects for what you have to offer. Qualifying prospects, or identifying true prospects by establishing both their serious interest and ability to become clients or by the opposite action of screening out the idle curiosity seekers and casual observers, is a well-known step to professional marketers, although it seems to elude many initiates to the Internet marketplace.

There are millions of casual travelers on the Internet and Web, but only the tiniest fraction of these are going to stumble over your presentations by chance or would be serious prospects for you even if they did happen across your presentation. If you depend on chance to bring the right prospects to you so that you may make your offers to them, you will be disappointed. The vastness of the Internet and its random pattern of roads and avenues (there is no main highway on the Internet; the superhighway metaphor is a delusion and not at all apt) make it unlikely that any large number of visitors will stumble across your site or your advertising and promotional copy.

In short, there is no single, major traffic stream along which you could erect a large billboard to be seen by millions driving by. The Internet and World Wide Web aren't even as well organized as the Yellow Pages, which provide master indices to businesses and other organizations. There are similar printed directories for the Internet, but their similarity to the telephone companies' directories is superficial, existing only in physical appearance. There are several dozen search services on the Internet that provide their services free to users, as referred to in the previous chapter, where it was described how they derive income from selling advertising space on their sites. These are usually banner ads with links to the advertisers' sites, including Yahoo!, Alta Vista, Lycos, Magellan, Excite, Web Crawler, and Infoseek, along with other, more specialized search services, such as Switchboard, that enable one to find individuals. The closest you can come to applying the billboard idea to the Internet is placing such banners on busy sites, sites that draw many visitors each day. (Unfortunately, a great many of those banners ads are much more analogous to the chewing tobacco advertisements painted on the sides of barns along little-traveled country lanes than they are to the huge neon signs in New York's Times Square.)

Without these search services, it would be difficult to find your way about, especially if you were looking for some specific site or information. To get a significant traffic flow to the site of your own "commercial," you must do something positive to create the traffic, as you can see others doing by the increasing frequency of notices on TV and in print, inviting you to visit the advertisers' e-mail and Web site addresses.

SUCCESSFUL INTERNET MARKETING

There are various hypotheses about how to use the Internet most effectively or in what mode it can be used most effectively. One hypothesis is that the Internet is a good marketing medium for only certain kinds of goods and services. Another is that it is a good medium for only certain kinds of or approaches to marketing. Perhaps both hypotheses, or even some others, are right, and the Internet is, indeed, a marketing opportunity of diverse aspects. Whatever the case, it is safe to say that if the Internet is an effective marketing medium, it is so for only those who learn to use it effectively in terms of their own needs. That is, for only those who have learned enough of Internet characteristics to match those characteristics to their marketing needs. But this is not peculiar to the Internet; it is a truth for all marketing, although it may be more significant a principle to observe in the case of the Internet, considering the factors just discussed. The basic steps to success are the same on the Internet as they are in any other medium, at least in principle:

- Find the words to describe what you offer, but phrase those in terms of direct and immediate benefits to the client. (The promised benefit is the true offer.) That is always the paramount way, and probably the only true way, of getting and sustaining interest.
- Determine and qualify, as precisely as possible, exactly who are the prospects you want to reach. Specify or stipulate these so that you are sure of precisely who you are trying to reach with your presentation.

- From this specification, find the avenue that enables you to single out and present your offer to those prospects. Even the most precise and clearest definition of your targets—your market—is of little use until you are clear on how you will reach these targets.
- Follow up and close. By far, the majority of sales efforts fail because of weak and ineffectual closes, and perhaps because so many misunderstand what *close* means. It is commonly mistaken to mean getting the order, whereas the close is *asking* for the order. This is an art in itself, but it must be mastered. It is crucial to sales success.

These items require some clarification and extended discussion. Let's look at them a bit more closely.

DEFINING YOUR OFFER

The common assumption made by many who are not marketing professionals is that an offer is a statement/description of the product or service the seller wishes to exchange for money, and it may or may not include other information, such as the price (although probably most who define the word *offer* as such a description would include the price in the definition). Defining your offer as a description of what you want to sell is a serious first mistake in sales technique. To achieve maximum sales impact, especially at the opening, the offer should be defined and presented as a description of what the prospect really wants to buy, the end result, a benefit. The prospect may not even be conscious of this true desire until you articulate it and bring realization (the "Aha!" effect) about. Everyone has unconscious desires, and one of the greatest marketing talents one can have is the ability—perhaps *instinct* is a better word—to identify those unconscious desires and express them in making a sales appeal.

Elmer Wheeler, long heralded as America's greatest salesman, had this talent. Probably his most famous dictum to all salespeople was "Sell the sizzle, not the steak," but he had other such wisdom to impart, such as "Make them thirsty if you want to sell them lemonade." On one occasion, he sold a large stock of out-of-style long john underwear by displaying them with a large sign that promised, "They don't itch."

There are three points to note here:

1. Identify the most motivating benefit you can think of.
2. Make it an emotional benefit.
3. Make it a promise, not an announcement.

Think of your service not in terms of what it *is,* but in terms of what it *does*—does for the client, that is. Examine your service in terms of what benefits it delivers and what problems it solves. Discriminate carefully between an announcement and a promise, because it is the promise that is the true offer.

"Automobile for sale" is therefore not an offer. At best, it is an announcement. "A comfortable and secure feeling on the highway" is an offer. "Diet plan for sale" is not an offer. "New, slim figure in 30 days" is an offer. "Your friends will envy you" is an even better offer. What the customer wants to hear, consciously or unconsciously, is what you propose to *do* for him or her: the *benefit* you promise to deliver. And it works in every sales situation, business to business as well as business to consumer-citizen. Your client is someone with problems to solve and desires to satisfy.

There must be a major benefit in the purchase of every product and service, or no one would buy it. In fact, there are usually several benefits, major and minor ones. You must distinguish the major ones from the minor ones, and select one as the main benefit. Focus is important.

Be clear in your own mind on what you are offering. You won't make it clear to others until you have it in sharp focus yourself. Think it out. Test it. Satisfy yourself that it is, in fact, something that the typical client prospect will want most ardently and by which he or she is likely to be motivated. The better the job you do with this—the more effectively you strike a nerve with your offer—the more motivated your prospect and the more successful your marketing effort will be.

THE UNIQUE SELLING PROPOSITION

Lately, it seems that more and more marketers are becoming aware of something expressed as a "USP." That originally referred to "Unique Selling Point" or "Unique Selling Proposition," but has since proved to be a highly versatile expression that can also stand for "Unique Service Proposition," "Unique Service Program," and other articulations of USP. The concept, however, is the same in all cases, and again, it is of special importance here because it is a key to attracting visitors to your site to see your presentation.

The idea is simple enough. Our society is one in which every product and service that is successful in winning public support and competition will grow rapidly, producing similar products and services. Perhaps all the versions of the product or service will be equivalent to each other in quality and value, perhaps not, but the buyer really has no way to know and is therefore dependent on what the seller says about the product or service. The seller who offers the product or service with some unique benefit has an advantage in having given the prospect a powerful reason to favor that product or service over competing products and services.

The unique item may be a characteristic of the product or service, but it may also be something else. Most common is the claim to offer the lowest price and the highest quality, or to point to some special feature. What is important is that the unique item represent a benefit to the buyer and that the benefit be an important one. Montgomery Ward offered the first unconditional money-back guarantee offered to mail-order buyers, and that was enough to win him a great many customers immediately. Joe Karbo was the first to lament how poorly he had been doing, verging on bankruptcy, until he discovered the marvelous product he was offering for sale, and he created a second USP by being the first to include in his advertising a certificate signed by his accountant certifying the truth of his claims of rising from poverty to wealth.

Of course, these were immediately imitated, when they proved to be successful marketing gambits, so a USP that is successful does not remain unique forever, and the alert marketer is always in search of a new USP.

One important note here: *Unique* needs definition. A USP need not be truly unique or truly one of a kind and unlike anything else in existence. It needs only to be unique as far as the client is concerned. If it is the first time the client has encountered it, it is subjectively unique. You may borrow ideas from anywhere, as long as no competitor has done so before you.

SELECTING THE MAJOR BENEFIT/MOTIVATION

In some cases, the major benefit is quite obvious, but more often you must work at finding the benefit that will be most motivating to prospects. But you must first be clear on identifying your prospects. For example, if I were to offer a seminar or training program in proposal writing, two possible benefits occur to me immediately: I might promise to teach the prospect how to learn to write successful—winning—proposals, or I might promise to teach the prospect how to win contracts.

DIFFERENT OFFERS FOR DIFFERENT PROSPECTS

Are the two benefits—promises, that is—of writing better proposals versus winning more contracts the same thing? If not, which do you think will be the more motivating?

Logically, it could be argued that they are the same because the end result of writing better proposals is winning contracts. But subjectively, from the buyer's viewpoint, they are two different benefits, and which I would use would depend on knowing to whom I would be making the offer and what their own overall interests and objectives were. Students of writing who wanted to learn proposal writing and those who write proposals and want to improve their proposal-writing skills would be one kind of prospect. Marketers who wanted to learn how to win contracts would be an entirely different kind of prospect. The former would probably be looking to learn how to become top-notch proposal writers, possibly to qualify for a proposal-writing job or promotion within the organization where they are employed, whereas the latter would be most motivated by the promise of winning contracts. That would dictate to me the slant I would have to use to make my presentation effective. Any presentation can, of course, be slanted in many different directions. But you must know who your marketing targets—your prospects—are. If you are appealing to the world at large, such as via a newspaper or magazine with a large circulation, your slant will attract the kind of prospect to whom it is appealing, but that will be a tiny fraction of the world at large. The alternative is to discover methods by which you can reach the individuals to whom you have slanted your promise. That is the challenge of Web advertising.

Of course, to pursue the above example, it is possible that you might attract both kinds of prospects, individuals whose interest was most stimulated by the promise of learning to write better proposals and those whose interests were most related to the outcome of better proposals or greater success in winning contracts. What then? Choose one and hope for the best? Promise both, making one the major promise and the other a subordinate promise? Decide which is the more important prospect? Or is the best answer dependent on still other factors, about to be discussed here?

PROBLEMS AS KEYS TO SUCCESS

Of one thing you may be sure: Everyone has problems of one sort or another, and your prospect is no different. But not all problems are of equal magnitude in the prospect's view, and it is a mistake to dilute or dissipate your appeal by basing it on the solution to some minor problem. Your offer must be one that has a major impact. If it is an offer to solve a problem, it must be to solve a problem that is important enough to be a major concern of the prospect, addressing a major concern or objective of the prospect.

Even then, having found the major problem or objective of your targeted prospect, it is a mistake to dilute your appeal by bringing in a host of solutions to minor problems. That distracts the prospect from your major point, distracting the prospect's attention from the main solution and weakening your argument overall. On the Internet, with all the wealth of attractive diversions and ease of switching to alternative presentations, it is more difficult than ever to hold the prospect's attention. You must work at it.

CHOOSING AND IDENTIFYING YOUR PROSPECTS

Targeting your markets means choosing your prospects, of course, as deliberate and conscious choices. But choosing your prospects is still not entirely arbitrary. You must decide who are all the possible prospects for the services you offer, which are the most promising prospects, and which are the prospects you can reach via the Internet. There are several possible kinds or classes of prospects and thus bases for analyzing the possibilities and making choices. Here are a few of the alternatives you may consider in making your analyses and developing your plans for targeting your marketing appeals:

- Prospects with some known specific kind of problem or need that you are well-prepared to solve or satisfy
- Prospects who are traditionally always in need of such services as you offer, probably as a regular need of their businesses
- Prospects to whom your services are especially well suited, a divine fit that happens occasionally
- Prospects to whom you happen to have some special access through your own past business acquaintances, family, friends, or other circumstance

If your consulting is a business-to-business type, as most consultancies are, you may be choosing your prospects by industry, size, or nature of the problems your services address, as three of the possible approaches to deciding who will be your best prospects. In any case, you must necessarily start with assumptions, which are probably based on your earlier experience and the market appraisal that earlier experience dictates.

What is most important is not that your initial estimate is accurate, but that you permit experience to be your teacher and set your feet on the right path. You must permit your experience—facts on the ground—to modify, adjust, and/or refine your initial estimates. But it is important, first, that you have a clear picture of who your prospects are. In today's industrial and commercial complexities, naming a general industry as a target is not definitive enough. Most modern industries are so complex and well developed that they are divided into many branching or subordinate industries. The electronics industry, for example, has become compartmentalized into such specialties as communications, weapons, avionics, audio, computers, and automotive electronics, and some of these are further compartmentalized. Too, there are different methods for classifying many industries, such as classifying them in terms of the kinds of customers with whom they deal. Some electronics companies, for example, do military work primarily, while others do strictly commercial work, but the latter class may break down into companies that produce consumer items to be retailed, those that produce standard items for other businesses or industries, and those that do only contract work, developing custom items. These definitions may have a profound effect on your marketing strategies on the Internet. You need to define the markets you have chosen to pursue with enough precision to enable you to organize a specific plan for reaching the buyers in that market.

DATABASE MARKETING

Modern facilities, the personal computer and database software, have made it possible to carry this concept of precise market targeting forward to logical extremes in what has come to be known as *database marketing*. That is a marketing approach predicated on building a comprehensive database of your clients, developing a meticulously detailed profile of each client. (There is, however, no reason that the concept cannot be applied gainfully to profiling prospects, as well as clients.) The theoretical extreme of the idea is to be able to make individual (customized) sales appeals to each client, based on the known interests and preferences of each client, which is market targeting carried to an extreme. While it would not be practicable to write up an individual sales appeal to each client if you are in a consulting field in which your contracts are usually too small to justify the expense and time required for such special efforts, it might be entirely practicable if your projects are larger ones, big enough to justify intensive, individualized sales efforts, such as proposals. Contract opportunities calling for proposals are a common enough example of this; they are individual sales efforts tailored to the specific prospect and need. (See Chapter 7 for discussions of proposals and related matters.) But aside from this, there is another way to use this database: You can identify some interest many of your clients have in common and design a special marketing effort for that segment or niche of your market. The database is the right tool for developing such data as will reveal common characteristics of any segment of your prospect population.

Your client list is, of course, a particularly valuable asset, and your prospect list is as valuable as the degree to which the prospects on the list have been qualified as candidates to become your clients. Still, while the two lists are separate entities, the distinctions between them are blurred somewhat by the nature of consulting as a contract business: You may have ongoing or continual contracts with some clients, while you may have only one contract and never a second one with other clients. That makes the latter client more a prospect than a client. And even in the case of those clients with whom you have had several contracts, during any period when they are not current clients, they are prospects. Thus, the distinction between the lists is of questionable significance. Perhaps all names on your database merit treatment as prospects.

Database marketing focuses attention on gathering data on each individual client, but because clients become—are—prospects for new sales and new projects, there is little reason to confine the data gathering to the client list. There is no reason for not building a database of prospects who have not yet been clients. The more you know about your prospects, the more likely you are to find the right appeal, the one that brings the results you want: sales. Use the facilities of the Internet, then, to facilitate the gathering of detailed information about your prospects.

Note the philosophical relationship between database marketing and the USP, for there is a relationship in that in database marketing your sales appeal approaches individual customization, thus becoming unique.

REACHING THE RIGHT PROSPECTS

The purpose in identifying the markets you chose is simply to guide you in reaching your chosen prospects with your offer and sales appeals. My own experience in supporting the selling of custom training programs at the Educational Science Division of U.S. Industries, for example, taught me to seek out the marketing managers as prospects. It was apparent that it was the marketing managers in most corporations who were the most ready to listen to what we had to say. That was probably because marketing managers are usually under the greatest pressure in their organizations—have severe and continuous problems to solve—and are thus most receptive to the possibilities of help of any kind, including that of outside consultants offering their services.

The Internet offers a great many opportunities to learn who your best prospects are and how to reach them. Whether it is or is not the ideal marketing medium per se, it is certainly a most useful marketing research tool for independent consultants. You can do more market research in a day on the Internet than you can do in a week by other, older means. You can identify suitable periodicals, associations, corporations, institutions, and even entire industries of whose existence you may not have been aware. You can subscribe to online newsletters and mailing lists, and get a flood of information flowing in regularly. I spend a few minutes each morning reading my e-mail, which brings me that kind of daily input. Most of it I erase as quickly as I skim it, but I save some posts and record them elsewhere on my system; some I erase only after making a mental note of something useful I read there; and some I respond to immediately or save for response later. It requires perhaps a half hour of my time to read through perhaps 40 or more messages, less time than I spend on the morning newspaper. And I usually have at least one or two opportunities every week to respond to someone seeking help and requesting information about rates and services.

Aside from being enabled to actually submit an occasional bid or proposal, I accomplish two things in doing this every morning: I learn useful information for immediate or future use in marketing, even getting sales leads, and I respond to certain messages, thereby continuing to make myself visible, which leads ultimately to specific business opportunities. It is time well invested. Note, here, that I use the Internet as part of an overall marketing plan and fundamental strategy (that of promoting visibility and professional image), a part that leads me to use all marketing media more effectively than I otherwise would.

That brings up the use of the Internet to achieve indirect marketing objectives, such as the market research referred to. For example, let us suppose that you wish to advertise in some specific periodical, but know little about that periodical or how effective advertising in it would probably be. You may use the Internet in a number of ways to overcome that difficulty: You may make inquiries of others on some mailing list or similar forum, for one thing. Two of the lists I am on are for small publishers, and members of the lists are constantly advising others on their marketing experiences and recommending marketing resources and methods. But I subscribe also to forums for independent consultants, and the exchange of information on these forums is equally supportive of mutual interests in marketing consulting services. Too, a growing number of periodicals are installing online versions of their periodicals, some of them closely resembling the printed versions, and you can study these and even make inquiries or place advertising orders from your desk via the Web sites of the periodicals.

FOLLOWING UP AND CLOSING

Having made your offer and appeal, should you now wait for the prospect to say something that amounts to, "Yes, I like what you say. Where do I sign to take advantage of your offer?" Occasionally, you will meet the prospect who reacts just this way, a prospect who is so convinced by and eager to take advantage of your offer that he or she presses you to consummate the deal. That is the exceptional case. Most prospects for anything more costly than a bar of soap or can of soup are not quick to decision, to commitment to spend a significant amount of money. They want to think about things. And the longer they think, the less likely they are to order. You need to exercise initiative here, to retain control. The marketer who is not in control is in a losing position. You must always remain in control. And the thing to do at this point, when you have completed your sales presentation, is to close.

WHAT IS CLOSING?

"Closing," in a most general sense, means getting the order, and many people are not aware that it has also a much different meaning in sales techniques. To the expert sales technician, "closing" means *asking* for the order. In many sales situations, and especially in those where you are in pursuit of a big-tag sale—the typical sales situation in a business that is not a one-call business—you must close (ask for the order) many times before you win the order. Rarely does even the prospect who is convinced and ready to buy exercise much initiative, not even that of asking you where to sign. You, as the salesperson, must retain the initiative and remain in control.

There are two reasons for closing:

1. A surprisingly large number of people will not say, "I'll take it," or words to that effect, even if they are convinced they want the item. Asking for the order then impels them to agree to the purchase. Closing, in that case, is used to overcome the prospect's inertia.

2. When the prospect is silent, as a seller you do not know whether the prospect needs a prompt to consummate the purchase or is still hesitant and not yet sold. Closing is then a way of finding out whether it is time to stop talking and start writing (the order) or do more selling.

Asking for the order is a somewhat subtle process. You do not say something such as "May I have your order, Mr. Jones?" It's easy enough for Mr. Jones to say, "Wait a minute. Let me think about this," and it is quite likely he will demur in some manner, possibly in this way. But it is more likely that he will shake his head, say "No," or otherwise terminate the discussion quite definitely. You certainly do not want that. Classic sales wisdom is to avoid ever phrasing a close so that the answer can be yes or no.

HOW TO CLOSE

The way to close—to ask for the order—is, in an indirect way, one that does not invite a yes-no answer and cannot be answered that simply, but presumes the order. Here, for example, are a few possible ways to do that:

- Would the beginning of next month be all right to start, or do you need me to get started sooner, Mr. Jones?
- Would you prefer our agreement on my letterhead or your own?
- Shall I meet with your staff as a first step or shall I develop the detailed work plan for your approval first?
- Do you prefer oral or written progress reports?
- Is my proposed delivery date okay, or do you need the program sooner?

Each of these compels the prospect to specifically demur, if not ready to approve the order, and many prospects who are fence-sitting at this point will be encouraged to accept the order and focus on the question posed by the close. It requires a more thoughtful answer than yes or no, and that is to your advantage, for the purpose in the first close is not to get the order; it is likely that you will not on your first try. The purpose here is to determine whether it is time to stop talking and start writing, to gauge the prospect's attitude at this point. It is easy to oversell by talking too much and too long, and a great many sales are lost by salespeople who have never learned that there is a time to stop talking and start writing the order. Closing helps you find that time. The prospect's evasion of agreeing to the order is a sign: It tells you that the prospect still has doubts and needs to be sold some more. It is a prompt to ask the prospect if he or she has questions and offer to answer them. It also helps avoid the finality of a "no" from the prospect, and you want to leave the door open for more sales effort when you find the prospect still wavering. In any case, it furnishes a basis for continuing the sales effort, where you might otherwise feel compelled to abandon it.

ADAPTING TO THE INTERNET

Of course, selling via the Internet does not permit the spontaneity of face-to-face selling, but the principles are the same. They need to be adapted to Internet characteristics and limitations. Ultimately, we shall have to develop those marketing methods that will make maximum use of the Internet's capabilities. For now, we must still probe and experiment, adapting what we already know about selling via other media as best we can to online conditions. If you have been conducting all discussions with the prospect online, you will still have to close, probably several times, perhaps even many times, by e-mail. The strategy and technique are unchanged, even working online.

It may be that the Internet is not well suited for the endgame in selling. Perhaps the Internet is much more useful as a medium for market research and lead generation, with closing done in an offline follow-up. It may be that for some independent consultants or in certain kinds of situations, the right approach is to arrange to meet personally with the prospect, after getting the contact established firmly online. Or it may be that some but not all sales can be consummated via online communication and correspondence. Be aware of the possibilities and alternative actions required to meet each situation.

One thing that we can do on the Internet is to plant seeds for future business growth. In that respect, the Internet offers great and somewhat obvious opportunities. First of all, the existence of the Internet as a vast and efficient communications entity has already inspired certain developments that will almost certainly ultimately change the way we do business. Two important developments that will be instrumental in bringing this change about are CommerceNet and EDI, the Electronic Data Interchange. For now, these are used primarily by larger organizations, so their significance to most independent consultants is mostly a potential for the future.

COMMERCENET

CommerceNet, based in the Silicon Valley area of California, is a cooperative effort of a large number of companies and other organizations joined in a consortium to develop the commercial capabilities of the Internet for electronic commerce. The long-range objective is to develop efficient exchanges and activities among customers, suppliers, and others to improve efficiency and reduce the costs of doing business. There is no question that EDI represents a great boost in online facility for procurement, as well as for other activities, although much of the needed development is in the future. In the meanwhile, more than 100 commercial, educational, nonprofit, and government entities currently are members of CommerceNet, and the numbers are growing.

The goal is to promote the growth of a communications infrastructure and marketplace that will be open, easy to use, suited to commercial use, and readily expandable. Among the many activities of CommerceNet are these:

- Operating an Internet-based Web server with directories and information to facilitate business-to-business transactions
- Accelerating the mainstream application of electronic commerce on the Internet through fielding member-driven pilot projects focusing on transaction security, payment services, electronic catalogs, Internet EDI, engineering data transfer, and design-to-manufacturing integration

- Encouraging broad participation from small, medium, and large organizations and offering outreach programs to educate organizations about the resources and benefits available with Internet-based electronic commerce

The Internet-based electronic marketplace will support business services that have depended on paper-based transactions in the past. From their computers, buyers will be able to browse multimedia catalogs, solicit bids and quotations, and place orders. Sellers will be able to respond to bids, schedule production, and coordinate deliveries—even make deliveries, in some cases—electronically. New information services will spring up to bring buyers and sellers together. These services will include specialized directories, broker and referral services, vendor certification and credit reporting, network notaries and repositories, financial services, and transportation services. Many of these kinds of transactions and services already exist and occur electronically on the Internet and other online systems, but they require dedicated lines or prior arrangements and are not yet routine, fully automated systems, as they are destined to be eventually. The use of an Internet-based infrastructure will reduce the cost and lead time for participating in electronic commerce and make it as practical for the smallest business as it will for the large corporation or other organization of great size.

An immediate benefit of this electronic marketplace will be streamlined procurement through online catalogs, ordering and payment, and reduced costs through competitive bidding. (One difficulty that may arise, in connection with making exporting and importing products via the Internet—information products, that is—will be difficulty of governments in imposing and collecting relevant taxes and duties.)

EDI: ELECTRONIC DATA INTERCHANGE

Electronic data interchange (EDI) is defined generally as the electronic transfer of business documents between computers, but in a more sophisticated and more highly automated system than has been possible in the recent past. An increasing number of businesses choose EDI as a fast, inexpensive, and safe method of sending purchase orders, invoices, shipping notices, and other frequently used business documents.

EDI is different from e-mail or sharing files through networks, modems, and bulletin boards. Those transfers of computer files require that the computer applications of senders and receivers ("trading partners") agree upon—use the same—document format. The sender must therefore use an application that creates a file format identical to your computer application.

With EDI, that agreement is not necessary. The EDI translation software converts the proprietary format into an agreed-upon standard. When you receive the document, your EDI translation software automatically changes the standard format into the proprietary format of your document-processing software.

EDI is thus a cost- and time-saving system. With automatic transfer of information from computer to computer, there is no need to rekey information. With no data entry, the chance for error drops to near zero.

There are many other uses for EDI as well. Universities use EDI to exchange transcripts quickly. Auto manufacturers use EDI to transmit large, complex engineering designs created on specialized computers, and large multinational firms use EDI to communicate between locations, for example. One of my business acquaintances is a real estate consultant, specializing in appraisals, and he has found it necessary to replace his aging 386 computer with a larger one, a Pentium, because he needs greater computer capacity to use the EDI network in connection with his work.

DIRECT MARKETING ON THE INTERNET

Most of the marketing activity directed to consumers is marketing that urges the consumers to take a preliminary action, such as visiting a store or picking up a telephone. It is somewhat passive, compared with what is known generally as *direct marketing.* (It is also known as *direct response* and *direct mail,* because mail is by far the main medium for going directly to prospects, resulting in what many call junk mail, unfortunately.) Direct marketing does not wait for the customer to come to the seller, either physically or through some form of correspondence. Instead, the seller goes to the prospective customer by mail, by telephone, or by knocking on the door, figuratively and literally. That is traditional direct marketing, although direct marketing efforts have been expanded in modern times to include those on TV and radio, in which you are asked to call a number and place your order, to be charged to your credit card. The goods are then shipped to you, usually by a parcel delivery service.

Both marketing philosophies and practices are plainly apparent in the efforts of marketers on the Internet. Direct marketing roots are plainly apparent in the many marketing campaigns carried on directly and indirectly (by advertising and by publicity or PR campaigns) via e-mail, newsletters, mailing lists, and other approaches that send literature directly to lists of people, as in direct mail. Advertising via malls and other sites on the Web, on the other hand, is much more reminiscent of billboards, print advertising, radio-TV commercials, and retail store locations.

The bulk of the marketing presentations on the Internet are those appearing on the Web. In the beginning, they were little more than billboards, but they have rapidly become more sophisticated, utilizing the computer's capabilities for hypertext branching, color, and even motion and sound. The major difficulty is that of generating enough traffic—attracting people to the site in great enough numbers.

Direct marketing depends basically upon statistical probability, presenting sales appeals to such a great number of people that winning orders from even a tiny fraction of those addressed represents a viable sales volume. So far, that is most difficult to do on the Web. However, some merchants do practice a form of direct marketing on the Internet. Some use the online equivalent of junk mail by bombarding the e-mail boxes, creating the same problem as in conventional direct mail, with this difference: A relatively small percentage of those receiving junk mail via the conventional postal services complain to the mailers and demand that their names be removed from the mailing lists, but a relatively large number of those using e-mail object strenuously to receiving this stream of unsolicited e-mail. Bulk e-mailers have turned to various measures to lessen or soften the reactions of objectors by using an apologetic tone, starting the message with some such statement as, "I have reason to believe that you will be interested in this message," or "This is the only message you will receive from us," or promising a simple way to have the recipient's name removed permanently from the mailing list.

A somewhat less provocative way to do this is to supply a copy of or offer a free newsletter, which promises useful information and advertising. That, understandably, tends to arouse a less violent reaction than a stream of unabashed advertising hyperbole.

Although in general all direct marketing is based on addressing a great many prospects with your sales appeals, there are many variables involved, and one of them is the number of prospects and the rate of response to your appeals. That is, the size of the target population you need for success in a direct marketing campaign online (as elsewhere) depends on what you intend to sell, the size of your average order, your campaign costs, and the response rates you realize.

Response is a carefully chosen term, for it has a different meaning in different marketing situations and different direct marketing campaigns. For a direct-mail campaign aimed at selling some consumer item of moderate cost, "response rate" means number of orders received as a percentage of pieces of mail sent out. But the direct objective of a campaign is not always to get orders; it may be to elicit another kind of response, such as sales leads. If yours is a practice that requires lead generation and follow-up to close sales, as most consulting practices do, you need leads. You need to get responses that hold the promise of enough interest in what you sell or do to be worth following up. Thus, you may be seeking only some follow-up expression of interest from respondents, such as a request for a copy of some free report you offer. Having written or selected a report that would be likely to have appeal to those you think are the most likely prospects for your service, each response is a sales lead of at least some qualification: The respondent has demonstrated interest in something within your field of specialization and so is probably worth following up.

One of the great advantages of mass mailing via e-mail is that the cost per addressee is much less than via any other avenue on the Internet, much less, in fact, than via any other method of reaching a large number of prospects. With the relatively small target population you are usually limited to with a Web site, a 0.1 percent response rate is not going to produce a great many orders. If you manage to reach only 5,000 prospects, a 0.1 percent response will produce only five orders. Still, that may be more than enough to make the campaign quite satisfactory, if those are consulting assignments. It may be that even one or two assignments would make the promotion a great success for you, if those assignments are large enough and profitable enough.

That is one reason that, while many advertisers on the Internet are disappointed with the results, others are quite pleased. It is also the reason that direct marketing via a Web site may work very well for you as a consultant, if your assignments are large enough to be profitable at a small response rate, and you have a high conversion rate—converting your leads to contracts.

PLANTING YOUR SEEDS ON THE INTERNET

The Internet and the Web offer at least a half dozen ways to make yourself and the services you offer highly visible to all you can reach along these avenues. It may be that some of the ways will work better for you than others, so you may regard trying all the ways as part of your market research, seeking to find those that work best for you. It's not possible to predict which are the best ways, for all cases and all individuals: There are too many imponderables involved for that. (For example, you may find an online newsletter to be right up your alley, whereas you dislike chat groups.) It seems best to try all the ways that are available, and let experience tell you which are the right ways for you—which are the most effective ways to plant your seeds on the Internet. Some of the methods will cost you time and money; some will cost you time only. Here are the principal tools or options open to you, some of which we have already introduced and discussed briefly:

- Mailing lists
- E-mail
- Newsgroups
- Home pages
- Newsletters
- Chat groups

Mailing lists are one of the most effective ways of making yourself well known to other subscribers if you are an active participant and not a mere lurker. Each subscriber is sent a copy of every post, but many lists offer a digest format in which you get a periodical compilation of posts from others.

Some mailing lists are public, and anyone may subscribe to them. Others are restricted to certain users. One thing that is true for all is that the list is in ASCII format, because all e-mail must be in that plain-vanilla form. If you use a word processor to prepare messages for sending to a mailing list, you must either prepare it in ASCII format or convert it to ASCII before you send it.

The two most prominent mailing list programs or systems are Listserv and Majordomo, although you may encounter other systems, including private ones. Subscription to a public list is simple: It requires only an e-mail request (technically, it's a command) to the administrative address of the list. In most cases, you may leave the subject line of the e-mail form blank and in the message area you type the command as follows:

Subscribe [list name] [your name]

For example, to subscribe to a Listserv list named CONS-L you would address your request to LISTSERV@VM1.MCGILL.CA and in the message area (you may ignore the "SUBJECT" area, since the list-manager software does):

subscribe cons-l [your name]

Actually, using your name in the message is optional, since your post carries your e-mail address.

To post your own messages to the list, you use a different address. You send your own contributions to the list to this address:

CONS-L@VM1.MCGILL.CA

The latter is the list address, as distinct from the administrative address. You use the administrative address to issue commands. For example, if you decide that you do not wish to receive any more messages from the list, you may cancel your subscription by addressing that administrative address again with the command in the body of the message: unsubscribe cons-l. Following is a small portion of a list so gathered, reproduced here exactly as reported:

- AMODLMKT Applied Modeling Issues in Marketing: mail the command info AMODLMKT to LISTSERV@UMSLVMA.UMSL.EDU
- BA315 BA315-MARKETING MANAGEMENT: mail the command info BA315 to LISTSERV@UMSLVMA.UMSL.EDU
- bcmarket-l Business and computing faculty marketing committee: mail the command information m-l to listproc@scu.edu.au
- bus_marketing "Coll Bus Marketing Faculty": mail the command information us_marketing to listpro
- bus_marketing "Coll Bus Marketing Faculty": mail the command information us_marketing to listproc@lists.Colorado.EDU

By now it should be apparent that e-mail is almost a universal solvent in marketing on the Internet. It is the major means for publishing newsletters, propagating the messages on mailing lists, providing a direct feedback link for communications between Web advertisers and respondents, delivering many electronic publications, and even transferring funds to pay for purchases.

E-mail is thus all but indispensable in online functioning generally and in online marketing. One basic principle in marketing is to make it as easy as possible for the customer to order or respond otherwise. That is why so many advertisements in magazines include postage-paid cards and simple checkoff items to place orders, for example. If a customer must go to even a little trouble to place an order, he or she is likely to procrastinate, and that often means that the order is never placed. The equivalent of that postage-paid card or envelope online is an e-mail form that can be used directly at the Web site to send an order or inquiry to the advertiser.

CHAPTER 5

Tactics and Strategies for Networking on the Internet

It is not practicable, and probably not even possible, to choose any single best method for all marketing on the Internet—even for some given profession, such as consulting. The best method is always one that best fits the individual situation. Marketing is an art, especially in the consulting field, where most, if not all, work is custom work that is carefully designed to fit the need. Many strategies and tactics are possible. Each need and each situation must be judged individually. As always, and especially where art, rather than science, is required, marketing requires *empathy,* the ability to understand your typical prospects' perceptions and desires, and thereby choose the right strategies and tactics for each case, whether you are addressing a market and developing leads or following a given lead and addressing a specific prospect.

This is a philosophy that is dictated by the nature of the medium, namely because you cannot address a truly mass audience here, where you could afford to miss a large portion of the market because you need to glean only a tiny percentage of it. In most situations in marketing on the Internet, you must deal with your audience on almost an individual basis.

PRACTICAL CONSIDERATIONS

There is no doubt that networking in one form or another is still a prime method for marketing professional services for most independent practitioners, despite some exceptions. Even if you limit yourself to networking as your sole or principal marketing activity, you are likely to find the opportunities to do so on the Internet and the World Wide Web to be too abundant and diverse to be able to take advantage of all of them. The Internet is a cornucopia of contact opportunities of all kinds and is fertile ground for imaginative strategies and tactics. There are ample opportunities for innovation; a resourceful marketer need never be at a loss for something to do next, especially if he or she has a talent for public relations or has some able and aggressive public relations specialist available.

THE ONLINE SOCIETY

In many ways, the Internet resembles a traditional community or, at least, the town hall of a traditional community. There are similarities, but there are also differences. The main cement that binds the members of the traditional small town or neighborhood together is physical proximity and common interests. In cyberspace, there is a different kind of proximity, resulting from ongoing communication with each other and common online interests. It may include a sharing of business interests, of political persuasions, of children and their problems, or of many other concerns that neighbors do not usually discuss in chance encounters on the street. The Main Streets or town halls of these online towns are the communications channels (newsgroups and mailing lists, for example) where the town inhabitants meet each other and chat, exchanging ideas and opinions and even doing business together. In the relative privacy and anonymity of online correspondence, we tend to be a little less guarded about many subjects that we would not discuss face to face with relative strangers. It is from these kinds of discussions that online personalities emerge and relationships are formed.

DEVELOPING YOUR PROFESSIONAL IMAGE ONLINE

Earlier, I prescribed two elements necessary to successful networking, actually the two prime *objectives* of networking: high visibility and prestigious professional image. Respect for your abilities and integrity is a must for you as a consultant, of course, but there is a third element that is also highly important: It is your personal image or persona, your personality as perceived by others. Important as it is to be respected professionally, a large part of success in networking—in marketing and business in general, for that matter—depends on being well liked personally. It is a factor that helps greatly in selling anything and is all but indispensable to the successful marketing of consulting services.

People are far more likely to buy from those they like. And while being well liked personally is in itself an important asset, it is also an important contributor to your professional image. Prospective clients, consciously or unconsciously, tend to place their trust in those they like, as they tend also to mistrust those they do not like or even those about whom they feel nothing but indifference.

I observed this quite clearly many years ago, when I was employed in an organization devoted to servicing the Magnavox television receivers, then a carriage-trade product. It was soon obvious that the most frequent complaints of dissatisfaction from customers, with frequent demands to send a service technician back to make some further adjustment, were from customers whose sets had been serviced by our less diplomatic and less outgoing technicians. The customers' confidence in and satisfaction with what the technician had done was obviously in direct proportion to how well they liked the technician, to his "bedside manner." The more congenial, friendly service technicians had fewer callbacks than did the other technicians. In fact, many customers felt so strongly about this that they requested that we send back another technician than the original one, whom, the customer was sure, "didn't know what he was doing," although we knew the technician to be entirely competent. Even the most calm and composed individual tends to be influenced heavily by emotions, even with deliberate efforts to be objective. This plays a role in business relationships, as it does in personal ones.

Despite the physical separation between correspondents on the Internet and the fact of relative anonymity, personalities do emerge in ongoing correspondence, and individuals do get to know each other and develop strong impressions. Online correspondence with someone in California (I am on the east coast) resulted in an ongoing relationship from which I have profited substantially, but it is only one of many such happenings. In the past few days I have received orders from a client in Canada and another in Germany, both from online contacts, and I have responded to initial inquiries from prospective clients in Portugal, India, and Dubai. You develop a personality and image in online correspondence that are as firmly established and as important as are your personality and image emerging from face-to-face relationships. That image can be a valuable business asset for marketing your services.

Among the chief ways to develop your image as a highly competent professional is to be an active participant in online events. It is time-consuming, but so is any effective marketing, and the major investments of your time will be early on and can decline later, once you are well established and busy taking care of your new clients. Being an active participant means giving of yourself, entering into the discussions enthusiastically with well-reasoned arguments and opinions, and offering complete rationales for those arguments and opinions. Try sincerely to be as helpful as you can—to answer others' questions and respond to their conversational gambits. Do this honestly, but diplomatically. Some people feel free to be painfully blunt and even tactless in the isolation of online correspondence. It is not a good idea, if you value your reputation and image. Your consistent sincerity will shine through, just as consistent insincerity does. Others are quick to detect brush-offs and elitism, and such things will not earn you any new friends, let alone new clients.

At the same time, try to be relatively low-key. Being highly visible and yet low-key is not an oxymoron. It is possible to do so. Discriminate between fact and opinion, between making it clear that you are offering your opinion only and believing what you say to be fact. Being vociferous may be taken as dogmatism, which can lead easily to injured feelings. Even when you are stating a verifiable fact, try to cite the source whenever possible and avoid sounding overly emphatic, again to avoid coming across as being highly dogmatic. If you are stating an opinion, make it clear that you are expressing an opinion.

That latter is especially important. You should be at pains to be as objective as possible in your statements and never overbearingly positive. You will encounter a few of the dogmatic, know-it-all types, of course; almost every group has one or two of that kind. Among the many adjectives that apply to their behavior are loud, vociferous, positive, sneering, patronizing, contemptuous, and condescending. Of course, this does not win them many friends, and you must take care to avoid exhibiting any such attitudes as these. You can avoid these by being objective and always careful to make it clear that when you are not supplying verifiable fact, you are expressing an opinion that may or may not be supported by the opinions of others. You will also further your image by remembering that you are trying to help others and not trying to show off how much you know or how wise you are. And, in keeping with that, try to have and show sincere respect for the contributions of others. That is very much bread on the waters: Respect for others breeds respect for you.

Only recently, on a mailing list I happen to sponsor, one participant managed to arouse a little acrimony (including several private messages of complaint to me from others) by being rather assertive in his statements. His statements were correct and the opinions he expressed well-founded, but his overly positive tone alienated others. By explaining this to him diplomatically in a private message and asking for his help, I managed to pour oil on the waters and the trouble has been put to rest. (In fact, the gentleman thanked me for alerting him to the problem and suggesting the cure.)

SCHMOOZING

Schmoozing is a word with many meanings and nuances, but in general it defines friendly, even intimate, conversation. But it also has an extended connotation, wherein it refers to stroking another, becoming overtly friendly, using great tact and diplomacy and even flattery to persuade and win others over. It is therefore an appropriate term to describe a general approach to networking effectively. Schmoozing is very much a part of networking, and skill in the art of schmoozing can carry you a long way along the road to productive and profitable online relationships in all kinds of groups and correspondence.

NEWSGROUPS

Newsgroups on the Internet number in the thousands, with many new ones being added almost daily, although many are short-lived, while the numbers of mailing lists, newsletters, Web sites, and other activities are also increasing steadily. (You can subscribe to the mailing list NEW-LIST@LISTSERV.NODAK.EDU to receive regular announcements of new mailing lists and newsletters to which you can subscribe. To subscribe to this mailing list, NEW LISTS, simply send an e-mail to LISTSERV@ LISTSERV.NODAK.EDU with the line SUB NEW-LIST, your first name, and your last name in the body of the e-mail. You can learn of the existence of new newsgroups by calling for a list as an option of most newsreader software.) Admittedly, a great many newsgroups are frivolous, have few subscribers, and are soon abandoned, but many are serious and well attended, addressing an almost infinite number and variety of subjects. Following is a small sample, and Exhibit 5-1 presents a screen of several newsgroups with misc.jobs.contract selected for reading. Follow-

Exhibit 5-1

LISTING OF MISC.JOBS.CONTRACT NEWSGROUP

Trumpet News Reader - [News]	
File Edit Special Group Article View Window Help	
US-MO St. Louis ORACLE developers, by R.Jones, 6 Oct 1995 02:40:59 GMT	401 of 948

bit.listserv.techwr-l	biz.marketplace.services.non-computer
biz.comp.services	biz.misc
biz.general	misc.business.consulting
biz.marketplace.discussion	misc.jobs.contract
biz.marketplace.non-computer	misc.writing
biz.marketplace.services.discussion	

Transtech, Inc.	US-IL-Chicago +++> Oracle SQL*Forms, Pro*C
NTES Jobs	US-CA Programmer Analysts - AS400 RP6, Learn JD Edw
KENDA Systems, Inc. - NY Office	U.S.NY.NYC Oracle DBA under Solaris [KENDA Systems
Ategra [Recruiter]	US-ALL Powerbuilder Client/Server Developer
Ategra [Recruiter]	US-MO-ST LOUIS DB/2 DB2 DBA's & Developers, Progra
NTES Jobs	US-CA Project Manager - 15+ years experience Refinerie
Kam Makhani	US-CA-SAN FRANSISCO- PROGRAMMER/ANALYST
Chancellor & Chancellor	Statistician, Los Angeles or San Francisco Bay, CA — ag
Chancellor & Chancellor	$4/hr Third Party Passthru (tm) for Contractors
Chancellor & Chancellor	Unix/C++/C Windows NT Client Server Engineer, Oaklan
R.Jones	US-MO St. Louis ORACLE developers

<<	>>	View/list	Format	Skip all	Post	Follow
Reply	Archive	Extract				

ing that is a list of newsgroup names to illustrate how specialized many of them are.

alt.a-monkey.cute	alt.anonymous.messages
alt.abortion	alt.art.pyrotechnics
alt.abortion.inequity	alt.art.scene
alt.abuse-recovery	alt.art.theft.scream.scream.scream
alt.abuse.offender.recovery	alt.asylum.netcop.wannabe
alt.abuse.recovery	alt.atari-jaguar.discussion
alt.activism.death-penalty	alt.atari.2600
alt.actor.dustin-hoffman	alt.babylon5.uk
alt.adjective.noun.verb	alt.bacchus
.verb.verb	alt.backrubs
alt.adopt.latvian.babies	alt.bad.clams
alt.adoption	alt.badgers.rose.rose.rose
alt.agriculture.misc	alt.bbs.internet
alt.agriculture.ratite	alt.bbs.lists
alt.airline.class.action.lawsuit	alt.bbs.lists.d
alt.airline.schedules	alt.beer.like-molson-eh
alt.alcohol	alt.belvoir
alt.aldus.freehand	alt.beneficent.daemons.bless
alt.aldus.misc	.curse.bless
alt.aldus.pagemaker	alt.beograd
alt.algebra.help	alt.bermuda.triangle.billing
alt.alien.research	alt.best.of.internet
alt.alien.visitors	alt.bible.prophecy
alt.animals.badgers	alt.bigfoot
alt.animals.bears	alt.bigfoot.die.die.die
alt.animals.dolphins	alt.bigfoot.research
alt.animals.felines	alt.bin.pictures.child.pornography
alt.animals.felines.lions	alt.binaries.autographs
alt.anonymous	alt.binaries.bbs.pcboard

As noted earlier, in most newsgroups, blatant advertising is a no-no. But a few are devoted to advertising such as the one illustrated in Exhibit 5-2.

Newsgroups appear to be patterned physically on the model established by the BBSs—electronic bulletin board systems—that were so pop-

Exhibit 5-2

ALT.BUSINESS.SEMINARS, A NEWSGROUP THAT IS AN ADVERTISER'S HAVEN (OR SHOULD THAT BE HEAVEN?)

```
┌─────────────────────────────────────────────────────────────┐
│                Trumpet News Reader - [News]                  │
│  File  Edit  Special  Group  Article  View  Window  Help     │
│  Seasoned Senior Exec. for Rent, by GeneStiuka, 6 Oct 1995 17:37:47 -0400    4 of 24 │
│  alt.building.jobs              alt.journalism.moderated     │
│  alt.business                  bit.listserv.techwr-l         │
│  alt.business.home.pc          biz.comp.services             │
│  alt.business.misc             biz.general                   │
│  alt.business.seminars         biz.marketplace.discussion    │
│  alt.journalism.freelance      biz.marketplace.non-computer  │
│                                                              │
│  Hugh Bryan                  ===>>> Free Lucrative Home Based Business <<<=== │
│  us000056@interramp.com      <<<<CHECK THIS OUT>>>>          │
│  Chris Boyd                  FREE sign up - The Best Opportunity in the U.S. │
│ ►GeneStiuka                  Seasoned Senior Exec. for Rent  │
│  Wally Glenn                 Re: ----->Fast Cash In A Flash<----- │
│  make money                  try me its easy$$$$$            │
│  **PAGERS**@dial156.concom.com Dallas to New York in 30 seconds │
│  Bernardo Brummer            Re: WANTED: Evaluators for a High Tech Turnkey Busin │
│  thbn@empnet.com             Ground Floor Opportunity in Australia │
│  amsi@wi.net                 SuccessSaver                    │
│  Marilyn J Carter            MLM Seminar - Eugene, Oregon USA │
│                                                              │
│  [  <<  ] [  >>  ] [ View/list ] [ Format ] [ Skip all ] [ Post ] [ Follow ] │
│  [ Reply ] [ Archive ] [ Extract ]                          │
└─────────────────────────────────────────────────────────────┘
```

ular and ubiquitous before the Internet appeared on the scene and began to dominate the online (cyberspace) world. (BBSs exist in great quantity yet, but many former BBS devotees have abandoned them in favor of the Internet.) Yet, despite some physical similarity, the newsgroup has somehow never achieved quite the degree of intimacy and sense of community that characterized so many BBS discussion groups and message exchanges (although many mailing lists do appear to have recreated that environment or something close to it). Most newsgroups have a somewhat impersonal aura about their exchanges of messages and online personalities, and show little sense of community. The typical participant does not find it easy to get a sense of belonging, as he or she may more easily do in a mailing list. Still, many newsgroups are quite active with enthusiastic contributors and can therefore serve a useful purpose in your networking.

Once you have found groups you believe to be right for your purposes—that is, are active and attended by those who seem to be good prospects for your services—you should become a "regular" in the discussions. Most important, you can earn special attention and respect by offering answers to those asking questions and showing sincere interest in the group. Many subscribing to these groups are individuals seeking help. The more you offer here, the larger you loom as an expert. Make it clear that your response is based on a partial grasp of the idea and is probably not a full answer. That would require a formal study, analysis, and synthesis. The latter, expressed with great tact, is the commercial message that you can deliver without drawing an antagonistic response.

An alternative is to make only a cursory response in an open message to the group, but make a far more detailed, personal off-list response to the individual who posted the query, using the e-mail option. There, you may be as commercial as you wish, since it is a direct communication to an individual. You can expand on your public response as much as you wish and invite further direct correspondence with the individual, whom you have begun to convert from a general prospect into a serious sales lead. You can soon estimate how much time and effort to devote to this by estimating how serious a prospect this is—that is, by qualifying the prospect.

Overall, this is a most efficient way to find serious sales leads and follow them up to qualify them and decide how much effort to put into efforts to close them. The advantage is that it is so easy and inexpensive compared with conventional methods.

MAILING LISTS

Many newsgroups have matching mailing lists, which are discussion groups that meet via e-mail. The newsgroup bit.listserv techwr-l, a newsgroup of technical writers, has a corresponding mailing list, TECHWR-L@LISTSERV.OKSTATE.EDU. The Publishers Marketing Association Forum <PMA-L@SHRSYS.HSLC.ORG> is an unusually busy mailing list that can be reached via the address LISTSERV@hslc.org with a request to subscribe. The mailing list is supplemented with a newsgroup, alt.publish.books. Another example is the home page http://www.govsolutions.com, covering the subject of proposals for government contracts, with the complementary mailing list Proposal-l@ari.net.

A few of the participants in these groups are also lecturers, consultants, publishers, and writers. Public speaking, consulting, publishing, and writing are career activities that are often companion activities. As a consultant with services to offer, it may be helpful to you to learn that these lists appeal to a number of specialists who have direct or indirect interests in writing and publishing. If you are a consultant who also lectures and writes, you should be interested in these other sites, newsgroups, and mailing lists. But even this does not cover all the possible fields of your interests as a consultant. There are also the subject-matter fields, and the diversity of professional activities is indicative of many fields.

If yours is a consultancy connected with computers, for example, your interests may be linked with any whose specialties are in any way connected with computers, such as schoolteachers, mathematicians, publishers, engineers, or physicians. Too, as a consultant, your own activity may be principally advising, practicing your craft on a client's site, lecturing, or some combination of these skills and activities, as my own are. In fact, you may or may not identify what you do as consulting, even if it is an activity that others offer as a consulting service.

This kind of consulting diversity may be true for the members of any list, such as that for proposal writers. While many subscribers to this list are proposal writers and managers on corporate staffs, there are also many freelance proposal writers, consultants, and assorted vendors who offer proposal-writing support services on the list. The publishers mailing list produces at least 30 to 50 posts each day and at least twice that on many days, but the proposal writers list is spasmodic: It may deposit a dozen posts in my electronic mailbox on some days, and then none at all for a number of days. But then some mailing lists start with a torrent of activity, which then slows to a trickle. A mailing list I sponsor for freelance writers, scribe (scribe-list-request@bellicose.com), surged with messages initially and then slowed to some activity every day, but also exhibits relative lulls and great spurts of activity, in what appears to be a random, unpredictable pattern, possibly linked to how busy the subscribers are with their writing activities at any particular time.

NETWORKING TACTICS

The newsgroups and mailing lists thus represent a great many kinds of prospects and potential business opportunities. Were I a publishing consultant of some sort, such as a publicist or a specialist in marketing books, that mailing list of small publishers would represent an excellent market target. But I am a writer of books and a contract writer, with a general interest in book publishing, selling to the mainstream publishers who can afford to pay substantial advances against royalties, so I am not trying to win book contracts from others on this list: I do not solicit book contracts there, directly or indirectly, although my signature file reveals that I do ghost for others and supply writing services in general. I have therefore had more than one inquiry into the availability of my writing services to support small publishers in producing brochures and other literature, which is the kind of business I seek as a result of my networking on these online channels of communication.

Since the small publishers mailing list (PMA, or Publishers Marketing Association forum) is the one in which I am most active and is the busiest one of all that I frequent, I will use it for examples, but the examples illustrate principles that apply to all such cases in both mailing lists and newsgroups, since both classes of communication are exchanges among the subscribers.

ABOUT "GIVING THE STORE AWAY"

A large number of the posts in the PMA mailing list are inquiries from individuals, asking for information from others in the same business and reporting their own experiences. (That is typical of all such lists and newsgroups.) If prospecting for sales was my objective here, I would be offering assistance to all on the list and answering as many questions as possible. (I do answer those to whom I think I have something useful or even some wisdom to impart, but only then.) Some consultants object to doing this, saying that a consultant cannot afford to give even a little information away freely. They call that "giving the store away," or giving away that which they have to sell.

I believe that is shortsighted and self-defeating. My experience has been that my principal activities as a consultant have been providing services, ideas, and hands-on know-how, even more than information. I have found that expert services per se are the principal benefit the client seeks *and pays for* in most cases. My advice may be welcomed, but it is my service that is most desired and most justifiably the basis for my fees, in the client's opinion. No matter how much information and how many ideas I conjure up and offer freely to any and all who inquire, my clients want my *doing* skills even more than they want any information I can provide. I can tell them everything I know and explain how I do what I do, and yet my clients would not be able to do what I do. I can improve their writing and even their sense of what works and does not work in any given marketing situation, but I cannot give them my ability to analyze situations and devise strategies, for I do not know myself just how I do it! I therefore am not really giving much away by being frank and open with what I know. (And even if I am giving something away, I am getting back much more than I gave away.)

There is another side to this: The "samples" you give away are elements of the "proof" in the proof-and-promise concept, bearing evidence of your skill and knowledge. Therefore, giving away some useful information and ideas in a mailing list or newsgroup discussion is giving away samples of the less important items of my services. (Do not major corporations give free samples of their products and services?) Freely giving away those samples results in more than one adequate compensation:

- It draws attention to you and gains prominence in the group for you, raising your visibility, as the specialist you are.
- It indicates your goodwill and good intentions, and earns you the appreciation of others.
- It suggests strongly that you are not motivated entirely by money, but are driven to do what your professional integrity motivates you to do.
- It demonstrates effectively what you can do to help your clients as their consultant, generating confidence in you and in your professional abilities.
- It lends you prestige overall as a sage in general and a fair-minded provider of support services.
- Finally, and certainly a not inconsequential benefit, is the boost such generosity gives to related activities and interests you may have. If you have written a book or two, or you offer seminars or formal classes, you can promote them effectively here by quoting from them, while adding to your own prominence and reputation. In con-

sulting, most related activities are mutually supporting or can be made so.

CHOOSING GROUPS AND LISTS

There are so many newsgroups and mailing lists already in existence that it is quickly obvious that you cannot find time for more than a relative handful of them, if you are to get any consulting work done. You need to think things out in choosing the newsgroups and mailing lists to frequent for networking and prospecting purposes. It's easy to make snap judgments, which are likely to be wrong and lead to wasting your time, if you do not search carefully beneath the surface.

I set out to provide to my paying clients one of the services I had for years provided for my employers: proposal writing that wins contracts. The expertise on which I based my consulting practice was in knowing the government market, winning government contracts, and, especially, in my marketing sense and professional proposal-writing skills as the main tool. I had long ago become convinced that strategies made the difference between the winning proposals and the also-rans, and I worked hard at devising strategies each time I undertook to write a new proposal. That strategy was always based on a USP of my own, although I had not yet begun to identify my special strategic approaches by that term. I devised USPs for the proposed program itself, much of the time, but I found cases in which a USP for the presentation was equally effective in commanding the client's full attention and winning the contract. For example, in a number of cases the requirement was so complex and so poorly explained in the Request for Proposals that I was forced to invest a major amount of time in devising charts that would enable me to understand the requirement and devise a solution. That done, it became sensible to use the charts to explain the program I proposed. The client, finding his or her own understanding of the project greatly enhanced, was impressed enough to select the proposals for award. The charts were thus presentation USPs.

Thus, it might at first appear that the right group for me on which to focus my marketing efforts would be that group devoted to proposal writing, which was introduced earlier. Would not prospective clients who wanted proposal help search out such a group?

Studying the audience in that group would soon disillusion me from any belief that they might be good prospects simply because they are engaged in proposal writing. They are themselves staff proposal writers, for the most part. Pursuing them might produce an occasional new client, probably when their own teams were overloaded and needed some extra help, but there are at least two reasons why relying on that group as a major market target for my services would be a mistake:

- The majority of those members of the group are staff proposal writers, rather than the managers and marketing executives of their organizations, and so would not be those most likely to have either the authority to award contracts or the tendency to go outside their own organizations for proposal-writing help. Quite the contrary, they would resist this as a perceived threat to their own positions represented by hiring proposal specialists under contract. (Experience verifies that this is a typical problem when working on a client's site alongside the regular staff: The staff tends almost always to regard the outside consultant as an insult, if not actually a threat.)
- The proposal-writing group's activity is sporadic, busy on some days and totally dormant for lengthy periods. Occasionally, some item or question raised by one of the subscribers to the list strikes a nerve and provokes some lively discussion for a day or two, but that is usually short-lived activity. Even if the participants were the executives and managers who hired or were responsible for hiring consultants, I would not be reaching them with consistency or frequency via these lists. Regularity and consistency of appearance are important factors—musts, in raising and maintaining a high degree of visibility for marketing purposes. In general, an appeal is increasingly effective when it has sunk into a prospect's consciousness through prolonged repetition. Choose groups that are consistently busy if you want to maintain that visibility.

This illustrates the need to analyze each situation (marketing is art as well as method, perhaps even more art than method), requiring careful analysis and measured judgment to reach maximum results. Reading the mail in that newsgroup and contributing to it occasionally are worthwhile activities in general, but they are a backwater in their possible contribution to my marketing. They are not likely to produce more than an occasional lead of value.

My activity in a busy technical writers newsgroup and mailing list is also of limited value as a marketing asset because the situation here is similar to that of the proposal-writing group: Many do write proposals, but most are staff employees, freelance technical writers, and suppliers, and are thus of only indirect value to me for marketing purposes. They have some indirect marketing value, as sources of information—marketing intelligence that may have some usefulness occasionally in pursuing leads—but that is largely chance and thus cannot really be assigned any figure of merit. Again, I might occasionally be called upon to help out an overloaded staff on a proposal project, but that is the likely extent of business to be culled from active participation in the group.

In short, then, you need to seek out the newsgroups and mailing lists subscribed to and attended by those who are most likely to hire consultants or, at least, find the idea of using consulting help an attractive one. In my case, it is the executives whose responsibilities include winning contracts—directors of marketing in large organizations and general executives wearing several hats in smaller organizations—whom I need to reach with my appeals.

That brings up another significant point in re marketing strategy: What are the organizations, as well as the individuals in the organization, on whom I wish to focus as market targets? If they are large organizations, I pursue those executives identified formally as managers, directors, or vice presidents of marketing. If they are smaller organizations or not-for-profit organizations, such as associations, labor unions, and government agencies, my targets will be the general top executives, perhaps the CEO (chief executive officer) or other top dog on Mahogany Row.

Aside from size, what are the characteristics of the prospects I think to be my best possibilities as future clients: Apparel manufacturers? Electronics developers? Drug wholesalers? Construction firms? Government agencies? Insurance agents? Software publishers? Trade associations? Professional societies? Restaurant chains? Banks?

The list could go on interminably, of course. Moreover, the permutations of kinds of industry, sizes of organizations, and other parameters for classifying prospects multiply the lists almost beyond imagination. Still, there must be a basis for choice, or you will grope blindly.

You will start (or have started) your consulting practice with certain assumptions that seem sound enough as premises, but probably they will prove to be less than completely accurate. Before long—probably in the first year—you will find yourself changing those premises according to your growing experience, as I was. Business histories are full of cases showing how companies gradually develop their businesses along different lines from the ones they adopted at the beginning. Be prepared always to adjust your concepts to the facts on the ground. They may lead you to places you never had in mind when you started. An amazingly large number of today's companies are in businesses that are entirely different from those in which they started. The giant Marriott hotel chain, for example, started in Washington, D.C. in 1927 as a root beer stand, but that is only one of many such stories.

The first consideration in marketing must always be given to that which leads most directly to the sale, the direct or primary lead. "Institutional advertising" and promotion, in which the advertiser is simply building an image and not even trying to provoke direct sales—Hughes Aircraft or IBM advertising in *Time* magazine, for example—have their place, but only for the large corporation and not for the independent consultant, who has a similar objective (image building and visibility raising), but cannot afford expensive advertising to achieve that objective. As an independent practitioner, you are probably always striving for the next sale as the direct objective of your marketing. Your paid advertising and promotion must thus be directed as much as possible to turning up specific leads, with building your image and visibility as important but secondary advertising activities and objectives.

Thus you should have and use a set of criteria to help you select the most promising forums to attend and in which to be an active participant. These should perform a function similar to that of qualifying a prospect: to qualify the group, newsgroup, mailing list, or other as one that represents a true market target for you. Here is a suggested set of six major criteria to consider in judging the suitability to your needs of the forum represented:

1. The main interest addressed by the group is completely compatible with the services you offer: Participants in the group are the kinds of clients you normally contract with, and the content of the discus-

sions addresses the typical kinds of client problems or needs your service responds to and supports.

2. A major portion of those participating actively in the group are the shakers and movers—managers and executives who have the capability to retain you and your services, with the authority to issue purchase orders and award contracts. (In some cases, the individuals may not have that direct authority personally, but are in such positions that they are able to influence and inspire the issuance of purchase orders and award of contracts.)

3. There is enough daily or weekly regular activity in the group so that you have ample opportunities to participate regularly and establish, reinforce, and maintain your presence in the group as a whole and in your contacts with the others of the group.

4. There are other consultants and vendors pursuing the same ends in this group, and doing so regularly. (The existence of some competition is a positive indicator, not a negative one, since it demonstrates that the group constitutes a market; the lack of competition suggests the reverse.)

5. You are comfortable with the volume of message traffic and the subjects discussed. You find ample opportunity to make your own contributions to the discussions and win recognition in the group.

6. You get encouraging results, such as leads and interested responses to your posts within a reasonable time and with reasonable frequency.

Items 1 and 2 do not need much elaboration beyond that which was said earlier, that the group or list must address the interest of those who would be the logical prospects for your services, well qualified to become clients.

Item 3 requires only brief comment, to wit: If the group's activity is irregular, treat it as a minor target, to be attended only when and if you have time to spare. You need to conduct marketing activity regularly, not spasmodically, so always give priority to the group that is doing something and interacting on a daily basis.

Item 4 may surprise you, since it encourages you to go where there is ample competition, direct or indirect, but the logic is plain: If there is no competition—that is, the activity has not attracted many others who wish to sell their services—it suggests that the target is not a very attractive one. (We assume that our competitors are as alert, as bright, and as hungry as we are.) It needs then to be scrutinized closely and with skepticism. Your competitors are not stupid. If they ignore a market possibility, it is because they do not perceive the possibility as a good one. Still, it is always possible that you know/have learned something about this market that no one else has yet learned, something that makes this market much more attractive than it appeared to be at first glance. After all, there is always someone who is first, and it could be you.

Item 5 is important. I have sojourned briefly in groups that appeared to be directed to some significant interest, but found the messages rarely useful for my purposes, often consisting of little more than gossip, jesting, and sounding off, rather than serious discussions. Don't waste time in such groups. Examine them closely, judge them critically, and act decisively to move on if they are not right for you.

Item 6 is the acid test. Even if and when all appears to be just right, in the end, the target may prove to be disappointing. If, after a reasonable effort, you get no worthwhile results—not even a few good leads or expressions of interest—it may very well be that you are wasting your time, despite your checklist and the early appearance of the target. Continue to look for other, better targets: The supply of candidates is almost endless. In most cases, the array of possible opportunities is quite great, and the problem is often deciding which represent the best opportunities. There are probably many more possible targets than you can cover, so you can afford to be and should be highly critical in choosing the most suitable ones.

GROUP RELATIONSHIPS AND IMAGE

Establishing friendly relationships with the greatest number of potential prospects is one giant step forward in establishing an image of professional competence and integrity. Both are critical to laying a foundation for a future business relationship. In BBSs—electronic bulletin board systems—and commercial online systems, such as CompuServe, America Online, and Prodigy, the forums are a principal attraction. They tend to become friendly "town meetings," with a great many humorous observations and good-natured jabs at each other as individual personalities emerge, despite the lack of face-to-face meeting and knowing what others look like physically. It's something of a phenomenon how well online pen pals come to know each other and how many firm friendships spring up between and among people who have met only in the relative isolation of conventional mail and e-mail. (Even marriages have resulted.)

There is another side to that coin: Sharp disagreements sometimes arise, and tempers flare, resulting in "flaming" others. Be cautious and try to perceive such problems arising before you get embroiled in them. They are not only distractions from your purposes, but are actually harmful to your image. Even when you believe that you are entirely justified in engaging in sharp exchanges, they make you appear to be disagreeable and argumentative to observers. Try to recognize immediately that such conflicts are emotional, not rational, and the only way to "win" is by avoiding such confrontations or, if you somehow do get drawn into one, withdrawing as soon as you recognize that you are in one of those situations.

CHOOSING/DEVELOPING A MARKETING STRATEGY

I have been pressing on you the overall strategy of building your image and visibility, while you seek leads by looking in all the right places. However, you need to concentrate on more direct, more narrowly focused substrategies as the means to accomplish this. The sheer size of the Internet, in terms of its many activities, as well as its millions of "citizens" (referred to by some as "netizens") is itself a problem in choosing or devising substrategies for marketing yourself: The Internet is a great encyclopedia that accepts and records inputs from just about anyone who can master the intricacies of uploading and downloading information, which is really no great feat. In one way, it is a means for gaining your promised 15 minutes of fame, as you would if you appeared on one of the more prominent talk shows aired nationally. That fame is fleeting, with many others waiting to replace you to gain their own 15 minutes of worldwide recognition. So it is not enough to gain that fleeting fame, not nearly enough: You must be like that entertainer who strives to leave the audience wanting more, even beyond the encore. You must find some means to perpetuate your appeal, to make that fame shine brilliantly every day thereafter and make the world—that is, that part of the world with which you are concerned, your prospects—remember you. There is the major challenge. That is what marketing is really all about: not just today's sale but tomorrow's market of clients who will return again and again and spread the good word of you and your services to others. In broad terms, the many newsgroups and mailing lists are probably the most abundant and most readily available means for making your name and messages known to prospective clients. However, there is another avenue that offers opportunities to do this on perhaps a more effective basis. That is the opportunity to publish your ideas on the Internet, so that you offer them to many readers, rather than only a few.

PUBLISHING ON THE INTERNET

The most prominent and numerous online business publications are the newsletters, many published by individuals. Some are published as profit-making ventures in themselves, for which a subscription fee is charged and/or commercial advertising space is sold. But a great many other newsletters are free to subscribers and published as a means of marketing the publisher's own services or other business ventures. (A few are focused on drawing their readers to the publisher's Web site, and readers are enjoined to visit the site.) That idea, a promotional newsletter, is nothing new: It has its direct counterpart in conventional paper-and-ink newsletters published by many consultants to advertise and promote their practices, usually with complimentary (free) subscriptions.

THE ELECTRONIC NEWSLETTER

Publishing an electronic newsletter is not especially difficult to do. In fact, publishing online is much simpler in many ways than conventional publishing on paper: For the basic/primary approach, used by most online newsletter publishers, you do no formatting, other than simple sentence and paragraph structures; there is no binding, printing, and mailing, other than sending things out electronically—by e-mail—and with the systems available now, sending your newsletter out to the distribution list can be automated and extremely rapid. It's almost painless. But not completely. There are some tasks that are onerous and challenging, even in the online milieu.

IS IT AS EASY AS IT SEEMS?

The easy part of online newsletter publishing, if you opt for the most basic approach, is the mechanical production and distribution. You use simple ASCII fonts and e-mail all copies directly to subscribers, preferably using a mailbot of some sort, which automates the mailing. However, you still have the problem of research: gathering the information to publish in each issue and organizing it into a proper presentation.

Don't underestimate the importance of those latter two functions: Despite the fact that the newsletter is free, and despite the fact that the presentation is by informal ASCII and via e-mail, if the content is ho-hum and the presentation is high-schoolish, the newsletter will not accomplish much for you. You must make a serious, professional presentation to be taken seriously as a competent professional who is worth listening to and being retained for specific support.

NEWSLETTER VARIABLES AND CHOICES

There are several variables to consider. One is the frequency of publication. In the fast-moving environment of online activity, newsletters tend to be weekly, rather than the usually favored monthly schedule of paper-and-ink newsletters. For online considerations, a month between new issues seems to be rather a long time. On the other hand, gathering new information and writing it up every week makes the chore of publishing almost a daily one. You must consider ways to accelerate and simplify this part of the job, if you are to maintain a weekly publishing schedule. (Of course, you may compromise and publish on a semimonthly or biweekly schedule, as many do.)

One way to simplify the data-gathering and writing job is to invite and use contributions from readers. Many subscribers will gladly contribute articles without expecting payment other than the exposure (advertising) and personal satisfaction they get as writers. Your job will then be simply to edit the contributions. You can get a large part of your material this way.

Another expedient is to swap material with other newsletter publishers. It's a common practice to authorize other publishers to quote directly from your own publication, as long as accurate attribution is made. Usually, this is on the basis of a mutual exchange. So you gain material almost painlessly by subscribing to others' newsletters and reading them for appropriate material to quote.

Still another idea is to use material that is not copyrighted, such as compiling directories of some sort for each issue—interesting Web sites, new reports, and mailing lists, for example. You can't legally pirate someone else's directory, but you can use their published information to compile your own directories and lists.

SOLICITING SUBSCRIPTIONS

You know by now that sending unsolicited advertising and promotional mail to e-mail lists is a no-no, despite the fact that it is being done every day. Some people object rather violently to even a single appearance of unsolicited mail in their electronic mailbox, and almost all will object eventually to a large volume of such mail, on the grounds that this is sent at their (the recipient's) expense. (Many pay by the minute for all online time.) The better course is to refrain from sending unsolicited e-mail. There are other ways to solicit subscribers.

One way is to be a contributor to others' newsletters. In this, you gain some publicity of your own, and you can announce the existence of and the means for subscribing to your own newsletter. Another way is to announce it in messages to as many relevant newsgroups as you can reach. Still another way is to announce it in articles you publish as contributions to Web advertisers. There are Web pages that invite articles, as newsletters do. Some are, in fact, virtual newsletters appearing as a Web site or as part of a site. One, for example, is the Electronic Money Tree at http://www.soos.com, to which I have submitted articles that appear regularly, along with a number of others. The opening frames of this Web site are presented in Exhibit 5-3.

Exhibit 5-3
OPENING FRAMES OF ELECTRONIC MONEY TREE SITE

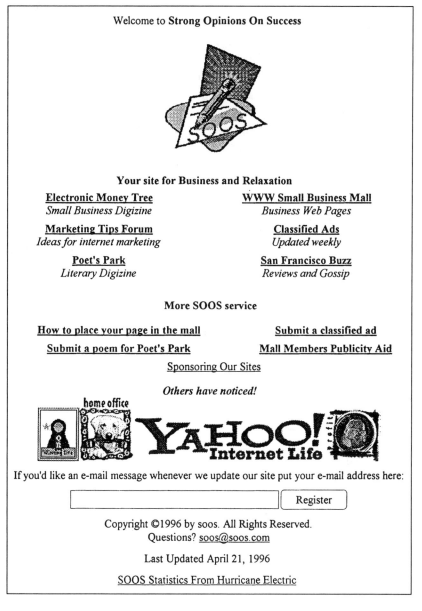

Welcome to **Strong Opinions On Success**

Your site for Business and Relaxation

Electronic Money Tree	**WWW Small Business Mall**
Small Business Digizine	*Business Web Pages*
Marketing Tips Forum	**Classified Ads**
Ideas for internet marketing	*Updated weekly*
Poet's Park	**San Francisco Buzz**
Literary Digizine	*Reviews and Gossip*

More SOOS service

How to place your page in the mall   **Submit a classified ad**

Submit a poem for Poet's Park   **Mall Members Publicity Aid**

Sponsoring Our Sites

Others have noticed!

If you'd like an e-mail message whenever we update our site put your e-mail address here:

[   ] [Register]

Copyright ©1996 by soos. All Rights Reserved.
Questions? soos@soos.com

Last Updated April 21, 1996

SOOS Statistics From Hurricane Electric

This is a multipurpose site, as you may note, advertising the Electronic Money Tree as a "Small Business Digizine" and offering several features, including a mall and advertising space. (Of course, on the screen, this site is presented in an attractive display of color.) The point is that this is yet another way to solicit subscribers, while also solving the distribution problem because the subscribers come to you via your Web site. (More on that in the next chapter.) Of course, that is the opposite of direct marketing because it asks the subscriber to come to you to read your publication, rather than the direct marketing method of going to the prospect.

It is possible, however, to have it both ways: You can invite people to visit your Web site and read a sample issue, and then, at the Web site, provide an invitation to subscribe to an e-mail edition of your newsletter.

That illustrates the enormous diversity of the Internet: It offers what at this point appears to be almost an infinity of options, limited only by your imagination. Do not, however, permit yourself to be limited by what others have done in the distant or recent past, or even what they are doing currently. Every idea you see, even the innovative and inventive one, is a springboard for your own new idea or twist on an older idea.

Let us go now, in the next chapter, to the Web and ideas for using it creatively and profitably in an interactive framework.

CHAPTER 6

Online Interactive Marketing

There is great commercial activity—advertising and promotion—via e-mail and e-mail-based products and services on the Internet. Despite this, it is the World Wide Web that is the great commercial hope of the Internet, as well as its most dramatic and romantic element. Whether it will or will not eventually prove to be the biggest and best advertising/ sales medium of all time, as so often predicted by enthusiasts, remains to be seen; the jury is still out on that issue. It is, however, at least an excellent marketing asset that can serve you very well as an independent consultant in need of an interactive marketing medium for networking and related purposes. Of all online media that are readily available for commercial applications, the Web is certainly the most prominent and most widely accepted. It offers certain specific advantages, some rather obvious, some not so obvious but real enough, nonetheless.

COLOR AND GRAPHICS

One major appeal for marketers is the capacity of the Web to present multimedia marketing presentations featuring colorful graphics. Although the Web can be used to present sound and motion too, these are still only sparingly in evidence; the major focus is still on graphics and color. The common strategy is obviously to use graphics and color to get and hold attention, a priority need for advertising and a first objective of any advertising or sales presentation. Your message must compete with many others, all vying to penetrate the prospect's consciousness. Unless you succeed in doing that, you can't deliver your message. However, the use of flashy presentations tends to be far too overdone far too often, evidently under the premise that generating admiration for the eye-catching display has a positive sales effect. The downside of this is that, for technical reasons (primarily the limited transmission capabilities of ordinary dial-up telephone connections) these presentations take so long to be painted on the screen that many visitors grow impatient and go on to other sites.

The problem can be minimized and even avoided. There are many other methods for getting a viewer's attention and holding his or her interest, most without the downside or at least with much less of a downside.

GETTING ATTENTION

In a straight text advertising or sales presentation, especially in black-and-white format, as in a newspaper, you usually rely on a headline, on words that somehow reach out and command the prospect's eye to stop and read. You devise headlines that you hope will do this, and you employ all possible measures to make the words themselves stand out, using any or all of several general methods and their derivative strategies:

- Large type
- Bright and/or varied colors in brief splashes
- Interesting and unusual type styles
- Various combinations of type styles
- Attention-getting words and phrases, such as "FREE," "NEW," "GET RICH"

Another method for catching a prospect's eye is the use of special visual effects—graphics and color in presenting photographs, drawings, cartoons, charts, and other devices. Graphics help you get attention and, with imaginative use of color, the graphics and accompanying words appear together instantaneously, as far as your eye can detect the tiny time lapses, so they almost leap from the page or from the screen. On the Web, the text can appear almost instantaneously, if it is from a stored standard font, but not the graphics. Most graphics and any text that is highly stylized and must be transmitted as a graphic crawls slowly onto your screen for those technical reasons referred to earlier. The more complex the illustration, the more data is required to paint it on a computer screen, and so the longer it takes to paint the presentation. That is another trade-off: complex and impressive graphics versus taxing the patience of the prospect waiting for them. Despite this problem, however, there are advantages in using the Web for advertising. In fact, recently some Web advertisers have been offering simpler graphics, illustrations that will form on the screen much more quickly, trading off visual impact for greater speed.

When I asked Richard Soos for permission to reproduce the first page of his Web site, The Electronic Money Tree (see Exhibit 5-3), he agreed immediately, happy to get the added exposure, but he remarked that his site offered little in the way of a graphic presentation. Its value lay primarily in the information it offers. That is a consideration to bear always in mind. He remarked that his Marketing Tips Forum is gaining fans rapidly: There is obviously hunger for information. Impressive graphics are fun to do and possibly gratifying, but in a practical sense they often provide less information and sales appeal than do the words and thus do not earn their way.

Actually, there are three variables that may be traded off in assessing the pros and cons of your options and what they offer in holding the reader's interest:

- The overall impact (including the visual impact) of the presentation
- The speed with which it can be presented to the viewer
- The amount of information that is conveyed to the viewer

Consider, in designing a Web site, the interaction or interdependency of the variable elements and the amount of information they convey, as well as the speed with which they can be formed.

Exhibit 6-1 shows the first page of the Marketing Tips Forum of the Soos site, where everyone is invited to post information and exchange ideas. A form for submitting ideas via e-mail is provided also, as shown in Exhibit 6-2. One may type ideas and other remarks in the comments space furnished and use the occasion to advertise one's own site and existence. (Soos reports that he has found his site to be highly successful and growing steadily.)

THE CONVENIENCE FACTOR

In marketing, as stated earlier, an accepted principle of sales technique is that you must make it as easy as possible for the prospect to become a customer—easy to order from you or otherwise respond as you wish, that is. That is why credit cards were probably the greatest boon to sales since Montgomery Ward introduced the unconditional money-back guarantee. Then came another step, the initiative attributed to Joe Sugarman of accepting credit card charges by mail and telephone. It was a daring idea at the time and an even greater boon to selling. Each of these steps made it easier for the prospect to order and alert marketers never to stop looking for and taking advantage of new devices to make responding easier. Along came fax, another advance in that aspect of marketing, and soon came such refinements as fax-on-demand (*fax-back*) to simplify the process even further. This is a service using a form of autoresponder that will fax specified documents to requestors automatically on request. That idea has been adapted to e-mail, and it is possible to have your literature sent out automatically by e-mail to anyone who makes an e-mail request in an "e-mail-back" kind of service.

E-mail, the Internet in general, and the World Wide Web have pushed that envelope of ease in ordering even further, combining and integrating many of these features, and thus providing customers a wide variety of choices. They, the customers, may then decide for themselves which is the most convenient and easiest method for ordering. Using the Web, you can offer prospects a variety of conveniences, even via fax transmissions for those who do not have their own fax capabilities. (However, virtually every computer sold in the past few years has included a fax modem, so that probably everyone owning a reasonably modern com-

Exhibit 6-1
PORTION OF MARKETING TIPS FORUM MENU

Marketing Tips Forum

Sponsored by:
WWW Small Business Mall
Support our sponsors!

[Post Message] [FAQ]

- Help for marketing my mall on Internet - **Morris Shamouni** *6/23/96* (0)
- Suggestions Welcome! Internet Marketing - **Alan Katz** *6/11/96* (0)
- Marketing on the Internet - **Phil Stimmel** *6/10/96* (1)
    - Re: Marketing on the Internet - **Michael Sealey** *6/21/96* (0)
- ~~~Developing a KILLER postcard~~~ - **Total Success Solutions, Inc.** *6/05/96* (0)
- Turning Browsers into Buyers - **Kirsten Bradley** *6/03/96* (1)
    - Re: Turning Browsers into Buyers - **Web surfer** *6/15/96* (0)
- Data entry business - **Doug** *6/01/96* (1)
    - Re: data entry business - **Web surfer** *6/1596* (0)
- Market your product or service with low cost video - **Hal Landen** *5/29/96* (0)
- Why not customize mouse pads for your business? - **Tamara** *5/24/96* (0)
- Help! Marketing on the Internet. - **Gary Tito** *5/06/96* (2)
    - Re: Help! Marketing on the Internet. - **Phoenix Business Services** *5/08/96* (1)
        - Re: Re: Help! Marketing on the Internet. - **Rich** *5/23/96* (0)
- **Two Overlooked Important Business Areas . . .** - **B.L.S.** *5/05/96* (0)
- Starting out selling Learning Machine - **Joe Holsen mindsync@netvoyage.net** *5/02/96* (1)
    - Re: Starting out selling Learning Machine - **Troy Smith** *6/07/96* (0)
- Manufacturer/Patent Holder Needs Help - **Robert Gleeman** *5/02/96* (1)
    - Re: Manufacturer/Patent Holder Needs Help - **Brian Rooney** *6/05/96* (0)
- Web Advertising - **KEITH Beaven** *4/29/96* (3)
    - Re: Web Advertising - **Bob Crowder** *5/01/96* (0)
- What Is Your Offer? - **Herman Holtz** *4/22/96* (0)
- NFL-Trudeau Marketing Group - **Barry M Sawyer** *4/20/96* (2)
    - Re: NFL-Trudeau Marketing Group - **Watch Dog** *4/26/96* (0)
- Trade Show Info On the Web - **Mary Gillen** *4/13/96* (1)
- Need help to get Internet traffic for our Web page - **Paresh Shah** *4/07/96* (9)
    - Re: need help to get Internet traffic for our Web page -**websurfer** *4/29/96* (0)
    - Re: need help to get Internet traffic for our Web page - **Mary Gillen** *4/09/96* (0)
- What's Your *1-Minute Commercial*? - **Mary Gillen** *2/16/96* (3)
    - Re: What's Your *1-Minute Commercial*? - **Hans Ebner** *2/28/96* (0)
- Using the Forum - **Richard Soos** *12/15/95* (1)

Post A Message!

Exhibit 6-2
FORM FOR SUBMITTING INFORMATION VIA E-MAIL

Re: What's Your *1-Minute Commercial*?

[Follow-ups] [Post Follow-up] [Marketing Tips Forum]

Posted by Hans Ebner on February 28, 1996 at 14:56:22:

In Reply to: What's Your *1-Minute Commercial*? posted by Mary Gillen on February 16, 1996 at 13:48:17:

This is a great idea. One of the problems I see with electronic commerce is that few folks can define what business they are in. hans

Follow-ups:

Post a Follow-up

Name:

E-Mail:

Subject: **Re: What's Your *1-Minute Commercial*?**

Comments:

Optional Link URL:

Link Title:

Optional Image URL:

[Submit Follow Up] [Reset]

[Follow-ups] [Post Follow-up][Marketing Tips Forum]

puter has a fax capability, if the owner's telephone line is connected to the fax modem.)

PROMOTIONAL OPPORTUNITIES ON THE WEB

When you have only a hammer, everything looks like a nail. We all see the world through our own biases, especially influenced by our career specialties. Multiple debates are raging over how to analyze and characterize marketing and commercial promotion opportunities on the Web, and the debaters tend strongly to interpret and frame Internet marketing and promotional opportunities in terms of their own special fields. So direct-mail mavens see the Web and its characteristics as a kind of a super-direct-mail opportunity, telemarketing specialists see the Web as a new kind of telemarketing possibility, door-knocker salespeople see the Web as a better way to knock on prospects' doors, and retailers see the Internet as a place to erect cyberspace malls and offer merchandise at retail. Most fail, however, to back up enough to get the broad perspective and see the Internet as something new and different, something that offers new and different possibilities, as yet unexplored and untapped.

It is true that the Internet has some resemblance to those other fields of sales and promotion, is perhaps even an analog of some other marketing media, but it is still unique in some respects. It is unique in its combination of elements from all those other fields and in offering both seller and buyer a chance to select the best choices. It is unique in its global span, so you can do business across the world as casually and as easily as you do business across your own city or neighborhood. And it is unique in its capacity for interactive marketing relationships on a much grander scale than across the counter in a retail establishment; you can interact on almost the face-to-face seller-buyer relationship with customers across the oceans on another continent. I have often exchanged e-mail messages with clients several times during a time period of only a few hours, so that we were close to having a spontaneous conversation to reach understanding and agreement, and without knowing where the other was in the world.

A GLOBALLY INTERACTIVE SYSTEM

One unique feature of the Internet generally—perhaps its most important feature—is that easy, even casual, global reach. And that global reach is a two-way proposition, truly interactive, as interactive as a personal telephone conversation. You can broadcast your messages in sound and full-color presentations, even with motion, to the entire planet, without studios, costly equipment, expensive air time, contracts with broadcasting systems, and all the associated costs of broadcasting sound and pictures globally via traditional television systems. You can do all this with a simple pc of your own or for a modest fee, using the system of a service provider. You can make this presentation to anyone with a pc and some service that gives them access to the Internet.

Interactive means, of course, dialogue—exchanges of messages, ideas, arguments, and offers. Some prospects will interact with you immediately when you make an offer of services that are relevant to the situation and the subject of initial discussion. That kind of prospect is likely to ask questions and press to see if you are flexible on pricing, will make a broader guarantee, will entertain a counteroffer, or is otherwise open to discussion and negotiation.

That is, of course, an entirely positive indication from a marketing viewpoint because it reveals an interested prospect who wants to do business with you enough to engage in serious pursuit of an accommodation. At this point, you have all but made the sale, essentially, and are in the negotiation phase.

That is the purpose of doing everything you can to evoke some kind of response from a visitor. Initially, it doesn't matter what the response is; the point is to get a response because that indicates some degree of interest in what you offer. It is a kind of qualification, moving that visitor from the status of unproved prospect or "suspect" up a notch to the status of interested prospect. But you don't have to wait passively for readers to decide to respond, and you should not, for that calls for initiative on the part of the prospect, and you will find initiative to be not the most common trait among your prospects. The initiative must come from you. (Note how the various contests conducted by mail include items that the contestant must do, pasting seals, clipping things, checking off items, and otherwise getting "involved," as the direct-mail psychologists put it.) You can suggest or invite queries and comments in your presentation, offering a form by which the visitor can respond with e-mail spontaneously, directly from your Web site. And you can then turn to e-mail to follow up those queries and comments that appear to be promising sales leads, and thus initiate a discussion that may very well soon develop into a negotiation and contract. But is it that simple?

PROACTIVE STRATEGIES

Here is where the difference between reactive and proactive strategies is critical. You can simply provide an e-mail form and a casual note that comments and inquiries are invited, with the fervent hope that visitors reading that message will use the form and make a comment or inquiry. That is, you can rely hopefully on the possibility of the visitor exercising a bit of initiative, if you wish, but the bulk of our experience is that few prospects, even those whom you may believe to be ideal or near-ideal prospects, will exercise a great deal of initiative. Most people do not often act; they react. They are much inclined to wait for someone else to take the initiative while they lie back and observe quietly. It's in the nature of humans to behave this way. Thus, the response rate will be rather a low one if you do nothing more than provide the means to respond and a general invitation to do so. To increase that response rate, you must do something to take command and somehow *provoke* or actively *induce* the prospect into responding so you can open a dialogue.

There are many things you can do to induce or provoke the prospect to respond. Here are just a few ideas:

- Offer something additional, either by e-mail or surface mail, such as a special report, a brochure with "10 Useful Tips" to something relevant to your field, or some other item worth having. ("Insider" information—tips—always has great appeal.)
- Offer a self-appraisal device such as a checklist or self-scoring questionnaire that will reveal to the user what his or her greatest strengths are as a marketer, writer, or whatever you think is a relevant or appropriate field. (These psychological profiles appear to have great appeal to everyone.)

121

- Provide a questionnaire inviting the visitor to rank your presentation or to express an opinion about some relevant subject. (Most people respond to an opportunity to express their opinions.)
- Invite the visitor to submit a question, to which you will respond at no cost to the visitor. (I have used this one rather successfully. And not only does it encourage feedback from the visitor, but it enhances your own image as a guru in your consulting field.)

FAST RESPONSE

There is no doubt that the time lapse between feedback from a prospect and your own responsive follow-up is a significant factor in the result. The visitor is interested at the moment, but that interest may very well flag rapidly with time. It is important to respond to the prospect as soon as possible—the same day or even the same hour, if possible. My own respondents often express their surprise and pleasure at getting such a fast result—same day whenever possible. That is an Internet strength of which we ought to take advantage: the ability to interact spontaneously even across the world.

You can often succeed in being able to respond this rapidly by person-ally monitoring your e-mail for responses and composing answers spon-taneously, or by using an autoresponder that will acknowledge inquiries or comments immediately by sending back literature in an e-mail version of the fax-back system used to send out literature automatically. (This again points out the advantage of being an independent entrepreneur who deals in small numbers in marketing.) Most e-mail software offers the option of notifying you immediately of arriving e-mail, so that you can respond spontaneously and virtually instantaneously.

Feedback from a viewer is usually a good omen. It tells you that the prospect is interested enough in what you offer to go to the trouble of responding and may be already seeking to see what the best terms are on which he or she can do business with you. Unfortunately, there are also prospects who are curious but not truly interested or, at best, only mildly interested. That kind of prospect will usually listen politely and without visible immediate reaction. If you allow the exchange to be as sterile as that, it is unlikely that you will close a sale there. Initiative on your part is needed to provoke or at least encourage true interaction with your prospect, in most cases. At the least, you need to take a first step in qualifying the prospect to determine whether this is or is not a true prospect, making it worthwhile to invest more time and effort in seeking a client here.

This is not a new requirement, nor is it peculiar to the online environment, although it is a somewhat different problem in marketing online than it is in marketing face to face. One of the challenges of selling has always been that of perceiving and doing something about the prospect's reluctance to consummate a sale. Even the most interested prospect, having listened attentively, perhaps even having asked questions and made remarks indicating some interest, will usually not say, "I'll take it," on his or her own initiative. A great many prospects appear to be 98 percent sold, ready to order, and yet they hesitate at the eleventh hour, at that critical point where you try to consummate the sale. Follow-up efforts to consummate the sale are best made immediately. Follow-up later, when the trail has grown cold, is far less likely to be successful.

CLOSING

For the seller, having brought the prospect 98 percent of the way to the true close, covering the remaining 2 percent of the route is a well-known obstacle: The prospect is quite characteristically resisting that critical point of making the decision—making a *commitment,* that is—victim of the all too common human tendency to procrastinate, and to put off making important decisions, especially. It is such a common problem in selling that many of the classic principles of selling are aimed specifically at solving that problem, at ways of trying to persuade the prospect to make the final decision, to finally say "yes" and sign the order. There are tools for doing that. In the language of the sales professional, those tools are called *closing.*

Closing is a word that is commonly used by laypeople to mean "getting the order." However, to sales professionals, closing means *asking for the order,* a meaning with much greater significance than that of consummating the sale. To the sales professional, closing is a means for determining when it is time for the seller to stop talking (selling) and start writing (the order). Everyone has heard about the hapless salesman who talks too much and loses the sale he had all sewn up only a few minutes earlier, before he said that one word too much. But how could he have known when it was time to stop talking?

He could have known if and only if he had asked the prospect whether it was time to stop talking and write the order. Not asking directly, of course, but by any of various means for doing so in effect. That is what closing is—asking the prospect for the order—and that is how to find out whether the prospect is ready to become a customer or needs to hear some more sales argument. When closing does not produce an agreement to the order by the prospect, it is usually taken to mean that the prospect is not yet convinced or has one or more questions that need to be answered or needs to be assured in some other way. It is then the seller's responsibility to find out what more the prospect needs to know and provide the needed assurance.

Closing is almost always an awkward sales interaction because it is a kind of Mexican standoff, where the two parties, seller and prospect, are at poles. This is an especially acute situation in print or direct mail, where only limited spontaneity is possible. But online marketing offers at least some degree of spontaneity in interacting effectively via e-mail because e-mail offers the opportunity for almost immediate response. (The furnishing of an e-mail input as a means for the visitor to a Web site to respond directly to the owner of the site has become a common practice.) That e-mail form is the primary means for making Web sites interactive between presenter and visitor, in keeping with that sales principle of making it easy for the prospect to buy—easy, that is, for a prospect to get more information, place an order, or respond in whatever way you wish to have the prospect respond, whether you are seeking orders directly or seeking to develop a list of leads for follow-up. But it does not necessarily involve a Web site presentation. I get leads as a result of my e-mail activity, as well as from my appearances on my own and others' Web sites and newsgroups. Only today I received a positive response from a prospect in Lisbon, Portugal, who had queried me several days ago and asked for an estimate, which I furnished the next day.

The many kinds of e-mail and other contacts are advantages of special value to those of us selling our services as consultants, because for most of us, consulting is not a one-call business: We are in a business in which, for most of us, our sales result only from multiple, successive contacts with our prospects, in both the initial mass approach, and later in following up the sales leads we have developed. In earlier times, I turned to telephone and mail to close consulting sales after exchanges with and presentations to prospects, often by mail. Later, the follow-up was by fax, as that came into vogue. Today, most of my follow-ups are by e-mail. The principles of making the sales and closing do not change, but the means for doing so do change, improving steadily, coming closer to true spontaneity, and costing far less per prospect. That last consideration, in itself, is one of the great advantages of doing business online.

COSTS

The latter consideration, lower costs, is of major importance today. Costs are still rising steadily, despite the relative slowing of inflation. Where once it cost me $130 dollars in postage to send out 1,000 letters or press releases by first-class mail, today it costs me $320 in postage, more than twice as much, for the same thing, plus all the increases in related costs of paper, printing, and labor. It has become almost prohibitively expensive for an independent consultant to make 5,000- and 10,000-piece mailings, which will cost at least $3,000 to $6,000 in materials alone, plus the labor, which may double that cost.

Therein lies one of the true blessings of the Internet and the Web. Using the resources wisely, you can carry out the sales promotions at a fraction of the cost of surface mail. But the Web's usefulness and convenience are not to the seller only: It is also useful and convenient to you as a visitor to the Web, seeking to make as many favorable contacts as possible to implement your networking efforts. It is another means for making your name known to others in a kind of PR, if you take full advantage of all the opportunities to make your existence well known. Once, not very long ago, I supplied a column to a number of periodicals in trade for advertising space. Printing the copies of the manuscript and mailing them out was more burdensome than writing the column, and I was growing so weary of that chore that I was beginning to wonder if I was realizing a net gain from the activity. Today, however, I send out copies of my column by e-mail, reaching a far greater number of publications than before. A few still go to print publications, but most go to online electronic publications, and all go by e-mail, comfortably, conveniently, swiftly, and inexpensively.

Of course, the publishers benefit too because they do not have to typeset my copy. They can move my e-mail to one of their own word-processing files, do whatever editing and formatting they wish, and insert the file appropriately in their publication, all within a few minutes!

In the case of Richard Soos with his Electronic Money Tree, visitors are invited to post their own marketing tips or comment on tips posted by others. That furnishes a no-cost way to make your presence and thoughts known to many others who visit and post there. Soos stipulates that his Marketing Tips forum may not be used to post unabashed advertising messages; he sells advertising space elsewhere on his site. But you can derive promotional benefits that are tantamount to paid advertising each time you contribute a few words to such a site. (At the least, in guest writing for other publishers, the author is granted a "resource box" at the end of the article, in which he or she is allowed a hundred words or so of identification and promotional copy.) To the owner of the site, there is an advantage in inviting visitors to respond because it is an attractive feature that helps draw visitors. That addresses one measure of success for a site, which is the number of "hits" (visits) experienced. Attracting hits is a major challenge and major objective of any site. One measure of its usefulness is the number of visitors it attracts.

WEB MARKETING VERSUS DIRECT MARKETING

Some people draw parallels between Internet marketing and direct marketing, as a way of analyzing and explaining philosophies underlying Internet marketing. If pressed to find an analogy, I would find Internet marketing, especially on the Web, to have more resemblance to classic retailing than to direct marketing.

The chief difference between direct marketing and classic (storefront) retailing is that the direct marketer goes aggressively after selected prospects, seeking them out, and makes sales offers, whereas the retailer and Web site presenter makes presentations designed to attract visitors— nominally prospects—to whom sales offers may then be made. It is aggressive versus passive or active versus reactive marketing.

Direct marketers use direct mail more frequently than any other method, and they rely heavily on mailing lists characterized by demographics or other factors (for example, the list is of subscribers to some publication or all on the list have some common factor in their history as buyers). These are the characteristics that they think distinguish individuals who are most likely to become customers. A home improvement contractor would therefore not mail appeals to apartment dwellers but would seek mailing lists of home owners within the contractor's chosen service area.

General retailers, such as department stores, rely on location and advertising, on announcing sales, especially, to create traffic in their stores. They advertise sales to the general public via newspapers and broadcast media, so the nature of their advertising sorts out the prospects, attracting those who are most likely to be interested in whatever was featured in the sale.

Web marketers must do very much the same thing as retailers do because there is, at present, no effective way to seek out individuals on the Internet with direct sales appeals, especially not in great quantity. Note the adjective *effective*. There are such approaches as "junk" fax mail and "junk" e-mail, but these are not generally acceptable in the cyberspace world, although a few entrepreneurs are using these methods, despite the opposition. However, their principal appeal is to others who are seeking to somehow use cyberspace for marketing, and so they represent a special case that is not a useful model for discussion. Even presented with great caution and diplomacy, a junk-mail attack on prospective clients via fax or e-mail will produce at least some resentment and negative backlash.

Internet marketers relying on Web sites must attract prospects to their sites, where they can then attempt to sell them, just as retailers must induce shoppers to visit their premises. The chief drawing cards of the Web site presenters are the offers of interesting and/or useful information, possibly highly specialized and rare information, and other inducements, such as free newsletters and reports. Shel Horowitz, for example, a small, independent writer/publisher of books on how to get the most for your money, whether spending for business or for personal interests, presents a Web page (http://www.frugalfun.com) that offers a cornucopia of money-saving tips. He advertises that Web site in the signature that accompanies all his posts on whatever forums he frequents.

Despite heavy representation of commercial interests on the Web, not all home pages and other Web sites are commercially inspired. There are also many personal home pages, vanity or hobby Web sites set up by individuals, and there are many sites set up and maintained by nonprofit organizations, such as universities, labor unions, government offices, associations, and a variety of public agencies. All contribute in one way or another to the whole of the Internet. There is, therefore, ample precedent for you to establish and maintain a site of your own, as either a personal, nonprofit site, as a business venture in itself, or as a direct or indirect marketing medium for your consulting practice. In fact, a site of your own is probably going to be most effective as an indirect marketing gambit, aimed specifically at helping you achieve your networking objectives.

The pros and cons of the various possibilities have more to do with costs than with appeal or effectiveness. All will support your self-marketing, directly or indirectly. But however you structure and orient your site, you face the same problem—that of attracting enough traffic to make your site produce results effectively. In the end, success still depends heavily on probability statistics, on numbers. Therefore, you will probably be best advised to design your site and what it offers especially to attract those you have previously decided would be your best prospects as clients.

THE TYRANNY OF THE NUMBERS

In all sales and advertising, you are at the mercy of the numbers. Despite tactical and strategic differences among the many types of marketing, Internet/Web marketing is no different from others in at least one thing: its basic dependence on statistics and the laws of probability. It is a given, of course, that you cannot succeed in winning an order from everyone to whom you present your offer, regardless of media or other variables. Your marketing success always depends on your ability to reach and sell a small percentage of a large number of prospects—traditional mass marketing—or a large percentage of a small number of prospects—an ideal always difficult to realize.

Therein lies the real problem of the Internet and the Web as means for effective advertising and marketing: The difficulty of reaching a large enough number of prospects online for mass marketing purposes has become painfully apparent. Relatively few marketers relying on Web sites to make their sales presentations have been able to achieve the goal of truly large numbers of readers, numbers on a scale comparable to that of traditional direct marketing. Marketers whose success depends on reaching great numbers of prospects and achieving a correspondingly large volume of sales have been, for the most part, badly disappointed. And while, as a consultant, you are not a mass marketer in terms of a need to sell to a mass market, you are a mass marketer in terms of the need to prospect a mass market in search of sales leads. In that sense, we are all mass marketers, for we all depend on finding enough sales leads among the millions of prospects to give us a viable base of income-producing activity.

MEASURING AND ESTIMATING NUMBERS ON THE WEB

When you advertise in the traditional media, your costs are linked directly to rates that are based on the numbers of prospects your offer will reach. In direct mail, the rates are based on both the characteristics of and the number of names and addresses to which you send your literature. Mailing lists are normally rented—usually rented, and rarely sold—at rates per thousand names. In print advertising, the rates you pay are based on the estimated or calculated number of readers. In broadcast commercials on radio and TV, the rates are based on the estimated size of the audience. In each case, the numbers are measurable or the data exist to enable fair estimates of the numbers.

None of these measures is readily available to calculate exposure of advertising messages on the Web, and the raw data for estimating the numbers is not highly accurate. Even the total number of Internet users and visitors is disputed, as noted earlier. In the face of this, a jargon has developed of *clicks, click-throughs, hits, visitors,* and other terms as a set of keys to measuring or estimating the numbers of prospects reached by Web presentations.

Each element on a Web page sent to a visitor is a *hit,* but only a file that actually arrives at a visitor's computer is a *qualified hit.* If you count only the page itself and not the separate elements on it, you are counting a *page hit* or *HTML hit.* A *visit,* on the other hand, is all the action or transaction by a single caller (identified by the caller's Internet address) for a period of time, generally 30 minutes.

A major advertising element on the Web is the *banner,* generally appearing at the beginning of a page. This is a representation of an actual banner, a general advertisement featuring some business organization's name. A mouse click on the banner will transport a visitor to the individual Web site of the owner of the banner, where the banner owner can address the visitor with whatever promotional information is desired. That—transport to the Web site—is a prime purpose of the banner. It is possible to detect and record a *click* each time a visitor clicks a mouse on a banner, so the click is itself a measure. If the visitor continues, proceeding to the advertiser's site, it is a *click-through,* a more significant measure.

RELEVANCE TO MARKETING CONSULTING SERVICES

Aside from being arbitrary and of uncertain significance, these measures and factors would be unimportant factors in your own marketing concerns, even if they were highly accurate measures. That is because they are indicators that are far more relevant to mass marketing than they are to the marketing of custom services, such as consulting. In any case, they are still exploratory and far from resolution as the final terms by which marketing potential and effectiveness are measured. However, regardless of jargon and methods of measurement, marketing success for you, as for others, depends upon several variables immediately: One is the rate of response—the percentage of prospects who are influenced by your presentation and become true sales leads and, eventually, your clients. That depends on the number of prospects you manage to reach with your presentation, but it also depends on the suitability of those prospects as targets for those services you offer.

In terms of response percentages, if you can persuade 5 percent of your prospects to buy what you offer and you need 500 sales to cover expenses and pay you a salary adequate for you to live on, you must make your offer to at least 10,000 prospects. Generally, in mass marketing, 5 percent is a high rate of response, and many if not most marketing campaigns must get by on only 1 or 2 percent response, and so must make offers to prospects numbering in the hundreds of thousands, reach that higher response rate, or somehow change the markup figure. That is, if you can get that higher response rate or raise the size of your average order, you can reduce the number of orders needed to make the campaign viable, so that you do not need to reach that great a number of prospects. Some marketing campaigns, for example, are successful with response rates of only a fraction of 1 percent.

INCREASING YOUR RESPONSE RATE

Increasing the number of visitors to your Web site is difficult and expensive, either in dollars or in terms of the time it requires you to devote to that task, so it can usually be done only on a gradual scale; whereas in direct mail, you can often find additional mailing lists and so increase the size of your market immediately. In Web site marketing, you don't have that convenient option of just ordering another couple hundred thousand names to address with your offer. You must bring additional prospects to your site, usually in a rather slow process, even when you spend a great deal of money to do so. So the real question becomes one of how can you increase the response rate? The answer to that depends on several major factors, at least these:

- How well the prospects' interests and needs match what you offer—the accuracy and effectiveness of your targeting
- The effectiveness of your sales appeal—how persuasive your offer is
- Some lesser variables and unpredictable factors, such as the season (if your services are in any way seasonal) and the state of the economy at the moment

You can't do much about those latter factors, of course, but you can determine what are the characteristics of the individual who is most likely to become your client, so you can seek out ways to find prospects with those characteristics, and you can discover what offers have the greatest sales appeal and greatest effectiveness in persuading prospects to become customers—that is, how to tailor your posts and sales messages to achieve the greatest success. That would help increase your response rate, thus reducing the number of prospects you must reach to develop good sales leads.

MAKING SALES VERSUS MAKING CUSTOMERS

There are many businesses that spend more to acquire a customer than they can profit from that customer's order. Most catalog sales are examples of that. It is always costly to make a sale to a customer, especially a first sale, and especially so when that first sale includes providing that customer with an expensive catalog. However, the catalog seller is not making sales; he or she is making customers. That is, the catalog seller is creating a basis for future sales that will cost very little to make because they will come from an established customer.

Other sales to the new client may include some that are ancillary to your principal service as a consultant, such as seminars and newsletter subscriptions. In short, a new client may be—should be—an asset worth far more to you than the proceeds of that first sale. Your principal marketing cost is winning the customer. After that, in the normal situation, your cost to make each new sale is a fraction of the cost of that first sale.

Too, with the marketing of consulting services so much dependent on word-of-mouth recommendations and referrals, every new client is a marketing asset as a possible route to other new clients acquired at little cost to you. These latter considerations make all the normal standards of mass marketing somewhat irrelevant, as far as you are concerned, if your service is such that your clients are good prospects for future sales and referrals to other new clients, as is probably the case.

DATABASED MARKETING

The considerations discussed point out rather dramatically the importance of advance planning, of having developed a business plan, in fact, of which you would have made a marketing plan the chief feature. (Many develop business plans as financial proposals, documents to persuade bankers and investors of the soundness of the business described. However, it is equally sensible to develop a business plan solely to formalize a program to conduct and build an independent consulting practice. In developing that plan, you would have identified and described the prospects whom you think would be your most logical marketing targets.)

In the past few years, the concept of databased marketing has taken hold, especially among those in the direct marketing field, although conceptually the idea ought to apply everywhere and to all marketing. That aside, the idea is probably especially significant in online marketing and may prove eventually to be a key to success in online marketing.

The central idea in databased marketing is to develop a database of customers that includes a wealth of information about each individual customer that bears on the customer's buying preferences, influences, and habits. You would gather and record in your customer database those customer characteristics and data items most likely to influence the customer's purchases. In business-to-business marketing, which is the kind of marketing most consultants must engage in, the typical needs and problems your service satisfies and solves should be major items needing definitions, for example. What you choose to gather and record will depend on what you sell and to what kinds of customer characteristics what you sell is most likely to appeal. If you are a computer consultant, you will want to record in each record the individual computer owned, type of software used, typical needs, and other relevant data. If you are a marketing consultant, you will want to gather and record data on each client's typical marketing methods, needs, preferences, and whatever else will help you sell your services to that client. If you are a wedding consultant, you will want to keep abreast of impending nuptials or families that include young people nearing marriageable ages.

Of course, although the idea of database marketing was originally born as a method for increasing one's effectiveness in maximizing sales to an existing customer base, you can extrapolate that to prospects, as well as to clients. It helps you directly in defining the best prospects for your service and thus helps you sharpen and focus your networking and your sales appeals, to individualize your marketing appeals, tailoring them to the prospect. If carried out well—that is, if enough data have been collected to represent true buyer profiles for each individual or organization in the database—you should be able to so customize and tailor your sales appeal that you no longer depend on large-scale probability statistics, but can close a large percentage of your marketing targets. Thus databased marketing ought to prove to be an effective way to compensate for the relatively small target population you are able to reach online.

What is necessary to use this marketing strategy, then, is to first prepare a sound business plan or, at least, a sound marketing plan and, especially, a well-detailed profile of your best client prospect, that individual or organization most likely to need such services as you can offer. You will need to design your database accordingly, with many fields to describe the prospect's business, routine needs (as relevant to your service), special needs, interests, places/ways to reach and acquaint with your existence and what you do, and any other data that is relevant, such as associations the prospect belongs to, newsgroups and/or other regular contacts the prospect maintains, and any other activity that helps you establish and stay visible to the prospect, as well as reach with sales appeals.

GATHERING DATA FOR A MARKETING DATABASE

A principal activity necessary to databased marketing is gathering the data for the fields in the database records. Obviously, anyone building a customer database uses normal customer records such as order forms, invoices, and correspondence to begin the database entries. However, to extrapolate the idea and build a database of prospects, large business organizations use contests, rebate programs, and free subscriptions to periodicals among the methods, thus inducing participants to furnish information that can be used to help build the database.

Some of these ideas can be used on a scale that is practicable for the independent consultant. If you choose to publish a free newsletter as part of your marketing program, use it with the needs of your database in mind: Ask those requesting subscription to furnish answers to a few simple questions, for example. Inquire of readers what features of your newsletter they like best. Solicit their questions, observations, and suggestions.

Other methods for building the information base are possible, of course. Lead the discussions in relevant newsgroups and mailing lists in which you participate. Make provocative observations to stimulate discussions from which you can abstract information you can use. Be highly active, not only to make yourself known, but to gather information for your future efforts. Do the same thing in writing articles for publication on Web sites. Invite responses to your own e-mail address.

Participate in as many of these activities as you can manage the time for, initially, until you discover which work best for you. Then you can begin to focus your efforts where they are most productive and eliminate those that are less rewarding.

Building a database will take time, but building a business generally takes time.

MANAGING THE VARIABLES

As a freelance writer, for a few years I focused my marketing attention and efforts on the federal government agencies that appeared to me to be fertile markets for contracts to help them in turning out some of the brochures, pamphlets, leaflets, manuals, and other "paper" that is a principal product of Washington, D.C. Despite a degree of success in finding such work among the government agencies, I soon learned that by far the most fruitful areas for contract writing services were (at that time, at least) in writing training and educational materials. There was a large amount of activity in that field and not a great many writers aspiring to work there. I was soon turning out many audiovisual scripts and storyboards, manuals, lesson plans, instructor guides, and similar materials for the Postal Service Training Institute, the Public Buildings Service, the Civil Service Commission, the Occupational Safety and Health Administration of the Department of Labor, and many other federal agencies.

Unexpected opportunities arise, but are not always obvious unless you are alert. One training job required me to turn out a manual on value engineering for one agency, which led to other value engineering assignments for other agencies.

These are examples of a principle offered earlier, that of being prepared to make major alterations in your objectives and plans, as you encounter practical, "on the ground" experience. The value engineering work was temporary, although there were a number of projects, but the training writing proved to be such a fertile field that it became almost a career in itself. The proper mind-set goes beyond being prepared to

135

accept changes to your original ideas of where your best markets lie: You should be alert and consciously weighing your original concepts and estimates against what you are experiencing and observing every day, deliberately seeking to improve your view of your markets. Serendipitous occurrences come about most frequently when your mind is most receptive to new ideas. Otherwise, they come and go and are hardly noticed, except in regretful retrospect.

My venture into presenting seminars on proposal writing and government contracting came about unexpectedly in that manner, when I agreed to assist a friend in delivering such a seminar. I was so dismayed by what I found to be utter nonsense in one or two presentations by others that I was all but compelled psychologically to develop and present my own seminars on the subject for years afterward. And even in doing that, I continued to learn and modify my approach continually, as I found that the conventional wisdom I relied upon initially was often inadequate. I had to develop new approaches frequently to solve marketing problems. (Ultimately, I realized that all marketing methods, no matter how well they worked for others, were valid for me only so long as they worked for my program, and often accepted methods had to be adapted to my need or dropped entirely in favor of another approach.)

When I began my program of presenting seminars on the art of writing successful proposals in pursuit of major government contracts, I used direct mail as my main marketing strategy to enroll attendees. I drew seminar registrants from many kinds of firms, from the largest to the smallest, who pursued government contracts, but I soon learned that I got my best results by sending my sales literature out to the small computer software development firms, much to my surprise. I had expected the small electronics firms to be the most responsive. However, the experience served to alert me to a fundamental truth about marketing, even in the government sector: Markets change, and last year's marketing wisdom—sometimes even last month's marketing wisdom—may be out of date and totally unreliable now.

In promoting my seminars, I found it difficult to locate ready-made mailing lists of the several kinds of firms that I found to be most responsive to my seminar announcements. I therefore set about compiling my own lists, using many sources, such as the names of firms I found in the *Commerce Business Daily,* a government publication (readily available on the Internet now) announcing government contract needs and awards.

I also found the names of firms running large help-wanted advertisements in the newspapers to be excellent additions to my lists. It was a laborious task, building the lists, but eventually I had a valuable asset in my own mailing lists, which I was free to use over and over without paying anyone else a cent. And, as I made mailings, I invited addressees to let me know whether they favored another date or location for my seminars, if they were unable to attend the ones currently planned. Responses to that special invitation were the basis for both planning future sessions and compiling premium mailing lists for the future.

I present a mini-seminar online today, as a marketing tool. It appears on a site devoted to consulting, sponsored originally by an acquaintance and sponsored now by Dun & Bradstreet. Notice of the site and the free mini-seminar on it is made in many other places online. Today, you can use a Web site to make an offer and plant notices of the Web site everywhere, but especially wherever notices would reach the attention of those you have identified as your best market targets. The site itself can offer information of special interest to those prospects, such as news of happenings in their fields of interest.

There are, in fact, a number of such Web sites, offering news and other information related to government contracting and proposal writing, tips on proposal writing, tips on marketing to government, and a wide variety of other such items. (One that I am especially familiar with is http://www.govsolutions.com, the owner of which also sponsors a mailing list of those engaged in proposal writing.) All offer a great deal of free information related to proposal writing and government contracting, and all also offer services for which they charge, such as special search services and listings. The nature of the information is designed to give visitors a good reason to return to check out the site regularly.

It is, of course, important to encourage casual droppers-by to become repeat visitors. The prospect of some new useful information each week is a powerful inducement to return frequently. The repeated exposure to your offer is one of the most powerful influences in converting prospects to clients. The more often they read your offer, the more it penetrates their consciousness, the more memorable your message is, and the more credible and persuasive it appears. And the more often or the lengthier the time over which they see your messages, the more solid and dependable you appear to be, another plus factor. Add that to a growing trust in you as an honest and sincere guide and counselor, and you have the basis for great marketing success.

WHAT ARE YOU WORTH?

A great many of us sell our services as independent consultants far too cheaply. For one thing, we permit others to dictate our rates by charging what we think most others charge—by what we think "the market" is for our services—without regard to whether we believe that we are worth more and ought to earn more.

We hear about some consultants who charge much more than we do, stratospheric fees, it appears, and they appear to get enough work to stay busy. We wonder how they do it. They must be superb salesmen and saleswomen, we conclude. How else to explain it?

In fact, they *are* sales experts, whether the services they provide are or are not any better or otherwise more valuable than those we provide. They are sales experts primarily in their ability to build the $5,000 image where you and I build $500 images. They make no secret of the high rates they charge, nor do they make a special effort to justify them. They simply take it for granted that theirs is a fair and justifiable rate for what they do, and they believe that the rightness of their rate is an obvious fact. That attitude is the key element in building the image you need: It is something of a cliché, but still a truth, that you are worth whatever you decide to be worth. You can decide whether you will provide a $5,000 service or a $500 service, and thus be a $5,000 consultant or a $500 consultant. It is an integral and important aspect of the image you project online, with inevitable consequences.

YOUR ONLINE WORTH IMAGE

The point was made again and again in these pages that one of the most important considerations of your online marketing program is the projection of a highly professional image. Charging too little for your time and knowledge does nothing to enhance that image of high-level professionalism. Quite the contrary, it militates against that image. Prospective clients will inevitably judge your professional status by the fees you command, as well as by any other standard or measure. To accept rates too low to be properly becoming to a professional image is to undo whatever good you have done before. Clients expect to pay rates commensurate with the image you have built (or with their impression of what your rates would be). In the traditional business world, professionals use external signs as symbols of a high degree of professionalism, as exhibited by they way they dress, the stationery they use, the elegance of their offices, and other such physical signs. In the online world, this translates into elegant and costly Web sites and an appropriate tone to all your messages, being careful that all your messages and posts are quite literate and objective. As a professional, you will never allow yourself to be lured into flame wars or other petty arguments.

Be careful in striving for this that your messages do not acquire a nuance of arrogance. You can prevent that by showing complete respect for others' opinions as your peers.

Obviously, charging high rates will cost you some clients and contracts, but greater income resulting from "more professional" (higher) rates should more than offset that loss.

FEES OR RATES?

Independent consultants tend to charge clients a *rate* of pay, most often an hourly one, rather than a fixed *fee* for a task or project. I believe that working by the hour is very much against your interest as an independent consultant in more than one way:

- It supports, at least by implication, IRS efforts to disallow independent consultants' tax position as independent entrepreneurs and classify them as temporary employees.
- It handicaps your ability to earn more than a mere living; that is, to benefit appropriately from the risks of independent entrepreneurship.
- It tends to inhibit the growth of your consultancy because you are restricting your income potential to the number of hours you are able to devote to billable work.

- There is no incentive to invest in training, equipment, or systems to make your work more efficient—to reduce the number of hours necessary to get a job done—for your client benefits, but you lose, and you lose doubly because you have invested money to reduce your income.

The hourly rate is a relic of a time before machines and automation, a time when work was valued in terms of individual human effort accomplished entirely by the individual. It is simply not appropriate to today's situation, but it endures because we tend to cling to the familiar ways we already know.

Despite all that, it does not mean that you cannot charge a standard hourly rate, if that rate is high enough. The rates independent consultants charge clients today are decidedly variable. This is a murky area of marketing, especially in marketing a custom service. Each consultant and his or her service are unique. It comes down to a basic business-policy decision: You opt for many clients at "popular" rates, or you opt for fewer clients—"carriage trade" clients—at high rates.

To opt for the higher rates normally requires investment up front, at least until word of mouth develops to build your high-priced image and support your rates. It costs money to build an image that justifies and enables you to command a high rate. Marketing on the Internet, you will need an impressive Web site, for one, and that will probably require the services of a Web site designer to create that Web site. You will find it wise to invest in activities to help you publicize your Web site, such as an online newsletter and sponsorship of a mailing list. Which is the right course? Which will pay you better? That depends on your ability to build that image necessary to command high rates and your willingness to do so because it adds to your risk of entrepreneurship.

YOUR INTERNET IMAGE

You can develop a presence on the Internet, as in any society. Of course, in a population of many millions, you are not likely to become known to all in that society. But Internet society is made up of many subsocieties, of course, as is general society, and you can become well known in some of those if you participate actively.

The point is to first select the subsociety or -societies in which you can be most effective in terms of your goals and objectives. That is rapidly becoming a complex task in itself, as the Internet continues to expand. I find, for example, that whenever I log on to my selection of newsgroups, I am confronted with a message asking if I wish to see the list of new newsgroups—that is, those that have originated since my most recent review of new newsgroups, which was probably some time in the previous few days. I am also a subscriber to a mailing list that announces new mailing lists, and I generally get several notices each week, almost daily, in fact, of new mailing lists to which I can subscribe if I find them of interest. The mailing list announcing new mailing lists is NEW-LIST@ LISTSERV.NODAK.EDU.

I have found the mailing lists to be more useful than the newsgroups, for my purposes, especially if they are highly active mailing lists. An active mailing list comes much closer to the BBS society than does the newsgroup, I find. The flow of information and exchanges is much more dynamic and immediate. You can get messages several times a day and correspond with some of the other subscribers to the list on a more or less spontaneous basis. And, as in BBS society, personalities emerge from the spontaneous exchanges, and friendships arise from both the exchanges posted publicly for all to read and from the personal messages you can receive and send when you've something to say to one individual that would not be of interest to the other subscribers.

In a short while, if you are active and make your own contributions to the discussions, you begin to acquire an online personality. In one mailing-list group I frequent, one subscriber has come to be viewed as a bit testy and even caustic, while he is also considered to be an astute observer. Another is regarded as something of a guru on the main subject of the list. Still another is deemed to be a calming voice of reason. One subscriber became the object of severe criticism because he made what he thought to be a humorous post, but many found to be offensive and an attack on another subscriber, who happens to be held in high esteem by most participants.

You must be careful in wording your messages. In face-to-face conversation, facial expression and gestures modify your words and help make your meaning and intention clear. Written words appearing on a screen stand entirely on their own and are usually taken quite literally. You can call someone an "old dog" and make it clear that it is an affectionate colloquialism when chatting face to face, but it will almost surely be found to be insulting if written to someone who is a stranger or virtually a stranger.

Remember, too, that when you post to a busy mailing list, you are posting to a great many people. It is not something to do carelessly. Think carefully about what impressions you wish to make. Before I send a post, I review and think carefully about what it says. Far better to remain silent than risk damaging the image I have worked to create. If I have any doubts about the wisdom of posting the message, I hold it in abeyance for a while and often decide then to abandon it as an idea best forgotten.

THE IMAGE YOU WANT

Here, the question of "giving the store away" arises again. On mailing lists, you often find subscribers asking questions similar to those you answer for paying clients as part of the service you sell. Should you provide an answer free of charge here, in the mailing-list group? On my desk this morning is an invitation from a publisher to write some audiovisual material on consulting, along the lines of an outline provided, as a warning to the consultant to avoid giving away information without getting paid for it.

I believe that, far from protecting your interests by such defensive policies, you can make yourself appear mean-spirited and damage your image severely. Information is one tool you use in providing your services, but certainly not the only tool nor even the most important one. You sell, also, your diagnostic service, using your analytic abilities and your ability to reason and develop solutions. The information is of limited use without those other abilities, so giving the information away is not yielding a great deal, but it does reveal to all that you do have relevant knowledge. Almost as often as not, the client does not know what his or her problem is, but knows only what the symptoms are. If information per se is all you have to sell, you are seriously handicapped in delivering a consulting service. More to the point, I believe that in many situations it is beneficial to you to give information away freely and is even a key to making effective sales presentations!

There is also a special consideration that bears closely on the question of giving information away in your online appearances, a consideration that has been noted and remarked on frequently by others commenting on the Internet as a marketing medium. It is this: The Internet, in its image as an information superhighway, is a great reservoir of information available to everyone at no cost, other than the cost of being connected to it. That fact establishes a psychological barrier to paying for information online: Frequenters of the Internet tend to be well-conditioned to getting the information they want free of charge. It is thus appropriate to offer free information online.

GIVING INFORMATION AWAY AS A SALES STRATEGY

Giving away information can be turned to direct advantage and may even be the platform for delivering a brief and effective sales presentation. The scenario is this:

1. Someone online who could easily become a client asks a question of anyone who chooses to respond.
2. You respond with some direct, but general, information that is appropriate.
3. You follow up by saying that you have some special methods or ideas that would undoubtedly be even more helpful, but it would be necessary to have more detailed information and do some analysis to diagnose the problem or need.

You thus have laid the groundwork for a potential sale by inviting the other to furnish more preliminary information or suggest responding to you privately. You can then follow up appropriately to see if you cannot now convert this inquirer into a client!

THE WORLD'S LARGEST MARKET

Government agencies at all levels, federal, state, and local, have established residence—multiple residences, in fact—on the Internet and Web.

Taken together, they represent the world's largest market for most services and commodities, and especially for consulting and related professional services. The federal government agencies alone contract for more than $200 billion worth of goods and services annually, and the thousands of other government agencies together account for probably about twice as much. In many ways, what has been said about addressing the public market is applicable to the government market, but there are also some special considerations in selling to government markets. That is a subject that merits a chapter of its own, the next chapter.

CHAPTER 7

Marketing to Government on the Internet

M‌ost people refer to the federal establishment centered in Washington, D.C., when they speak of "the government," but we actually have thousands of governments in the United States, as classified by the U.S. Census Bureau. They include the 50 state governments and their agencies, and the governments of those thousands of counties, cities, towns, and townships, plus some miscellaneous territories and districts. Most, if not all, are very much in evidence on the Internet, in one guise or another. Together, they represent a huge market, existing and potential, for the industrious independent consultant, who may very well devote his or her entire consulting career to government markets, as many entrepreneurs and even large companies do.

THE UBIQUITOUS GOVERNMENT PRESENCE ON THE INTERNET

According to an article in *The Washington Post* ("Doing Business on the Internet," by Karen D. Schwartz, July 8, 1996), almost all agencies of the federal government are involved in commerce of some kind on the Internet. (In fact, federal presence on the Internet has continued to grow steadily since that announcement was made.) That should come as no great surprise for at least two reasons: One is because it is the federal government that inspired and still supports the Internet, as a result of the government-sponsored ARPANET, of the U.S. Advanced Research Projects Agency, the National Science Foundation, and other federal programs. Another is because federal agencies spend more than $200 billion annually in commercial activities, primarily in procurement of supplies and services, although even federal procurement is only a small part of what government does and presents on the Net.

Federal procurement represents a very large market—actually a large number of markets—but still is only a fraction of the total commerce in our society and of the total represented on the Internet. Nevertheless, it is still too large to ignore, and certainly an alert marketer, especially an independent practitioner, should not overlook or ignore it. Even that small fraction of the huge federal procurement budget devoted to buying the services of independent consultants represents a multimillion-dollar market for our services. Add to the federal procurement budgets the collective procurement budgets of state and local governments, and we are talking about a total market of more than $600 billion annually in all government buying in the private sector. It is thus inescapable that government purchasing will be a major factor in Internet commercial activity, as it has been in the traditional commercial transactions of the country.

Already, substantial growth in electronic commerce—online transactions—is apparent, and this growth is inevitable. Government has long had a goal of reducing the flood of paper and now "paperless transactions" are a reality that is destined to grow under the impetus of steadily increasing online facilities. Despite our too-human reluctance to abandon the established and familiar situations and practices, we are slowly turning to electronic/digital documents to implement and record our transactions (commercial and other).

MARKETING RESEARCH ON THE INTERNET

Access to online information about procurement needs of and marketing opportunities in federal, state, and local government markets is already abundant and it is still increasing. In fact, marketing and other information generally about all government organizations at federal, state, and local levels is at flood stage on the Internet and the Web (not to mention information about a great many foreign governments and quasigovernment organizations). You can now do a great deal of your research—perhaps all or nearly all of it—into all these markets without leaving your desk. We will sample just a little of it here, to illustrate the process and the content.

Exhibit 7-1 presents a listing of what is in the current day's issues of the federal government's procurement journal, the *Commerce Business Daily* (CBD). This publication, in electronic form, is available at several places on the Web, most often via paid subscription. In this figure, the CBD is presented on the Web by courtesy of Loren Data Corp.

Government contractors and subcontractors scan the CBD every day, seeking information on what the government's agencies see as needs, for the satisfying of which they invite vendors and contractors to submit bids or proposals. Exploring a given item, as synopsized in the CBD, you will find instructions for requesting the detailed information you need to order a copy of the solicitation package or *bid set,* that detailed information necessary to pursue and compete for the contract. For example, if you click your mouse on R-SOL TELECOMMUNICATIONS TECHNICAL SUPPORT, you come up with a few items, such as those of Exhibit 7-2. Further, clicking the next item checked in the illustration, you come up with Exhibit 7-3, the actual solicitation notice. That brief text advises you that a proposal will be required (the notice specifies that it is an RFP or Request for Proposals) and will give you enough information to enable you to determine how relevant the requirement is to what you do and tell you whether you are interested enough to pursue the opportunity further by requesting a copy of the solicitation, usually a thick packet of materials, including the following, as a minimum:

- A letter from the procurement official expanding on the synopsis and furnishing some relevant information in brief
- A statement of work, explaining in some detail what the government seeks, what is required (information to be furnished in the proposal), and special injunction or warnings, some indication as to how proposals will be evaluated, and several fill-in-the-blank forms

Exhibit 7-1

DAILY NOTICES OF THE COMMERCE BUSINESS DAILY

COMMERCE BUSINESS DAILY ISSUE OF JULY 9,1996 PSA#1632

The CBD Index Page has been accessed ▓▓▓▓▓▓ times since September 25, 1995.

- NEW: *Starting Monday, May 13, CBD Synopses with references to Web pages now have hot links*
- *World-Wide EDI(sm)FAQ*
- *Search today's CBD.*
- *What's New 5/10/96*
- *Subscribe to the CBD electronically and have it delivered to your e-mail everyday.*

SOLICITATIONS

- A - Research and Development *(4)*
- B - Special Studies and Analyses - Not R&D *(7)*
- C - Architect and Engineering Services - Construction *(7)*
- D - Automatic Data Processing and Telecommunication Services *(2)*
- F - Natural Resources and Conservation Services *(5)*
- G - Social Services *(4)*
- J - Maintenance, Repair and Rebuilding of Equipment *(18)*
- M - Operation of Government-Owned Facilities *(1)*
- N - Installation of Equipment *(1)*
- Q - Medical Services *(10)*
- R - Professional, Administrative and Management Support Services *(10)*
- S - Utilities and Housekeeping Services *(25)*
- T - Photographic, Mapping, Printing and Publication Services *(56)*
- U - Education and Training Services *(3)*
- V - Transportation, Travel and Relocation Services *(6)*
- W - Lease or Rental of Equipment *(2)*
- X - Lease or Rental of Facilities *(3)*
- Y - Construction of Structures and Facilities *(38)*
- Z - Maintenance, Repair or Alteration of Real Property *(94)*
- 10 - Weapons *(1)*
- 12 - Fire Control Equipment *(2)*
- 14 - Guided Missiles *(2)*
- 15 - Aircraft and Airframe Structural Components *(31)*
- 16 - Aircraft Components and Accessories *(29)*
- 25 - Vehicular Equipment Components *(3)*
- 28 - Engines, Turbines and Components *(14)*
- 29 - Engine Accessories *(3)*
- 30 - Mechanical Power Transmission Equipment *(5)*
- 34 - Metalworking Machinery *(2)*
- 36 - Special Industry Machinery *(1)*

Exhibit 7-2
ITEMS LISTED FOR SUPPORT

R - Professional, Administrative and Management Support Services

SOLICITATIONS

- <u>CONSTRUCTION MANAGEMENT SUPPORT SERVICES FOR</u>
- <u>LOGISTICS SUPPORT SERVICES FOR DISTRIBUTION,</u>
- <u>NETWORK TECHNICAL SUPPORT AND TECHNICAL PROJECT</u>
- <u>SHIPHANDLING SIMULATION SERVICES</u>
- <u>MANAGEMENT OF FITNESS CENTER</u>
- <u>DESIGN AND CONSTRUCTION MANAGEMENT SERVICES FOR THE</u>
- <u>ENGINEERING AND TECHNICAL SERVICE</u>
- <u>MICROCOMPUTER TECHNICAL SUPPORT PERSONNEL</u>
✓ • <u>TELECOMMUNICATIONS TECHNICAL SUPPORT</u>
- <u>RADIATION SAFETY OFFICER</u>

<u>Today's CBD Index Page</u>
Created on July 8, 1996 by Loren Data Corp.—<u>info@ld.com</u>

- The relevant statutes and regulations cited and, in some cases, reproduced in the bid set
- A few fill-in-the-blank forms required by various federal statutes

LEADS FOR SUBCONTRACTS

The listing of purchasing intentions and invitations for bids and proposals is the main objective of the CBD, but the CBD also offers other valuable marketing information, such as the frequent listing of contract awards. See Exhibit 7-4 for a listing of the service classifications in which contracts are awarded.

Each of these listings will advise you of prime contracts awarded, to whom they were awarded, and for how much money. Few contractors do

Exhibit 7-3
SYNOPSIS OF SOLICITATION NOTICE

COMMERCE BUSINESS DAILY ISSUE OF JULY 9, 1996 PSA#1632

National Park Service, Gateway National Recreation Area, Building 69, Floyd Bennett Field, Brooklyn, New York 11234-7017

R—TELECOMMUNICATIONS TECHNICAL SUPPORT SOL 1443RP177096004. Due 081696. POC Mark Davidson, Contracting Officer, 718/338-3415. The work on the contract resulting from the solicitation shall consist of the contractor supplying telecommunications technical support personnel on an intermittent basis from date of award through September 30, 1996. One person will be required for an average of thirty-five hours per week. This contract will also contain four one year options with the same personnel and hourly requirement. The place of performance will be Gateway National Recreation Area with sites in three of the boroughs of New York City (Brooklyn, Queens and Staten Island) and Monmouth County New Jersey. The offeror will be required to submit a technical as well as a cost proposal with the technical proposal carrying more weight. All responsible sources may submit a bid which will be considered. (185)

Loren Data Corp. http://www.ld.com (SYN# 0068 19960708\R-0009.SOL)

R - Professional, Administrative and Management Support Services Index Page

---

everything required to carry out the project awarded in a prime contract, so prime contractors winning large projects usually subcontract some elements of the projects, sometimes even many elements. (As much as one-third to one-half the prime contract may be performed by subcontractors.) The awards section of the CBD is thus a valuable marketing research resource to determine which awards and prime contractors appear to be good prospects for subcontracts. Many individuals and small companies survive on such subcontracts alone, which may be far more profitable than are the prime contracts.

Opening up one such item (Exhibit 7-5) reveals a synopsis that identifies the contract, the contracting officer, the amount of the award, and the name of the successful proposer. This is therefore a sales lead.

Exhibit 7-4
PARTIAL LISTING OF AWARDS TO PRIME CONTRACTORS

AWARDS
- J - Maintenance, Repair and Rebuilding of Equipment *(3)*
- L - Technical Representative Services *(1)*
- R - Professional, Administrative and Management Support Services *(1)*
- S - Utilities and Housekeeping Services *(1)*
- Y - Construction of Structures and Facilities *(4)*
- Z - Maintenance, Repair or Alteration of Real Property *(6)*
- 10 - Weapons *(5)*
- 12 - Fire Control Equipment *(2)*
- 13 - Ammunition and Explosives *(3)*
- 14 - Guided Missiles *(2)*
- 15 - Aircraft and Airframe Structural Components *(10)*
- 16 - Aircraft Components and Accessories *(8)*
- 17 - Aircraft Launching, Landing and Ground Handling Equipment *(2)*
- 19 - Ships, Small Craft, Pontoons and Floating Docks *(1)*

AIDS TO ALL GOVERNMENT MARKETING RESEARCH

Researching all the markets every day can be a full-time job, demanding much too much time for an independent practitioner to undertake alone. There are, however, many services available to help you do the research, find the opportunities, and even help you write the proposals. Exhibit 7-6 reproduces a couple of Web pages exemplifying this kind of service. As is typical of Web pages, certain services and information are free, designed to attract visitors who are likely to become prospective clients.

Exhibit 7-6 reveals a set of support services focused on federal government agencies. Another vendor of marketing support services offers wider-ranging coverage, as shown in Exhibit 7-7, offering help in marketing to governments at all levels, but also covering other markets, as shown in Exhibit 7-8. Exhibit 7-9 is the opening page of Florida's Web site for suppliers. The various links listed will transport you to the information indicated. You need to do a great deal of exploring, but there is

Exhibit 7-5
TYPICAL SYNOPSIS OF AN AWARD

COMMERCE BUSINESS DAILY ISSUE OF JULY 10, 1996 PSA#1633

Office of Naval Research, 800 North Quincy Street, Arlington, VA 22217-5660

A—RELIABLE DETECTION AND ANALYSIS OF COGNITIVELY-ASSOCIATED EVENTS IN FREE-RUNNING BRAINWAVES POC Mrs. Sarah F. Wiley, ONR 252 (703) 696-8554. CNT N00014-96-C-0109 AMT $384,978.00 DTD 062896 TO HNC Software, Inc., San Diego, CA 92121 (0190)

Loren Data Corp. http://www.ld.com (SYN# 0353 19960709\A-0004.AWD)

A - Research and Development Index Page

pay dirt to be found, if you persevere. North Carolina offers a somewhat more detailed first page on its Web site, as shown in Exhibit 7-10. Here, again, you can invoke various links to explore detailed information. California lists its requirements on a daily basis on the Web, as shown in Exhibit 7-11. Beside the code and descriptive name, the number of such needs is listed. On July 9, 1996, the date of this listing, there were 15 requirements for consulting services, for example, as the figure indicates.

Exhibit 7-12 reminds me of how much easier marketing research is on the Internet than it was using the classical legwork of yesteryear. A number of years ago, I developed a directory of federal, state, and local governments' procurement systems, along with relevant data, such as the various minority and small-business programs of each state. I collected all this information laboriously, using surface mail and the telephone, and plodding about to find the various state and local agencies where I would make my pleas to the officials, seeking information about their purchasing departments and business opportunities. I recall Delaware as being the most difficult one, one that never did respond to my most desperate pleas and compelled me to use indirect and roundabout methods to gather the information. Looking back at that problem and my difficulties in solving it at the time makes me especially appreciative of the Internet and its great facilities for market research in general, and that of government organizations especially. Taking maximum advantage of these facilities should

Exhibit 7-6

A TYPICAL ANNOUNCEMENT OF

SUPPORT SERVICES OFFERED

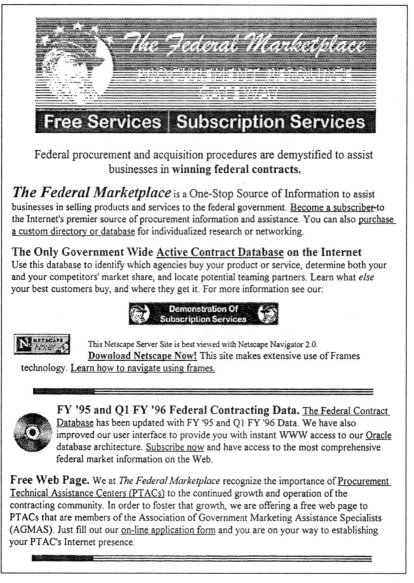

Federal procurement and acquisition procedures are demystified to assist businesses in **winning federal contracts.**

The Federal Marketplace is a One-Stop Source of Information to assist businesses in selling products and services to the federal government. Become a subscriber to the Internet's premier source of procurement information and assistance. You can also purchase a custom directory or database for individualized research or networking.

The Only Government Wide Active Contract Database on the Internet
Use this database to identify which agencies buy your product or service, determine both your and your competitors' market share, and locate potential teaming partners. Learn what *else* your best customers buy, and where they get it. For more information see our:

Demonstration Of Subscription Services

This Netscape Server Site is best viewed with Netscape Navigator 2.0.
Download Netscape Now! This site makes extensive use of Frames technology. Learn how to navigate using frames.

FY '95 and Q1 FY '96 Federal Contracting Data. The Federal Contract Database has been updated with FY '95 and Q1 FY '96 Data. We have also improved our user interface to provide you with instant WWW access to our Oracle database architecture. Subscribe now and have access to the most comprehensive federal market information on the Web.

Free Web Page. We at *The Federal Marketplace* recognize the importance of Procurement Technical Assistance Centers (PTACs) to the continued growth and operation of the contracting community. In order to foster that growth, we are offering a free web page to PTACs that are members of the Association of Government Marketing Assistance Specialists (AGMAS). Just fill out our on-line application form and you are on your way to establishing your PTAC's Internet presence.

(Continued)

Exhibit 7-6

CONTINUED

Free Services

News & Information

- Overview Of The Federal Market
- Sales Opportunities
- Federal Procurement Update
- Professional Announcements
- News Forum
- Reader's Guide To *The Federal Marketplace*

Regulation & Legislation

- Federal Acquisition Regulation (FAR)
- Cost Accounting Standards (CAS)
- Recent Legislation

Procurement Resources

- The Procurement Assistance Jumpstation
- The State & Local Procurement Jumpstation
- Procurement Technical Assistance Centers
- Home Page Development & Business Capabilities Directory
- SIC Codes
- FIPS State and County Codes

Subscription Packages

FM BRONZE -- $75 annually

For $75 a year you get all of the features listed below. You can search the active contracts database by SIC code, contractor name, and product and service code. If you want a more sophisticated search capability, you'll need to subscribe to FM SILVER, which features ContractSearch™, the ultimate federal marketing tool. Subscribe today.

Topics

- Selling To The Federal Government
- Bids & Proposals
- Financial Aspects Of Contracting
- Legal Aspects Of Contracting
- Small Business Assistance Programs
- Electronic Data Interchange - EDI
- Small Business Innovative Research - SBIR
- Government Forms

Databases

- About *The Federal Marketplace* Databases
- Query by SIC Code
- Query by Product/Service Code
- Query by Contractor Name
- 8(a) Contractors

Directories

- Federal Procurement Offices
- SBA District Offices
- SBA Regional Offices
- Federal Offices Of Small And Disadvantaged Business Utilization
- Freedom Of Information Offices
- GSA Business Center Regional Offices

FM SILVER -- $400 annually

You get everything above **plus** our latest service, ContractSearch™. Utilizing the power of Oracle software, ContractSearch™ allows you to uncover the details of approximately one half million contract actions. And it's been updated with **Q1 FY '96 data**. Form your own sophisticated search queries using up to 20 data elements. Find out exactly which agencies are buying from your competitors and discover how much money these contracts are worth. Discover lucrative bid opportunities well in advance of your competitors by pinpointing contract termination dates. This is a powerful research capability, and it's not available anywhere else on the Internet. Subscribe today.

Exhibit 7-7
A WIDER-RANGING SET OF
SUPPORT SERVICES OFFERED

Purchasing / Procurement HomePage

The Most Links to Purchasing Sites on the Internet

brought to you by:
William (Bill) Christensen, C.P.M.

AWESOME!!
PURCHASING
LINKS

Government Purchasing	University Purchasing	Purchasing Organizations
Purchasing Info Resources		Products/Software/MRO
Purchasing HomePages		Purchasing Consultants
NEWS	Purchasing Seminars & Training	Careers

155

Exhibit 7-8
OTHER MARKETS

Purchasing/Procurement Links
Government Sites

- State of Florida Purchasing Info Center
- State of Maine - Div. of Purchases
- State of North Carolina
- North Carolina Local Gov't Purchasing
- Washington State

- National Purchasing Institute

- State and Local Gov't Guide
- The Procurement Assistance Jumpstation
- Federal Acquisition Jumpstation
- Solutions Consulting Group - government & other links
- FedWorld Information Network—Federal Government documents
- US Chamber of Commerce
- White House Home Page
- United States Postal Service - Purchasing

- International Commerce—government web pages - Asia, Australia, Canada, Europe, New Zealand, U.K., and U.S.
- Purchasing Australia
- Poland

E-mail to Bill Christensen
Return to Home Page

greatly reduce the cost of pursuing government contracts. It is that cost which has been one of the factors inhibiting small business from making the effort to compete for government contracts, but that is less of a consideration now for those using the Internet facilities effectively.

Interesting to note, also, is that at the time I was busily collecting all government procurement information I could find, I filled a large cardboard carton with the documents I had collected in my odyssey. The car-

Exhibit 7-9
A WEB PAGE FOR FLORIDA'S PROCUREMENT SYSTEM

FCN PURCHASING
ONE STOP SERVICE CENTER

● **State Contracts and Agreements**
SNAPS, State Contracts.

● **Purchasing Applications & Databases**
SPURSview On The Net, Database of Recycled Commodities.

● **Purchasing Manuals & Forms & Guidelines**
Purchasing Manual, Purchasing Forms, Surplus Guide, Standards Guide.

● **Vendor Information**
Vendor Guide.

● **Announcements & Bulletins & Reports**
Newsletter, Phone Directory.

● **Related Links.**
NIGP, FAPPO, RESPECT, PRIDE, NASPO.

● **SPURS Information.**
Multiple Invoice-to and Multiple Account Code Release Package.

You are user **006517** since Feb 09, 1996

| purchase | | FCN Search |

FCN Homepage   Help   Overview   What's New

These pages are maintained by Stelios Manias: WebMaster

ton was one that had originally held 5,000 sheets of paper for my printer. Today, I could do that search in a few hours, or a day or two at most, and fit all the data I collected on a floppy disk or two that I could carry in my shirt pocket.

Finally, there is Maryland, my own state of residence, whose purchasing and supply service is part of its Department of General Services, as shown in Exhibit 7-13.

Exhibit 7-10
HOME PAGE FOR NORTH CAROLINA'S PROCUREMENT SYSTEM

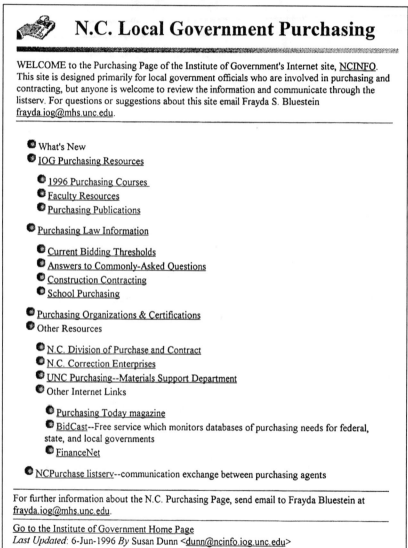

N.C. Local Government Purchasing

WELCOME to the Purchasing Page of the Institute of Government's Internet site, NCINFO. This site is designed primarily for local government officials who are involved in purchasing and contracting, but anyone is welcome to review the information and communicate through the listserv. For questions or suggestions about this site email Frayda S. Bluestein frayda.iog@mhs.unc.edu.

- What's New
- IOG Purchasing Resources

  - 1996 Purchasing Courses
  - Faculty Resources
  - Purchasing Publications

- Purchasing Law Information

  - Current Bidding Thresholds
  - Answers to Commonly-Asked Questions
  - Construction Contracting
  - School Purchasing

- Purchasing Organizations & Certifications
- Other Resources

  - N.C. Division of Purchase and Contract
  - N.C. Correction Enterprises
  - UNC Purchasing--Materials Support Department
  - Other Internet Links

    - Purchasing Today magazine
    - BidCast--Free service which monitors databases of purchasing needs for federal, state, and local governments
    - FinanceNet

  - NCPurchase listserv--communication exchange between purchasing agents

For further information about the N.C. Purchasing Page, send email to Frayda Bluestein at frayda.iog@mhs.unc.edu.

Go to the Institute of Government Home Page
Last Updated: 6-Jun-1996 *By* Susan Dunn <dunn@ncinfo.iog.unc.edu>

Exhibit 7-11

CALIFORNIA'S LIST OF PROCUREMENT INTENTIONS

Department of General Services
Office of Small and Minority Business

California State Contracts Register
Daily Advertisements

Categories

- 01 JANITORIAL MAINTENANCE (20 items)
- 02 PRINTING AND PUBLISHING (2 items)
- 03 INSECT EXTERMINATION (6 items)
- 04 TRANSPORTATION AND WAREHOUSING (3 items)
- 05 CONSULTING (15 items)
- 06 SECURITY (1 items)
- 07 DATA PROCESSING (5 items)
- 08 MAILING (2 items)
- 09 REFUSE AND SEWAGE DISPOSAL (10 items)
- 10 ARCHITECTURAL AND ENGINEERING (2 items)
- 11 PHOTOGRAPHY AND REPRODUCTION (2 items)
- 12 EQUIPMENT SERVICE, REPAIR OR INSTALLATION (18 items)
- 13 EQUIPMENT RENTAL AND LEASING (7 items)
- 14 AUTOMOTIVE/AIRCRAFT REPAIR, RENTAL AND LEASING (1 items)
- 15 GARDENING AND AGRICULTURE (12 items)
- 16 MEDICAL/HEALTH CARE (9 items)
- 17 OFFICE LEASING (5 items)
- 18 CONSTRUCTION (106 items)
- 19 MISCELLANEOUS SERVICE CATEGORY (29 items)
- 20 COMMODITIES (0=items)

- Commodities (DGS Procurement Division) NEW

OSMB Homepage DGS Home Page

Updated Tuesday Jul 09, 1996

State of California, Department of General Services
Send Comments to rroa@dgs.ca.gov

HOW GOVERNMENTS BUY

In the private sector, an organization may buy whatever it wishes from whomever it wishes, by any lawful means it wishes. In government purchasing, because the agency is spending public money—taxpayers' money, that is—there are specific statutes and formal regulations that have the authority of law governing purchasing activities. These must be

Exhibit 7-12

DELAWARE STATE'S DIVISION OF PURCHASING

State of Delaware

Division of Purchasing

Robert P. McWilliams, Director

Division of Purchasing
P.O. Box 299
Delaware City, Delaware 19706

Phone: 302-834-7081

Fax: 302-836-7642

Welcome to the Delaware Division of Purchasing!

Our Mission Statement

Selling to the State of Delaware

Annual Contracts

Vendor Registration Application

For General Information:

Phone: 302-834-4550

Government | Education | Econ Development | Tourism
Delaware Facts | What's New | Internet Help | WWW Sites
This page is maintained by the Webmasters of OIS (webmaster@ois.state.de.us).
Last Modified: February 14, 1996.

---

observed and complied with, of course. As a contractor you are much better equipped to compete in the marketplace if you understand what these laws and regulations are, philosophically and specifically. I have found that knowledge of the statutes and purchasing regulations can make the difference between winning and losing sales to government agencies. It is akin to being purer than Caesar's wife: Often you find it highly advantageous to know the procurement regulations better than the agency's procurement officials do, if you use that knowledge with great tact and diplomacy.

Federal government purchasing is regulated by the Federal Acquisition Regulations (FAR), and other governments have their own purchasing

Exhibit 7-13
MARYLAND STATE WEB PAGE

Welcome to the

Parris N. Glendening, Governor
Gene Lynch, Secretary

Michele Tucker Rozner, Deputy Secretary

✹ **Recent DGS Press Releases** ✹

✹ **View and Download Procurement Information** ✹

All DGS Procurements and other related information can be found on The DGS Bulletin Board by having your modem dial (410)333-5116 (N,8,1 up to 14,400 kbps)

More information about DGS:

● General Services Overview
● Facilities Planning, Engineering and Construction
● Procurement and Logistics
● Maryland State Agency for Surplus Property
● Minority Business Enterprise
● Real Estate

Helpful Links:

● Maryland Electronic Capitol
● Search the State Telephone Directory
● Download Directory Files
● Certified Minority Business Directory
● Vital Records Information

161

regulations and practices. Most purchasing regulations are similar to those of the federal government and despite the fact that lower-level governments do not buy nearly as much as the federal government does, many have volumes of purchasing procedures and regulations of a size that rivals those of the federal government.

There are thus many similarities among government buying practices at all levels, and there are some differences, although the similarities are much greater and more significant than the differences. The philosophical/political basis is the same for all: It is based on the principle of open competition, affording all of us equal opportunities to compete for government business, while still affording government the opportunity to seek the most advantageous buying agreements. That is basic in the concept of competitive bidding, with bids opened in a public forum and awards to the lowest bidders. All our governments recognize this as the guiding principle of government procurement of supplies and services. In fact, the systems are based largely on a uniform procurement code developed some years ago by a special committee of the American Bar Association.

COMPETITIVE PROPOSALS VERSUS SEALED BIDS

From the viewpoint of a contracting official, the ideal purchasing system would be based entirely on sealed bids and all contract awards made to the lowest bidders. That is the simplest system, the least expensive way to make purchases, and the surest way of buying at the lowest prices.

Unfortunately, the lowest price does not necessarily represent the best value, especially where the contract does not cite precise specifications that are well recognized and verifiable, as in the many cases of awards requiring custom services, such as the design of some new equipment system. In fact, a price that appears to be unreasonably low raises the suspicion of unacceptable quality, or unacceptable standards of performance, in the case of service contracts. Where the circumstances are such that this is a real concern—for example, the research and development of a new aircraft for the military—sealed bids are not a satisfactory method of selecting a contractor.

Value is always a major concern. The need for the maximum in the quality and reliability of many services and products often far exceeds the need for lowest prices. That is why government agencies normally use sealed bids only to buy standard commodities and services, where quality varies little or the government has a set of specifications to mandate and can verify that the product or service meets those specifications. For those other cases, where quality, safety, reliability, and other factors will necessarily vary widely from one supplier to another, the government buys via what it calls *competitive proposals* (formerly called "negotiated procurement"). This is a system under which an agency invites proposals and performs technical and cost analyses of each proposal to assess which of the offers it receives in response to an invitation best serves the interests of the government, all factors considered. In this kind of procurement, the agency is not required to award the contract to the lowest bidder, but can make its own judgment on relative merits of the proposals offered, can judge which proposals are acceptable, and can then negotiate a contract with one or more of the proposers to reach final decisions and make the best deals possible. Note the latter point that even having found one proposal to be acceptable and preferable to all other proposals, the government still can enter into negotiations, and often does. (Typically, the agency will call for what the trade refers to as a "BAFO," for "best and final offer," and use that as the basis for final negotiations.)

In fact, to make the technical evaluation as objective as possible, the evaluation team is not permitted to know the costs until they have assigned technical scores to the proposals. Costs must be submitted in a separate proposal, so contenders submit two proposals, a technical proposal and a cost proposal. Of course, proposers are enjoined from revealing costs in their technical proposals, although evaluators may do some reading between the lines and make their own inferences and estimates of costs thereby.

Although the details of implementation may vary somewhat from one government to another and even from one agency to another, this philosophy is basic to all public (government) procurement. It is important to understand this fully so that you price *realistically*. Pricing too low can be a disastrous mistake: The low bidder in these situations is often considered to be low to be credible, and thus is judged to have misunderstood the requirement and is unqualified to do the work. An excellent technical proposal can be thus nullified by a poor cost proposal. (If you have some reason for being exceptionally low-priced, it is necessary to explain this in some manner so your price is not taken as evidence of not understanding the requirement and therefore issuing a "nonresponsive" proposal.)

Probably the most significant difference between purchasing practices of federal government agencies, on the one hand, and state and local government agencies, on the other hand, is a physical one of assignment of purchasing authority and responsibility. Federal government purchasing is highly decentralized into many contracting offices, with most large government offices and branches of agencies having their own contracting offices, while state and local governments tend to centralize such activity. The United States is divided into ten regions, and most (not all) federal departments and other agencies maintain a major office in each region, although an agency may also have other offices within each region. In most cases, each regional office and many other offices have their own purchasing offices and contracting authority. With additional contracting authorities within regions, there are a great many contracting offices in the federal system. A given department may have dozens of contracting offices. (Still, there are also some centralized supply centers in the federal system, such as the Federal Supply Service, the Defense Logistics Agency, and central supply centers for the Department of Veterans Affairs and the U.S. Postal Service.) Contracting with the federal government is correspondingly decentralized—you must contract individually with each separate contracting office. With this kind of decentralization, assiduous use of the Internet in searching out each of the thousands of government agencies and offices enables you, even as an individual, to do marketing research on a national and even international basis. It gives you the same reach in marketing research as that of a large corporation and enables you to do market research you could not even dream of doing without the online capability.

This is important even in the case of state and local governments. Federal purchasing is heavily decentralized, but state and local governments tend to centralize their purchasing in a single purchasing and supply department, which is usually physically located in the capital of the state (county seat or city hall, for local governments). Agencies of the local government (and in many cases even a relatively small local government has a surprisingly large number of agencies) usually can contract individually for supplies or services only via the central office. (In some special cases, local government agencies can contract through the federal government and shop at the Federal Supply Service stores.) You may, for example, persuade the roads and highways commission of a state or local government agency to retain you. Although it will have to do the contracting via its central purchasing department, you would have had to sell yourself to the commission first. Thus you would have had to know that the commission existed and where/how to make your solicitations to it.

In a practical sense, this does not make a great deal of difference in procurement systems and selling to them. You normally pursue state and local contracts very much in the same way that you pursue federal contracts. And there are the same basic truisms, especially that one which says that the smallest business, such as the independent consultant, is as much entitled to pursue and win government contracts as is the largest supercorporation.

It does work that way. Obviously, as an independent consultant, you cannot hope to win a $200 million contract to design a top-level management system for the Pentagon. You must bid for contracts that are demonstrably within your capabilities, but individuals are winning government contracts every day, as I once did. It is an open market, made even more so now by the online facilities that you can employ to help you in your marketing to government agencies.

SPECIAL PROVISIONS

Every government has its own small-purchase statutes, which authorize simplified and speedy purchasing actions as exceptions to the formal contracting processes. The rationale is a simple one: It costs a government a great deal of money to solicit bids and proposals, conduct competitions, negotiate contracts, and make final contract awards. Therefore, a simplified procedure for small purchases is justified and is employed. It usually involves a government purchase order, instead of a formal contract, and little or no competitive bidding. In the federal government today, a small purchase is any purchase not exceeding $25,000; in state and local governments, that ceiling figure on small purchases is usually a considerably lower one.

There are a few other situations that invoke special exceptions to the normal practices of open competition and equal opportunity for all potential suppliers. The chief one is the *selected source,* from whom buying is often referred to as *sole sourcing.* There are three major rationales for justifying sole sourcing, which is negotiated but noncompetitive procurement, since the contractor is chosen without competition:

- What the agency wants to buy is unique and not available elsewhere— that is, the selected source has a unique capability, such as a unique and proprietary software program of which the agency has need.
- The selected source has special experience or a unique capability that enables it to deliver what is needed at much lower cost than another supplier who would have to develop the special capability.
- The source has submitted an unsolicited proposal with an original idea that the agency thinks to be valuable and wishes to accept.

THE "VIRTUAL CORPORATION" ADVANTAGE

A major consideration in evaluation of the proposal in many procurements is the credentials of the staff proposed as the principals to be employed in the service offered, if you compete for a project in which you will need employees or associates to form a team. Lately, a team of associates, especially independent specialists, formed to carry out a project that requires a staff, is sometimes referred to as a *virtual corporation.* That term was inspired by the reach of online communication and the ability it provides to search efficiently and on a global scale for associates, and to coordinate activities with associates at distant physical locations so that all can act in concert, well coordinated.

These are important considerations in marketing. Not only does the global reach of the Internet make it possible for you to search worldwide for the best qualified candidates when searching for associates or co-bidders with impressive credentials for the project, but it makes the virtual corporation practicable and credible. Moreover, procurement philosophy in government procurement is changing in favor of contracting with teams, rather than with single organizations. (So far, this has applied to major procurements, but the principle is now well established.)

That is not the only advantage the reach of the Internet offers you in contending for government contracts. Much of success in winning government contracts is dependent on the quality of the proposal offered, and so the pursuit of associates who can help turn out a quality proposal is another important factor in marketing to government agencies. Here, again, the Internet can be used for swift and convenient correspondence to broadcast an appeal for associates, submit information, provide samples, and otherwise facilitate the entire process. Where once I had to send people out to distant places to interview prospects for projects and gather the information needed to prepare proposals, today you can do it all without leaving your office—and in hours, rather than in days. Where once I had to spend hours on the telephone and/or advertising in newspapers to let it be known that I invited inquiries from prospective associates, now you can post notices in several places on the Internet and get responses a few hours later. Another highly important factor in the selection of a winning proposal is the quality of the staff—that is, the credentials offered in the resumés of the proposed staff. Again, the reach of Internet access enables you to gather a team whose resumés are impressive and so contribute substantially to the success of your proposal.

On balance, being part of a virtual corporation offers some benefits of both employment by a corporation and the independence of self-employment.

BIDDERS LISTS AND REGISTRATIONS

Contracting offices that solicit bids and proposals frequently or on a regular basis establish and maintain bidders lists and mail out solicitations to those who are on their lists and considered to be good prospective contractors for whatever the solicitation seeks to buy. The list of standard forms available in the federal system includes a Standard Form 129, *Application for Bidders List,* which you may file to indicate what kinds of contracts you wish to pursue. The state and local governments have their own equivalents of this form, although it is often an element of a larger form used as a vendor registration. In the federal system, one may choose to file a 129 form or not; it is not required by federal agencies that a contractor be registered with them in any way. All the states request that a prospective contractor fill out and file their registration forms, and in many states, filing a registration is mandatory to compete for contracts of the state government.

Exhibit 7-14 presents a copy of the registration form for pursuing contracts with the State of Florida. It can be downloaded from Florida's Web site, but must be mailed in. Note, however, that the form is still very much oriented to online activities and calls for entering e-mail addresses and URLs for Web sites, if any. Exhibit 7-15, on the other hand, an application to be placed on the vendor list for the State of Washington, also provides for the entry of similar information, but can be filled out and filed from your own computer, if you have a suitable browser. That availability of forms that can be completed and filed directly from Web sites is a rapidly growing feature of the Internet, making Web sites truly interactive. Taking advantage of this requires that the browser you are using is capable of interacting with the forms, and perhaps of downloading them, in some cases, but most of the leading browsers of today are equal to the task.

PROPOSAL STRATEGIES

There are those who believe that winning government contracts depends on having "connections." That is one of the several widely propagated myths about government contracting, probably circulated by those who have been unsuccessful in competing for government work and have a need to find an exculpatory explanation for their failures. Still, there is a tiny seed of truth in this myth, as there is at the base of most myths: It is true that in the case of the very large contract, one that represents a significantly large economic asset for a region, senators and congressional representatives will fight and use whatever powers they have to win such multimillion-dollar contracts for their own states and districts. That is of no significance to you as an independent consultant vying to win a small contract of a few thousand dollars for your services. I can assure you, from my personal experience, that you can win such contracts regularly if you put forth effective effort. You do not need "connections" of any kind. You do need to have a sharp pencil for sealed-bid procurements and proposal-writing talent for negotiated procurement.

Exhibit 7-14

VENDOR REGISTRATION FOR THE STATE OF FLORIDA

STATE OF FLORIDA

DEPARTMENT OF MANAGEMENT SERVICES

VENDOR REGISTRATION APPLICATION

CHECK ONE: ___NEW APPLICATION ___REVISED VENDOR RECORD
(FILL IN FEID # OR SS # AND ANY INFORMATION TO BE CHANGED)

ALL U.S.A. FIRMS THAT ARE ESTABLISHED AS AN INDIVIDUAL, SELF-EMPLOYED OR SOLE PROPRIETORSHIP MUST PROVIDE EITHER THEIR SOCIAL SECURITY NUMBER OR FEID NUMBER. ALL OTHER BUSINESSES SUCH AS CORPORATIONS MUST PROVIDE THEIR FEDERAL EMPLOYER IDENTIFICATION NUMBER. NON-U.S.A. FIRMS MAY OR MAY NOT HAVE A FEDERAL EMPLOYER IDENTIFICATION NUMBER AND IF NOT, A NUMBER WILL BE ASSIGNED BY THIS OFFICE. I.INSERT FEDERAL EMPLOYER IDENTIFICATION NUMBER OR SOCIAL SECURITY NUMBER BY WHICH BUSINESS IS CONDUCTED.

F__ __-__ __ __ __ __ __ __ (OR) S__ __ __-__ __-__ __ __ __

(OR) N_____ (TO BE COMPLETED BY DIVISION OF PURCHASING)
__ CHECK IF NOT A U.S. FIRM __CHECK IF A FLORIDA BASED FIRM

II.
SHORT NAME IF YOUR COMPANY NAME IS COMMONLY SHORTENED OR ABBREVIATED PLEASE PROVIDE US WITH THAT INFORMATION.(EX.NATIONAL FOOTBALL LEAGUE; NFL)
COMPANY NAME THE NAME ISSUED MUST BE THE LEGAL NAME BY WHICH BIDS WILL BE SUBMITTED AND TO WHICH CONTRACTS MAY BE AWARDED.
PARENT OF DBA DOING BUSINESS AS (DBA), PARENT COMPANY ETC.
MAILING ADDRESS: DELIVERY ADDRESS, CITY, STATE, AND ZIP PLUS FOUR IS THE ADDRESS TO WHICH INVITATIONS TO BID WILL BE MAILED.
CONTACT PERSON AND PHONE NUMBER PLEASE LIST THE CONTACT PERSON IN CHARGE OF BIDDING FOR YOUR COMPANY.

SHORT NAME _____
COMPANY NAME _____
DBA OR PARENT COMPANY NAME(IF APP)_____
MAILING ADDRESS _____
CITY_____COUNTY_____
STATE_____ZIP __ __ __ __ __-__ __ __ __ COUNTRY(IF NOT U.S. FIRM)_____
REMITTAL ADDRESS(IF DIFFERENT FROM MAILING ADDRESS)_____
CITY_____COUNTY_____
STATE_____ZIP __ __ __ __ __-__ __ __ __ COUNTRY(IF NOT U.S. FIRM)_____
PHONE NUMBER(__ __ __) __ __ -__ __ __ __ FAX NUMBER(__ __ __) __ __ -__ __ __ __

III.BUSINESS DESIGNATION (SELECT ONE CODE THAT APPLIES TO YOUR COMPANY)
1__CORPORATION, PROFESSIONAL ASSOCIATION OR PROFESSIONAL CORPORATION

5__NON-CORPORATE RENTAL AGENT

2__NOT FOR PROFIT CORPORATION

6__GOVERNMENTAL ENTITY(CITY, COUNTY, STATE, OR U.S.)

3__PARTNERSHIP, JOINT VENTURE, ESTATE OR TRUST

7__FOREIGN CORPORATION, FOREIGN NATIONAL OR OTHER FOREIGN ENTITY

4__SOLE PROPRIETORSHIP OR SELF EMPLOYED

IN THIS SECTION SELECT ONE IN CATEGORY IV, AND IVA IF APPLICABLE
PLEASE SELECT THE CLASS THAT BEST DESCRIBES YOUR COMPANY.(NON-MINORITY, SMALL BUSINESS-STATE OR FEDERAL; NON-CERTIFIED MINORITY; AND (IF APPLICABLE BLACK, HISPANIC, WOMAN, ASIAN/HAWAIIAN, NATIVE AMERICAN)

IV. MINORITY CLASSIFICATION   IVA. ARE YOU APPLYING FOR MINORITY CERTIFICATION(YES__NO__)
A__NON-MINORITY   H__BLACK
B__SMALL BUSINESS-STATE   I__HISPANIC
C__SMALL BUSINESS-FEDERAL   J__ASIAN/HAWAIIAN
D__NON-CERTIFIED MINORITY BUSINESS   K__NATIVE AMERICAN
E__GOVERNMENTAL AGENCY   M__AMERICAN WOMAN
F__NON-PROFIT ORGANIZATION

TO APPLY FOR FLORIDA MINORITY BUSINESS CERTIFICATION, CALL (904) 487-0915 TO REQUEST APPLICATION
V. PLEASE SELECT GEOGRAPHICAL AREA IN WHICH FIRM CONDUCTS BUSINESS:
GEOGRAPHICAL AREA: ENTIRE STATE: ABLE TO SUPPLY ALL COUNTIES IN FLORIDA
DISTRICT(S):ABLE TO SUPPLY ALL COUNTIES WITHIN THE DISTRICT SELECTED

(Continued)

Exhibit 7-14
CONTINUED

COUNTY: SELECT APPLICABLE COUNTY OR COUNTIES
TO BE CONSIDERED FOR STATE CONTRACTS, YOU MUST ACCEPT RESPONSIBILITY FOR DELIVERY TO AT LEAST AN ENTIRE DISTRICT.

CHECK APPLICABLE LINE
__ ENTIRE STATE
OR

__WESTERN DISTRICT	__NORTHERN DISTRICT	__CENTRAL DISTRICT	__SOUTHERN DISTRICT
03__BAY	01__ALACHUA	05__BREVARD	06__BROWARD
07__CALHOUN	02__BAKER	08__CHARLOTTE	11__COLLIER
15__DIXIE	04__BRADFORD	09__CITRUS	13__DADE
17__ESCAMBIA	10__CLAY	14__DE SOTO	22__GLADES
19__FRANKLIN	12__COLUMBIA	25__HARDEE	26__HENDRY
20__GADSDEN	16__DUVAL	27__HERNANDO	43__MARTIN
23__GULF	18__FLAGLER	28__HIGHLANDS	44__MONROE
30__HOLMES	21__GILCHRIST	29__HILLSBOROUGH	50__PALM BEACH
32__JACKSON	24__HAMILTON	31__INDIAN RIVER	
33__JEFFERSON	38__LEVY	35__LAKE	
34__LAFAYETTE	42__MARION	36__LEE	
37__LEON	45__NASSAU	41__MANATEE	
39__LIBERTY	54__PUTNAM	47__OKEECHOBEE	
40__MADISON	55__ST. JOHNS	48__ORANGE	
46__OKALOOSA	61__SUWANNEE	49__OSCEOLA	
57__SANTA ROSA	63__UNION	51__PASCO	
62__TAYLOR	64__VOLUSIA	52__PINELLAS	
65__WAKULLA		53__POLK	
66__WALTON		56__ST. LUCIE	
67__WASHINGTON		58__SARASOTA	
		59__SEMINOLE	
		60__SUMTER	

VI
SOLICITATIONS: PLEASE SELECT THE TYPE OR TYPES OF SOLICITATIONS YOU WISH TO RECEIVE. YOU MAY SELECT MORE THAN ONE(1) TYPE OF SOLICITATION. IF SELECTING THE SAME TYPE FOR ALL COMMODITIES/SERVICES YOU NEED ONLY CHECK 1 AND/OR 2, IF SELECTING DIFFERENT TYPES FOR COMMODITY/SERVICES, PLEASE INDICATE BY CIRCLING APPROPRIATE NUMBER BY COMMODITY/SERVICES.

I WISH TO RECEIVE SOLICITATIONS FOR: (CHECK ALL THAT APPLY)
(1)STATE TERM CONTRACTS: REFER TO SOLICITATION ISSUED BY THE DIVISION OF PURCHASING WHICH RESULT IN THE AWARD OF USUALLY ONE (1) YEAR AND INDEFINITE QUANTITIES. LOCAL GOVERNMENTS (COUNTIES AND CITIES) MAY PURCHASE COMMODITIES USING THE TERM CONTRACT. TO BE CONSIDERED FOR STATE TERM CONTRACTS YOU MUST ACCEPT RESPONSIBILITY FOR DELIVERY TO AT LEAST AN ENTIRE DISTRICT.
(2) AGENCY INVITATION TO BID: REFERS TO SOLICITATIONS ISSUED BY INDIVIDUAL AGENCIES AT THE LOCAL LEVEL, OR NON STATE TERM CONTRACT ITEMS WITH THE DIVISION OF PURCHASING.

LIST ALL COMMODITY AND/OR CONTRACTUAL SERVICE NUMBERS THAT YOU WISH TO RECEIVE SOLICITATIONS FOR:
PLEASE REFER TO ATTACHED CATALOG BEFORE COMPLETING THIS SECTION.

12 ___ - ___   12 ___ - ___   12 ___ - ___   12 ___ - ___   12 ___ - ___
12 ___ - ___   12 ___ - ___   12 ___ - ___   12 ___ - ___   12 ___ - ___
12 ___ - ___   12 ___ - ___   12 ___ - ___   12 ___ - ___   12 ___ - ___
12 ___ - ___   12 ___ - ___   12 ___ - ___   12 ___ - ___   12 ___ - ___

*ADDITIONAL CATEGORIES MAY BE LISTED SEPARATELY AND ATTACHED.
PLEASE RETURN TO:
DIVISION OF PURCHASING
DEPARTMENT OF MANAGEMENT SERVICES
SUITE 301 4050 ESPLANADE WAY
TALLAHASSEE, FL 32399-0950

SIGNATURE:_____ TITLE:_____

TYPE
NAME:_____ DATE_____
E-MAIL
ADDRESS:_____
URL_____

Exhibit 7-15

VENDOR REGISTRATION FOR
THE STATE OF WASHINGTON

Application for Placement on the DIS/OITO Vendor List

Instructions: Complete this online form and press the *submit* button below, or you may fax it to (360) 664-0495:

State of Washington

Department of Information Services
Office of Information Technology Oversight

PO Box 42445
Olympia, WA 98504-2445
(360) 902-3557

Company Name: [_____]

Contact Name: ○ Ms. ○ Mrs. ○ Mr.
[_____] [____] [_____]
First   MI   Last

Title: [_____]

Address: [_____]
[_____]
[_____]
[_____] [____] [____] [_____]
City   State/   Zip/Postal Country
            Province

Telephone: ([____]) [____] - [____]   Fax: ([____]) [____] - [____]

Electronic Mail: [_____]

This company (○ is/○ is not) Washington State Office of Minority and Women's Business Enterprises certified.

Instructions: Review the commodity code list below and check item(s) of equipment, software, or services your company is capable of providing. Your company *may* receive a Request for Quotation (RFQ) or Request for Proposal (RFP) for commodities which the buyer determines fit these codes.

(Continued)

171

Exhibit 7-15
CONTINUED

If you are using the online form, and wish to select more than one commodity, just click your mouse in multiple boxes.

Vendors who are not classified as *information technology* providers, please call the Department of General Administration, Office of State Procurement at (360) 902-7416 for information on other goods and purchased services. Or visit their web site at <u>GA Home Page</u>

☐ Accessorial Equipment - Color Monitors: 7037
☐ Accessorial Equipment - Impact and Other Printers: 7039
☐ Accessorial Equipment - Laser Printers: 7038
☐ Accessorial Equipment - Monochrome Monitors: 7036
☐ Accessorial Equipment - Other: 7035
☐ Accessorial Equipment - Plotters: 7034
☐ Applications Programming: 9279-V45
☐ Central Processing Unit (CPU, Computer), Digital: 7021
☐ Communications Security Equipment: 5810
☐ Computer Programming: 9279-V30
☐ Data Base Design: 9279-V50
☐ Data Communications Modems: 7018
☐ Data Communications Processors: 7017
☐ Data Processing Terminals: 7016
☐ Front-end Communications Processors: 7015
☐ Input/Output and Storage Devices - Disk (Laser and Magnetic): 702
☐ Input/Output and Storage Devices - Other (Memory, Mass.Storage,
☐ Input/Output and Storage Devices - Tape: 7025
☐ Large Mainframe Computer Systems: 7010
☐ Minicomputer Systems: 7011
☐ Nonportable Microcomputer Systems: 7012
☐ PC Service and Maintenance: 7014
☐ Portable Microcomputer Systems: 7013
☐ Punch Card Equipment: 7040
☐ Software Testing: 9279-V35
☐ Software, Large, and Minicomputer: 7030
☐ Software, Microcomputer: 7031
☐ Systems Programming: 9279-V40
☐ Telephone and Telegraph Equipment and Service: 5805
☐ Teletype and Facsimile Equipment: 5815

SUBMIT	RESET

Use the *SUBMIT* button to mail your completed form to DIS/OITO. Or use the *RESET* button to empty the form and restart.

Return to the <u>Supplier Registration</u> section of the *Doing Business* pages.

Comments:

PROPOSAL-WRITING TALENT

If you believe that that proposal-writing talent is principally writing talent in general, you need urgently to read the following material. Writing talent helps greatly, of course, but marketing talent helps more . . . a great deal more. The successful proposal writers have an instinct for marketing, a sense of what motivates and sells, and the best proposal writers also have the writing talent that makes the most powerful and most impressive presentation of the ideas that come from having marketing talent.

That is expressed as succinctly as I know how to express it so that the message is delivered clearly enough to make its major point known. There is no question in my mind that the secret of success in proposal writing is marketing first and writing second. Let's discuss what appears to me to be the most important element of all: marketing strategy.

I am convinced that the chief ingredient of success in government contract competition is *strategy—strategies, in fact,* for more than one kind of strategy is involved. There are five kinds of relevant strategies, all of which we shall get to in a moment. However, here again the advantages of the online environment count for something. The access to so much information is a great aid to gathering intelligence about your competitors and thus enabling you to make reasonable inferences about what their capabilities are and what they are likely to offer. These are items you need to assess in developing your own strategies, of which there are the following five to consider:

1. **Technical or program strategy.** The appeal of the program you offer to satisfy the client's need or solve the client's problem, such as originality, efficiency, effectiveness, or other outstanding trait you offer as an advantage benefiting the client, while satisfying the need effectively.

2. **Cost strategy.** How you justify the costs you estimate and make them appear to be the most modest possible for the job that is to be done with complete satisfaction of all requirements. (Although the evaluation team will not know your cost estimates while evaluating your technical proposal, it will [a] develop some idea of what the program you propose is likely to cost, and [b] later, when it does know the costs, weigh them against your technical proposal and its logic.)

3. **Competitive strategy.** How you appear against probable competitors and make yourself appear superior to them in your qualifications, your program, and your presentation.
4. **Presentation strategy.** The impact of your proposal, the manner of its presentation to achieve maximum impact, and the clarity with which you convey all your key points.
5. **Capture strategy.** That strategy or combination of strategies you rely on to win because you think they are responsive to the client's most important concern. That is the major strategy on which you place the major emphasis of your entire proposal.

You will need at least two of these: a capture strategy and at least one of the others on which capture strategy is based. Which of the others that will be depends on your analysis of the situation—what you think to be the most critically important consideration of the client. Is it price? Quality? On-time delivery? Maintainability? Backup or follow-on support? Other?

Here is where success is likely to depend on your judgment and your marketing intelligence. If your information and/or instinct leads you to believe firmly that the client is concerned most about costs—has a severely limited budget, for example—clearly you must focus on cost as your major capture strategy and not dilute it by stressing less important factors.

The most serious and most common mistake many proposers make is to try to overpower the client by offering superior strategies in all areas, hoping something will catch on. This has the effect of diluting all the arguments and obscuring focus so that there is little credibility. Here, briefly, are a few notes and ideas to consider in connection with various proposal strategies.

TECHNICAL OR PROGRAM STRATEGY

Perhaps your client is the bold and innovative type who welcomes new ideas. Then again, he or she may be the cautious, conservative type who definitely favors the familiar, tried-and-true approaches. It is important to have some good feeling for this when deciding how you will approach designing and proposing your program. The right approach can put you in the lead immediately for the contract, but the opposite is also true, of course. You must know your client. Here again, take advantage of the research capabilities of the Internet to gather some intelligence on the client's past activities that reveal the client's tendencies in purchasing. Remember that no matter how big or how monolithic the organization, humans—often a single human—make the decisions.

Even if you do not know your client, the intelligence you want may be in the RFP and its statement of work. Read all the pages of the solicitation carefully, and read them many times. You rarely pick up the more subtle, between-the-lines information on a first or second reading, but only after many readings. It was a ninth or tenth time reading that sometimes provided us with the key to success. These readings may also provide clues that can be followed up with online research.

At the same time, use logic—common sense. In helping a company compete for a U.S. Navy contract for a teleprinter communications equipment to be used aboard ships, it became clear that most other competitors for the contract would be offering versions of their standard commercial items, assembled to form a teleprinter system. My own client agreed to focus on this as a weakness in competitors' designs and so attacked them indirectly by offering a "monolithic" design, with only the keyboard as a separate unit, citing the many advantages of such a design for a piece of equipment to be used aboard a ship. This turned out to be a winner, both as a good design strategy and as an effective competitive strategy.

COST STRATEGY

If you are able to offer an extraordinarily low price, you must justify it, for reasons explained earlier. Make it clear that you know that your price is suprisingly low, but you are offering it quite deliberately and with full consciousness that your price is lower than might be normally expected. Explain why you are able to offer such an unusually low price, while maintaining high quality in your product. Otherwise, the client will suspect that you are underpricing the job, either because you do not really understand the problem and what must be done to solve it, or because you plan to cut corners and provide a shoddy solution to the problem. The client may very well then declare your proposal to be "nonresponsive" or technically deficient.

There are, of course, other cost strategies possible. You might try to talk value to justify your price, the "bang for a buck" argument. Or you might suggest a lower-cost alternative to the way the client has suggested the work be done. Again, there is risk here, if what you suggest is contrary to what the client has implied as his or her perceived proper method for doing the job. Be clear in stating this as an alternative and not your primary response.

COMPETITIVE STRATEGY

Be aware that you are always in a competitive situation and do not underestimate your competitors. Assume that they know as much as you about all the relevant matters and are as capable, as imaginative, and as hungry as you. Do not suggest, not even by the most indirect means, that they are inept. Never knock your competitors—not directly. Do so, if at all, only subtly and indirectly by such devices as explaining in great detail the special qualifications you bring to the project, qualifications that are essential to success and not easily to be found elsewhere. (An example was given earlier in discussing the proposal approach to developing a standard teleprinter for the Navy.) Let the client then infer from that what you wish to have inferred and cannot state bluntly.

PRESENTATION STRATEGY

Even the best ideas can miss the mark if the client fails to appreciate them fully as new, bold, innovative, advanced, or whatever you desire and believe to be their chief distinguishing characteristic. That is where effective presentation strategies can make a great difference. Take great care to make your proposal physically attractive and quite professional looking. Use graphics to drive home your major arguments. They do not have to be great art to be professional looking and effective: Clean, expressive tables and charts are highly acceptable and, if well designed to lighten the burden on textual language, are appreciated by the reader. Well-designed tables and charts are those that convey information much more easily and swiftly than can be done by text alone. Always study and evaluate your nontextual presentations in this light. Remember that the client usually has a large number of proposals offered and probably would not hesitate to put yours aside, if it is difficult to follow, and go on to another one. The client may or may not ever get back to your proposal. (Here is where the writing talent helps the most, probably.)

You can be, and probably should be, much bolder in presentation than in design. Use innovative ideas, such as supplying a 3- by 5-foot wall chart as an attachment to your proposal or printing a flowchart explaining the entire project on the cover of your proposal. (I have even persuaded clients to use foldout covers to do this, with good results.) Even though government RFPs usually warn against elaborate proposals, cautioning readers that they may be interpreted to reflect a lack of cost consciousness by the proposer, tastefully designed proposals do have an effect in suggesting your attitude and the professionalism that will characterize the work you do for the client. ("Elaborate" is a judgment or opinion, not a precise fact, and so far I have never known of a proposal rejected on that basis.)

BIDDING STRATEGIES

It might appear, from what I have written here, that the development and use of strategies are applicable only to proposal presentations—negotiated procurements—and not to the making of sealed bids. That would, in fact, be true if all sealed bids were truly black-and-white issues of comparative costs, with no doubt whatsoever about which is the lowest bid. That is not always true. There are many cases when it is not easy to determine which is the lowest bid.

The problem here is that not every sealed bid specifies a completely defined end product or set of services. Sealed bids can be requested to establish fixed rates for certain kinds of products or services and yet be nondefinitive for estimating purposes because total quantities are undefined. That is, in fact, freely acknowledged by the client in labeling this an indefinite-quantity contract. That is especially the case in the task-order or "call" contract, in which you have committed yourself to furnish certain categories of labor, as required, when the need arises, at rates that are fixed for the term of the contract. When the agency has a need, it will issue a task order for you to estimate, using the rates established by contract. Your estimate, then, is based on number of items or amount of time for each labor category required to satisfy the need or, for some cases, the kinds of labor required to perform the task, if more than one class of labor/kind of specialist is required to get the job done.

Here, as examples, are three possible cases of indefinite-quantity contracts, which may or may not be also task-order contracts:

- An indefinite-quantity contract (a common kind of contract) to supply consulting services. Let us suppose that the client wants editorial services, and the client wants bid prices for writing, editing, proofing, and composition, especially as follow-up services after the initial project.
- The writing of a computer program with flat rates quoted for follow-up maintenance services, with no estimate of how many hours of such service may be required. Minimum quantities to be bought are estimated, but there are no estimates of maximum quantities. You therefore do not know the probable total size of the contract overall and so have some difficulty in judging what effect it might have on your overhead or staffing needs, as one immediate consideration.
- Bid rates for a variety of computer specialists whose specialties may be in computer languages, machines, types of software, or functions. Again, at best, only minimum guaranteed requirements are specified.

Some contractors may buy in to the contract, quoting a low price for the original work and planning to operate at a break-even price or even to take a loss on the first phase, but to then make profits on the follow-up services. The basic work is a throwaway proposition, entered into to win the contract; the follow-up rates are the basis for "getting well."

One of the advantages of doing business with government agencies is, by constitutional right, being able to demand free access to information that is in the public domain. You can, if necessary, specifically invoke the Freedom of Information Act, but that should not be necessary in most cases. You can discover how much of each class of labor the client used in the past under some earlier or current contract, for example, and even what rates were charged for those classes of labor, and that can be very important marketing intelligence to guide you in pricing competitively. Again, online convenience makes this much easier to do now than it was in the past.

Let us suppose that you are asked to bid hourly rates for each of the following functional categories:

System Analyst
Senior Technical Writer
Journeyman Technical Writer
Editor
Word Processor Specialist
Proofreader
Illustrator

With only minimum guarantees of quantities of work, it's difficult to judge in advance how much of each class of labor you are likely to be called on to provide. However, if this is a contract that has been in effect before and is now up for renewal, you can make some excellent estimates of future needs because you have the right to request and get that information described above.

OTHER HELPFUL INTERNET RESOURCES

There are many other helpful resources on the Internet in addition to those listed earlier, including two that I believe to be unusually helpful and appropriate, with respect to proposals and contracting with governments.

There is the Web site of the Association of Proposal Management Professionals (APMP), for one. The association has branches in several cities. The membership is made up of both individuals on corporate staffs and independent proposal consultants, including writers and specialists in relevant fields, such as marketing, desktop publishing, and computer programming.

The URL of the APMP Web site is http://www.apmp.org.

Another useful site of great interest to anyone pursuing government contracts and interested in proposals may be found at http://www.govsolutions.com/.

Each of the aforementioned sites offers links to many other interesting and useful resources on the Net. The latter site, for example, includes links and instructions for subscribing to the proposal-l mailing list, which is circulated among working proposal writers and other interested parties. It is a somewhat intermittent mailing list, with periods of great activity and periods of little or no activity. But then it has many lively discussions and exchanges of information. It includes, for example, reports from various subscribers on the latest uses of desktop publishing facilities in connection with proposal writing and the growing requirements of clients for the use of such facilities in preparing proposals. There is today a trend toward delivering proposals on computer disks, as well as in print between covers, and this subject receives serious attention at these facilities. No doubt, delivery of proposals online, via e-mail, will become more and more commonplace in the future.

A problem, with regard to delivery of electronic editions of proposals, is that of widespread incompatibility among the various word processors. Probably the two most-used word processors for Windows are Microsoft's Word and WordPerfect, and it is possible to send encoded files in any word processor format by e-mail, attaching the file. However, neither of these word processors can read the other without conversion. The universal font is ASCII, the American Standard Code for Information Exchange, but that is a plain-vanilla font that permits virtually no refinements of styles and formats. So despite a large degree of hardware compatibility among desktop computers today (with the exception of the Macintosh line), that compatibility does not exist to the same degree among software products.

It should be clear, by now, that while the Internet offers a great many advantages in marketing for the independent consultant, it is also a complex maze of opportunities and avenues that need to be explored. Certainly, it will be difficult to learn by wandering about the Internet aimlessly, trying to learn by random experience. It makes sense to approach this with some kind of plan, at least a general one. Let us have a look at that next.

CHAPTER 8

An Integrated Online Marketing Plan

If you are an enthusiastic marketer touring the Internet and sightseeing its wonders, you may feel like a kid allowed to roam free in a candy store and help yourself as you wish. So many goodies of information at hand everywhere and countless opportunities to chat with people and search out sales prospects. All of this within easy reach and in abundant supply. What to grasp first, what to fill your pockets with, what to sample immediately, what to preserve for later? Why not a little of everything? Sample it all and choose favorites later?

Of course, it is not at all feasible to grab blindly and sample opportunities left and right, although you may find yourself doing just that the first time or two that you probe and experiment in Internet cyberspace. Whether that apparent abundance of marketing opportunities is truly as great and diverse as it appears will vary with the individual—with how it interfaces with your own prior marketing experience and ideas of how to best market your independent consulting services. All the pages that have gone before this one had, as one major goal, to put all the complex of activities on the Internet into some kind of perspective that will enable you to perceive the system overall. The Internet is a Topsy: it just grew, almost at random, from its origins as ARPANET, the creation of the U.S. Advanced Research Projects Agency. That original net grew rapidly by adding other nets to create today's system by agglutination, and so today the pattern of the system overall is not easy to visualize, because there is no grand plan and no central focus; it just is. It is far too easy to grope about, probably enjoying the scenery encountered in random explorations, but accomplishing little because there is no order or organization to your marketing effort without a plan.

In any situation, to do what has to be done in building a comprehensive marketing program, you must plan a coherent marketing program. That is no less true—is even more true, in fact—in coping with the complexities of the online world of commerce. The need for an organized plan for marketing on the Internet is greater because there is less inherent order in the online world of the Internet and because the Internet is new and growing wildly. You must sort out the complex of activities so you can decide on a manageable number and kind of sites, resources, activities, strategies, and avenues of marketing attack. Even the largest organizations must set a limit on the number of marketing activities to which they can be committed. In the traditional business world, some of the choices are implicit in the situation: A retail establishment, for example, must advertise and somehow attract traffic. Although it may also attempt a catalog or mail-order campaign, as some do, or even a radio- or TV-based direct marketing campaign, its main marketing effort is dictated by the nature of its business.

Marketing online is still so new that you may have trouble deciding what the nature of your business dictates to you as the most promising main marketing premises, let alone the approach or media to choose as starting points. You do know a few things up front, even if your practice is new or yet to be launched, and probably a few more things if you have been in practice a while. Here are a few starting premises or alternatives that you must choose to arrive at starting premises:

- Yours is a service business.
- You have/plan to have one or more ancillary products or services.
- It is/you plan it to be of a business-to-business or business-to-private-individuals nature.

- You usually/plan to win your clients directly with clients or you usually get your business via some kind of broker or other middleperson.
- You do/do not yet have some typical price range in which most of your projects fall.

If you are newly established, you may not have all these decisions made, but you ought to know what are the likely items or, if you could go as easily one way as the other on some of these items, which you would prefer. You do need to formulate some kind of marketing plan or at least set a few goals and establish your beginning premises whether you are or are not established, because you are entering a different milieu in marketing online and your methods must be compatible with what you can accomplish practicably online.

Because you are an independent and not a large organization seeking financing from lenders or investors, your business plan need not be an elaborate document with charts and spreadsheet projections, but will be primarily a marketing plan, despite the need to define your business in that plan. Your needs in that respect are relatively simple and can be met informally, but you do need a few starting definitions or ideas of how you are going to carry out at least the following eight steps:

1. Get the data you will need.
2. Set realistic sales goals.
3. Profile best prospects.
4. Define market targets.
5. Formulate your offer.
6. Position yourself.
7. Conduct tests.
8. Measure results.

If you have been practicing successfully before you met with and addressed the Internet as a milieu in which you will operate, you may have already made the most basic of these decisions—the profiles or definitions of your best prospects (item 3), the environments in which you are most likely to find them (item 4), and the appeals to which they are most responsive (item 5). Those may or may not be suitable for marketing online, and it may be a major mistake to assume that they are. When I marketed my government-contracting/proposal-writing seminars by mail, I built my mailing lists largely from the help-wanted advertisements, where I could easily find the computer software developers that had always been my best prospects and I could usually judge the size of the firms from the advertisements they ran. Online, it is a different proposition: Even if I could build such lists online, bulk mailing to e-mail addresses is a no-no that would almost surely hurt me much more than it would help me. If I wish to reach such prospects online, I have to discover other ways to find them and to reach them with my offers. (I was also compelled to go online or lose some of my clients who had gone online and were using cyberspace for communication and other functions of their own businesses.)

One way to do this is via the right newsgroups. Another is via mailing lists and newsletters, as discussed in preceding chapters. Another is by a Web site of my own, and still another is via visits to others' Web sites and posting articles there. (On the other hand, I also used the awards section of the *Commerce Business Daily* in the past to glean names and addresses that seemed to me to be those of viable prospects for my seminars, and I could do that online too, since the CBD appears there.)

Even now, after years of online activity and experience, I am constantly being surprised by learning how little I know of the medium and how often I can be dead wrong in my assumptions regarding it. Here is an example.

I have for years published and marketed a series of how-to reports by mail, and today, recognizing the trend to electronic publishing, I have converted these little reports into collections I sell as disk books. To date, my most successful approach to attracting prospective buyers has been publicizing my work and offering a free report (as a lead-generating device) through a column I furnish every month to a large number of electronic (online) periodicals that are published as e-mail or as presentations on others' Web sites. I found, to my surprise, that in at least one case, a very popular periodical that carries my column is published both on CompuServe, as well as on the Internet. I encountered it on CompuServe myself this morning, and I have indications that some of my columns are finding their way onto America Online, as well. So it appears to be wise to experiment and pay close attention to what is happening as a result of your experiments (which are dignified a bit, in the direct marketing world, by calling them tests).

Let's look at how to do some of those things I listed a few paragraphs ago as necessary steps in planning your online marketing.

Getting the Data You Need.   Nothing is more important in marketing than marketing intelligence, information that is relevant to your marketing needs, goals, problems, and—probably most important—marketing strategy. You need to do your marketing research initially to get a grasp of what the market prospects are so that you can construct a sensible marketing plan, but gathering marketing intelligence is a never-completed task. You must keep up with events that affect your markets, for all markets change, and more than one business failure, even of large corporations, has been due to complacency and failure to keep abreast of the markets. So, to a quite large degree, sales success hinges on the quality—accuracy, relevance, and quantity—of the information on which you base your marketing decisions.

Fortunately, there is no greater information *resource* than the Internet, with its numerous search engines and links. Where I once made many telephone calls, wrote letters, and posted queries on bulletin boards to gather information for an article I was writing on barter, I can now get all that information—and even more than I collected by those methods—within minutes by the simple act of searching the word *barter* on the Internet. With complete access to the Internet, there is no valid reason for not knowing what the condition of your market is at all times. You can always get general information on short notice—spontaneously—and it may or may not include all the details you need for any specific case, but it is usually detailed enough to enable you to then go to the telephone, fax, or e-mail to track down the final details you need or get in touch with people you want to find.

Setting Sales Goals.   You are the only one who can set your own sales goals—what work load you are prepared to handle, what backlog of orders suits you, what your services require in the way of time to plan, and other items that you will take into account in setting your sales goals. Take it as an article of faith that you must have specific sales goals, or how will you be able to judge how well you are doing? You may wish to set these goals in terms of number of projects, number of clients, or dollar volume of sales, but the last-named is probably the most sensible parameter along which to set your mileposts. You do want to have some array of clients because it is much too risky to have your practice heavily dependent on one or two major clients, but the most significant goal, especially in the beginning, is a dollar goal, because dollar volume is the one figure you can set reliably as a necessary minimum for success. You can easily calculate the minimum dollar volume of income you will need to pay yourself an adequate salary and meet all other business expenses.

Profile the Best Prospects. You need to have some standard by which to search for sales leads and judge their suitability. If you are already established in a practice you built before you added the Internet to your resources, you presumably already have a best-prospect profile defined. It may or may not be suitable for use here, depending on a number of variables. One of these is the possibility that the Internet has opened new doors for you—clients elsewhere in the world, for example. One of my acquaintances, self-employed and basically a one-man enterprise (although he sometimes shares projects with an associate) has become a world traveler as a result of acquiring clients throughout the world. For him, a Web site has been productive, although it is only one of an assortment of aggressive marketing approaches he uses. He does not depend on any single marketing approach, but has a carefully integrated array of mutually supporting marketing initiatives, most of them activities in cyberspace and all based on seeking those matching the client profiles he has developed over the years.

The profiles are, of course, dependent on the practicality of finding and appealing to, on the Internet, those who match the profiles. Keep the Internet facilities and connections in mind as the environment in which you must work and the tools you must use, as you develop that profile. You must be sure that you profile the kind of individual or organization that can be reached via the Internet.

Define Market Targets. This may or may not be quite the same as profiling your best prospects. You will have to decide which is the most appropriate term to use in your planning. Whichever term you use, you will have to decide whether you seek individuals or organizations as your clients, even if the individual represents an organization. *Profiling* is probably the more appropriate term, with some of the characteristics to define as elements of the profile being the size, industry, location, product, and other items that describe the organization. More important than your choice of terms is the accuracy and suitability of the characteristics you define, as the keys to finding your best prospects. In marketing training, some years ago, I found the individuals responsible for sales the most receptive ears in the corporations I visited, and so I tried always to seek out those individuals first.

Formulate an Offer. Bear in mind that an offer, as defined earlier in these pages, is the promise to deliver some specific benefit. You must assume that responses to your offer reflect the respondent's desire to gain the promised benefit, and that means that the number of responses depends on how accurately you have judged the desires of your selected target population. Sometimes, what appears to be a minor modification in the wording (for example, "Five Acres" versus "Five Acres and Independence") can make a major difference in response. The offer is often the most important thing to test because it can be the key to maximizing response, sometimes even more so than the price.

Position Yourself. Positioning yourself or your service is the art of establishing the client's image of you or your service, shaping what the client sees. The chief ingredient is the promised benefit. I did not want my clients to see me as the means to writing better proposals or more skilled proposal writing; I wanted them to see me as the means to winning government contracts. The proposal was a tedious and inconvenient necessity that I would take care of. It was better mentioned as inconspicuously as possible, but, in that manner, as the proof, not the promise. But that is not all there is to positioning. Your prospective client must also see you as highly competent, thoroughly professional, totally dedicated, and scrupulously honest and sincere. Nothing less than the latter will do for any consultant in any consulting field.

Conduct Tests. Testing has been discussed earlier. Plan to test all your material and efforts for their effectiveness. Results are not absolute; their value lies in being comparative measures. Make the tests comparative so that you can choose the best, and strive constantly to improve the results. In the beginning, you can make drastic changes and should do so if early results are truly disappointing. However, once your marketing begins to show good results, make small, gradual changes in your efforts to further improve results. Testing can and often does produce results that surprise. You may, for example, discover (as many have in the past) that *raising* a price increases sales volume. (Too low a price may raise doubts about credibility of claims to quality.) You may also discover that your client profile is all wrong. (One of your tests ought to be addressed to validating your profiles.)

Measure Results. Measuring results on a comparative basis is probably best done by constructing a simple matrix, such as that of Exhibit 8-1. This form enables you to compare results from different efforts. The

Exhibit 8-1
FORM FOR LOGGING RESULTS

COPY/ ORGAN	RESPONSES	NO CLOSES
TOTALS:		

first (leftmost) column is used to identify either the copy—different offers, that is—or the organ in which you transmitted the offer—for example, a Web site, a newsletter, or a mailing list. Of course, you measure only one parameter at a time, so you use this form for each parameter you choose to measure. You might, for example use this to measure the results you get from newsletters, newsgroups, and mailing lists, in one use. In another, you might measure the results you get from different copy you use to present your offer or for different offers you make.

MUTUALLY SUPPORTING ACTIVITIES

With these matters thought out and decided upon, you can address your market with some vision and begin to assemble a marketing plan in which the activities are carefully integrated to be mutually supporting and synergistic, producing a result that is greater than the simple sum of your efforts. One of the problems of any self-employment in a service business, including independent consulting, is that of feast-and-famine cycles. It is difficult to survive the famines, especially when they are lengthy ones, and it is difficult to satisfy all the obligations during the feasts. The latter are the less troublesome problems, of course. The great marketing difficulty for many independent consultants is finding some means to smooth out the variations of activity, and one way to do that is to diversify your activities, while making them mutually supporting.

Consulting, public speaking, and writing are three skills that seem to go hand in hand, judging by the great number of individuals who do all three: consultants who write and lecture, writers who consult and lecture, and public speakers who consult and write. In my own consulting practice, these proved to be mutually supporting in that each of these activities was a direct aid, and even a catalyst, to winning assignments for the other activities. For example, my seminars and my writings—books, articles, and newsletters—were directly responsible for the winning of many consulting clients and assignments. However, my newsletters not only supported the marketing of my consulting services, but they also supported the sale of books and reports I published myself, and they supported the seminars I presented. Perhaps it is even more significant that these multiple activities smoothed out the roller coaster of feast-and-famine cycles of consulting work. When I had a famine period, it gave me time to work on a new book or produce new reports and market them, or I could use the time thus made available to present seminars more frequently. That, in many ways, was the greatest benefit of developing a marketing program of several integrated facets.

In fact, I regarded my seminars, newsletters, and other activities as ancillary consulting services, rather than "other" services, and I used these activities in that manner to provide the same help to listeners and readers that I provided to clients. I found it easy enough to view my audiences and readers as clients. In fact, I looked upon these other activities as forms of group consulting, analogous in principle to group therapy. In a seminar, for example, each attendee could exercise at least a partially active role, rather than being completely passive as a listener. The attendee could become a client by asking questions or asking for recommendations. Thus, for the price of admission to the seminar, each individual could get both general and specific consulting services. I applied the same philosophy to my newsletters and other publications: They were or could easily be used as group consulting, since I invited inquiries and promised responses. In fact, I do that today on my own Web site, and every day I get questions from visitors to the site, using the e-mail facility provided there to ask me questions, to which I always respond.

Applying this idea to the online environment of the Internet requires some adaptation, perhaps along the lines of my own adaptation. Of course, the Internet is not a platform for seminars and lectures in the traditional sense, although it may be used to help market these. However, the newsletter for which a subscription fee is charged is a feasible idea, as is the publishing of books and reports, and is used by some consultants. It is probably possible to devise an online seminar too, and that may be an idea worth exploring. It certainly is feasible to market ancillary services in general online. The important thing is to choose activities that are mutually supportive, not only in their combined effect on marketing, but also mutually supportive in other ways, such as providing ideas for each other. For example, questions raised by a reader of my newsletter might inspire a new report or even a book.

With enormous arrays of activities possible on the Internet, the major hazard lies in the possibility of undertaking too many initiatives and thus being unable to concentrate efforts. Careful consideration should be given to choosing activities that will support each other in all respects. The first step is to establish a center of gravity, a main marketing element, around which the entire marketing system of elements can be assembled and integrated. For many, this is a Web site.

WEB SITE OR OTHER BEGINNING?

Creating and maintaining a Web site is proactive, aggressive marketing. That is a major factor in its favor, and many believe that a Web site is a necessity as the most productive online marketing medium. There are, however, numerous other means to market online, and a Web site may or may not be right for you as the center of your marketing.

To make a Web site viable—to make it productive in and of itself, as well as a center or basic element of your marketing—you must manage to attract enough visitors to it to constitute a nucleus. It probably will not be sufficient of itself to achieve all your marketing goals, at least not for some time, but it can be a firm anchor for your marketing campaign. It should be apparent by now that attendance at a Web site must be built over some period of time. You must support your site by advertising it everywhere and attracting the right kind of visitors, those who qualify as prospective clients, in sufficient numbers to make the statistics work for you. All advertising depends on the statistics of probability, on reaching enough of the right prospects with your message. A Web site requires initial investment and maintenance costs, so you must ask yourself whether the time and money is best spent here or might be better spent on other avenues of online advertising and marketing your services. Might you not get even better results with smaller expenditures by using other means of online advertising? It comes down to finding the best way to reach a maximum number of prospective clients. But does "best" mean lowest cost per prospect/sales lead or does it refer to the suitability of the kinds of prospective clients you reach?

One consideration in weighing the pros and cons of a Web site is finding the point of diminishing returns. A large and costly Web site will presumably attract more visitors than a modest site will. Or is that a fact? Experience suggests that the large and costly site will attract only a few more visitors than the small site. That then suggests that a modest site, used as a focal point for an integrated and mutually supporting set of marketing initiatives, would be more productive than a large splash on the Web.

In short, what makes marketing sense for a large corporation may or may not be a sensible approach for you as an independent consultant. As such, you are presumably limited in time and money for marketing. To create an impressive Web site and support it on a large enough scale to give it a fair chance for success requires a substantial commitment of your money and time. It may be assumed that such a major commitment as this would close out, at least for a time, your options to explore, test, and evaluate other approaches to Internet marketing. There are approaches that you can explore, quickly and easily, both individually to evaluate the potential of each and collectively to form a mutually supportive, integrated program. Following are five general kinds of facilities, all already mentioned and discussed at least briefly, that I have found to be helpful in marketing services and believe to be worth investigating and considering as key elements in your own marketing program. I would suggest considering a Web site after you have explored these alternatives and gained some experience with them. With this experience, you will be far better equipped to make decisions regarding your use of a Web site, either independently or as the focus of a multielement program.

- Mailing lists
- Newsgroups
- Others' Web sites
- Newsletters
- Direct e-mail

These activities have the virtue of being easy and inexpensive to investigate and test, before deciding on having an inexpensive Web site as a base, supported by those other activities. They are also the means for exploring and investigating the Internet to learn the system and to research all online market possibilities. Collectively, they will almost surely do more to circulate your name and raise your visibility than the best site would if it were your sole means for disseminating your messages and offers. At the least, experience with these will give you a much broader foundation of knowledge on which to base your judgment about the use of a Web site.

Probably the biggest advantage of using these is that they lend themselves to integration into a system. If you engage in a Web site, plus a mailing list, plus a newsletter, plus contributing your ideas to a few other sites and/or newsletters, you can use each to mention the other activities, while using each also to do specific advertising of your services, at no cost and with no danger of being attacked by others for spamming. Wherever using e-mail is an element of your participation, as in mailing lists and responding to others' presentations via e-mail, you can use your automatic signature file to post an advertising appeal. You can also create and use a signature file in posting messages in a newsgroup. And when you submit articles for publication on others' Web sites and your own or others' newsletters, you can include a resource box, which is much like a signature and can carry an advertising or sales message. These media furnish a double opportunity to advertise, by both the content of your writings and by the signatures or similar files you can attach.

I have personally found all of these approaches useful in marketing online. Taken together as an integrated system, they have been more productive than is the modest Web site I maintain, and I find it worthwhile to make the time available to attend to all as lines of communication and information. These are also assets in that they offer prospective clients several easy and convenient ways to reach me. Bear in mind that many of those using the Internet use e-mail only and never travel the Web. You can communicate with them only via media that are dependent on e-mail, although in some cases they may have access to the newsgroups also. Thus, if you depend entirely on a Web site of your own for marketing online, you are excluding a significantly large portion of the total Internet population.

MAILING LISTS

The mailing list is my favorite online tool for marketing generally and for other purposes, such as networking and keeping up with relevant activities. It can be a powerful medium for establishing and maintaining contacts and building your own image within that community represented by the list, while it is also a highly productive source of useful information. Mailing lists, as you now know, are a form of discussion group using e-mail as the medium for communication and discussion. Mailing lists are based on some special interest and a great way to establish widespread contact with others of linked interests.

The number of mailing lists is large and grows steadily. A 1995 tome on the Internet places the number at about 5,000. A more recent publication places it at 11,000. At the time this is being written, one search program claims access to the listings of 54,740 Listserv, Listproc, Majordomo, and other (independently managed) mailing lists. It provides, as a rough index, categories of arts, business, computers, culture, education, health, humanities, music, nature, politics, news, recreation, religion, science, and social interests.

The actual collection of messages and retransmission of them to subscribers are automated functions, managed by one of several programs. There are a number of such programs, probably the most frequently encountered are Listserv mailing lists, although Majordomo lists and Listproc lists are also very much in evidence.

One mailing list to which I subscribe and to which I referred a few paragraphs ago, is that of the Publishers Marketing Association, a group of small, independent publishers, many of them writers and self-publishers. This is a Listserv mailing list. The return path, the address to which you send your messages to be added to the general message traffic of the list, is shown in the first line of the following, a typical header of each message received, identifying the sender and providing a return address:

```
Return-Path: <owner-pma-l@SHRSYS.HSLC.ORG>
Date: Mon, 15 Jul 1996 11:47:20 -0400
From: JanNathan@AOL.COM
Subject: LIST COMMANDS
Sender: Publishers Marketing Association Forum <PMA-L@SHRSYS.HSLC.ORG>
To: Multiple recipients of list PMA-L <PMA-L@SHRSYS.HSLC.ORG>
Reply-to: Publishers Marketing Association Forum <PMA-L@SHRSYS.HSLC.ORG>
```

The message sent in this post is a list of commands that Listserv will recognize. They enable you to exercise several options available, such as switching your subscription to a digest form or suspending mail.

Note one important line here, the first, which gives a different Listserv address from the return address given earlier. That is because mailing lists have two addresses: one to receive and forward all mail, the other to handle all administrative matters, such as these commands, which, the message makes clear, must be sent to LISTSERV@hslc.org, the administrative address:

SET PMA-L DIGEST—to get this list in digest form
SIGNOFF PMA-L—to remove yourself from the list
REVIEW PMA-L—to get a list of subscribers
SET PMA-L NOMAIL—to remain on the list but not receive mail
SET PMA-L MAIL—to reverse the NOMAIL setting
SET PMA-L REPRO—to receive your own postings from the list
SET PMA-L NOREPRO—to reverse the REPRO setting
HELP—to receive the help file

SUBSCRIBING TO A LIST

To become a subscriber to a list, you send your request to the administrative address and place a simple command in the message area of your e-mail. Instructions for subscribing vary, and it is necessary to follow them precisely. Usually, the instruction is to address your application to the list's administrative address and place a simple message in the body of the e-mail along the lines of "subscribe [your name] [list name]". Here, for example, is the announcement of a new mailing list (NEW-LIST@ LISTSERV.NODAK.EDU is a mailing list that advises me on new mailing lists as they are born) with instructions for subscribing. It is itself a Listserv mailing list, but the mailing list it is reporting on here is a Primeserve mailing list, as is made plain in the instructions for subscribing.

Return-Path: <owner-new-list@LISTSERV.NODAK.EDU>
Date: Sun, 14 Jul 1996 21:48:49 -0500
Reply-To: "Jeffrey M. Cooper" <JCooper@Primeserve.com>

Sender: NEW-LIST - New List Announcements <NEW-LIST@LISTSERV.NODAK.EDU>
From: "Jeffrey M. Cooper" <JCooper@Primeserve.com>
Subject: NEW: FREESTUFF - free offers and opportunities list
To: Multiple recipients of list NEW-LIST <NEW-LIST@LISTSERV.NODAK.EDU>

FREESTUFF on list-request@primeserve.com

FREESTUFF is a list dedicated to the discussion and sharing
of free offers and opportunities. List members are encouraged
to submit and share any free offers they come across. This
list is not limited to free Internet or computer-related offers.
ANY free opportunities or offers are welcome.

To subscribe, send the following command in the BODY of mail
to list-request@primeserve.com
sub freestuff
or subscribe freestuff

Owner: Jeffery M. Cooper JCooper@primeserve.com
http://www.primeserve.com/

Use this information at your own risk. For more information and disclaimer send e-mail to
LISTSERV@LISTSERV.NODAK.EDU with the command INFO NEW-LIST in the body.

To illustrate the wide difference in activity among the mailing lists, the freestuff list contributes messages intermittently, an average of not more than a half dozen per month. The pma list, however, fills my mailbox with up to 75 or even more messages on most business days.

FINDING RELEVANT MAILING LISTS

The mailing list cited above, NEW-LIST@LISTSERV.NODAK.EDU, notifies me of new lists. It does not tell me what lists are out there already, but there are many sources on the Internet that will provide that information; it is available in great abundance. A few brief examples follow.

Exhibit 8-2 is the first page of a six-page list of mailing lists that I printed from a Web presentation. This one happens to be on human resources matters. Note that each entry provides subscription information.

Exhibit 8-2
A FEW MAILING LISTS DEVOTED TO HR INTERESTS

INTERNET LISTS OF INTEREST TO HR PRACTITIONERS
December 1995

This information is provided courtesy of Dave Perry, Rider University, Al Doran, York University, Ontario, Canada, Karl Sparks, Mt. San Jacinto College, Gerry Crispin, SPHR, and Terri Haase, University of Southern California

AMINT-L: International Programs Committee(Academy of Management)
  Listserv Manager: Carolyn Dexter, DBI@PSUVM.PSU.EDU, FAX 717-948-6456)
  LISTSERV@PSUVM.PSU.EDU
  subscribe AMINT-L Your Name

APP-ORGCOMM: Applied and Organizational Communication(Academy of Management)
  Listserv Manager: John Hollwitz, JCHOLL@CREIGHTON.EDU, FAX 402-280-2143)
  MAJORDOMO@CREIGHTON.EDU
  subscribe APP-ORGCOMM firstname lastname

BENEFITS-L
  a list for benefits administrators, not limited to higher education. Frequently very conceptual, but vital for those of us confused by the current scene in benefits. Maintained at Middle Tennessee State University.
  listproc@frank.mtsu.edu
  subscribe BENEFITS-L (your name)

BPR (Buss Process Re-engineering)
  mailbase@mailbase.ac.uk
  JOIN bpr (your name)

BPSNET: Policy and Strategy network
  Listserv Manager: Jim Stephenson, STEPHENSON@WHARTON.UPENN.EDU, FAX 215-898-0401)
  STEPHENSON@WHARTON.UPENN.EDU
  subscribe BPSNET Your Name

BUSETH-L: Business Ethics Computer Network
  Listserv Manager: Bill Baumer, UCSBILLB@UBVM.CC.BUFFALO.EDU, FAX 716-645-2127)
  LISTSERV@UBVM.CC.BUFFALO.EDU
  subscribe BUSETH-L Your Name

CARDEVNET: The CarDevNet focuses on Career Development issues
  cardevnet-request@world.std.com
  subscribe end

Exhibit 8-3 is one page out of a four-page list of mailing lists for those with journalistic interests. Again, instructions for subscribing are given.

Exhibit 8-4 lists some Listproc mailing lists on subjects in the area of economics.

I uncovered these and many other lists with only a casual search, using the Lycos and Alta Vista search engines, which are two of many readily available search engines on the Internet/Web. Other well-known search engines are Magellan, Web Crawler, Excite, Infoseek, and Yahoo!, and there are still others, some general purpose, others special purpose. Yahoo! is something of a pioneer on the Internet and extremely well known consequently. I happen to favor AltaVista, but each has its own characteristics, and all are effective in turning up information on the Internet.

TIPS ON USING MAILING LISTS

You can learn how to use mailing lists effectively and efficiently through trial and error, or you can learn by paying close attention to readily available instructions and avoid grief. Here are few basics you ought to be aware of before you begin.

Bear in mind at all times that there is no privacy on a mailing list: Your posts to the list will appear in the mailboxes of every subscriber and be displayed on every screen. Be sure that what you send to the list is something that you want to broadcast to all and something that is of general interest. If you opt to respond to a post, you can do so via the return path, which means it will be broadcast to the list in most cases (although on some lists, the return address is that of the sender, not the list), or you can send it privately to the sender. The example shown below, the header of one of my own messages to the pma list, illustrates this, since it shows the "return path," to send a message to the list, and the "from" line. Anyone receiving this could choose to reply to me privately and should respond in that way if the message is not of interest to others on the list.

Return-Path: <owner-pma-l@SHRSYS.HSLC.ORG>
Date: Tue, 23 Jul 1996 11:19:03 -0400
From: Herman Holtz <holtz@PALTECH.COM>

Exhibit 8-3
A FEW MAILING LISTS COVERING
JOURNALISTIC MATTERS

- Send e-mail to `listserv@ubvm.cc.buffalo.edu` with the following message: `subscribe ACWNYS-L <your first and last names here>`
- **Subscribe now**
- **Hyperjournal**
  - A discussion list devoted exclusively to electronic journals, especially those which publish on the World Wide Web. It is concerned with all aspects of the production and publication of electronic journals, particularly those managed by academics themselves.
  - Send e-mail to `Mailbase@mailbase.ac.uk` with the following message: `Join hyperjournal-forum <your first and last names here>`
  - **Subscribe now**
- **JPL-L**
  - Electronic publishing mailing list
  - Send e-mail to `LISTSERV@LISTSERV.CLARK.NET` with the following message: `subscribe JPL-L <your first and last names here>`
  - **Subscribe now**
- **K-16LINK**
  - Technology and writing, K-16
  - Send e-mail to `LISTSERV@UGA.CC.UGA.EDU` with the following message: `subscribe K-16LINK <your first and last names here>`
  - **Subscribe now**
- **Medialist**
  - A listing of newspapers, magazines, tv stations and other media outlets that accept e-mail
  - Send e-mail to `MAJORDOMO@WORLD.STD.COM` with the following message: `subscribe MEDIALIST <your email address here>`
  - **Subscribe now**
- **MNNYACW-L**
  - Metropolitan New York Alliance for Computers and Writing
  - Send e-mail to `Listserv@ccvm.sunysb.edu` with the following message: `sub MNYACW-L <your first and last names here>`
  - **Subscribe now**
- **NFICTION**

Exhibit 8-4
MAILING LISTS COVERING ECONOMICS SUBJECTS

Previous Next Up Contents

Previous: * Listserv Mailing **Next:** * Majordomo Mailing **Up:** MAILING LISTS

* Listproc Mailing Lists

Listproc is roughly the Unix version of listserv. Commands for subscribing and unsubscribing are identical (see the above directions for listserv). However, mail containing the commands is sent to "listproc" rather than to "listserv" (some listprocs masquerade as listservs, but this distinction is meaningless for simple commands such as subscribing and unsubscribing).

PEN-L Progressive Economists Network
pen-l@anthrax.ecst.csuchico.edu

RISKNet - Discussion of Risk and Insurance issues
RISKnet@mcfeeley.cc.utexas.edu

Econlaw - An economic analysis of law
econlaw@gmu.edu

Forensic Economics
forensiceconomics-l@acc.wuacc.edu

Statistics Canada's Listserver
statcan@statcan.ca

Cliometric Society list on Teaching Economic History
econhist.teach@cs.muohio.edu Archives of this and all lists by the Cliometric Society can be found at <http://cs.muohio.edu/>.

Cliometric Society list on Macroeconomic History
econhist.macro@cs.muohio.edu

Cliometric Society list on Economic History Dimensions of Global Change
global.change@cs.muohio.edu

Cliometric Society list on Economic History News
eh.news@cs.muohio.edu

Cliometric Society list on Economic History Discussion
eh.disc@cs.muohio.edu

Cliometric Society list on Economic History Research
eh.res@cs.muohio.edu

Cliometric Society list on Students and Instructors of Economic History
econhist.student@cs.muohio.edu

Cliometric Society list on Teaching and Research in Business History
h-business@cs.muohio.edu

Subject: Re: Childrens pubs
Sender: Publishers Marketing Association Forum <PMA-L@SHRSYS.HSLC.ORG>
X-Sender: holtz@paltech.com
To: Multiple recipients of list PMA-L <PMA-L@SHRSYS.HSLC.ORG>
Reply-to: Publishers Marketing Association Forum <PMA-L@SHRSYS.HSLC.ORG>

Think before you respond. Remember an earlier discussion, pointing out that in e-mail there are few subtle clues as to your hidden or between-the-lines nuances or indicators of irony and lampoons; readers will therefore usually interpret your words in their most literal sense. Unless you are a skillful enough writer to make the nuances of your message unmistakably apparent, shun all efforts to be subtle or practice a fine irony.

Bear in mind, too, that e-mail is not free to all who use it. There are many who pay for each message or for all online time, so every message they send and receive costs them something.

If you have a query about unsubscribing, changing to a digest format, or other such matter, be sure you address the list's administrative address and not the general address, so that your message does not go out to the membership at large.

YOUR OWN MAILING LIST

Sponsoring or "owning" a mailing list is an effective marketing approach used by many consultants. One of these is Carl Kline, of National Consultant Referrals, Inc., with a Web site also at http://www.referrals.com. As Carl points out, running a mailing list is not only effective, but economical. He reports, in part: "Within two months, I had over 600 subscribers." He observes, also, "Effectiveness is easier to measure than with other media because you get instant and timely feedback from your market target."

Kline explains some of the mechanism of going about starting a list, along with some of the technical problems:

Usually, you or your ISP, using a software program called a list server, maintains the mailing list you sponsor. For example,

National Consultant Referrals, Inc., created and sponsored "consulting-tools." All subscribers e-mail messages to a central e-mail address. If the software works correctly and the sender conforms to the format required, it takes the message and distributes it to all the subscribers. That is a big "IF." The problem is twofold. Part of the time the software can be a problem and part of the time, it is the participant. Because the software/hardware, called an autoresponder, has to be precisely addressed and may be programmed with little regard to ergonomics, the malfunction is caused by "human error."

You can own your own domain, as National Consultant Referrals does, set up your own server, and handle the whole thing yourself. However, it is not necessary to get that involved, unless you want to; you can utilize technical services that are readily available, either from your ISP or from one of the many services available. As in all things, the reliability and quality of the services offered vary widely, and you would be wise to shop as carefully for these services as you would for a home, automobile, or other important major purchase. If you do not now have an Internet/Web access service provider, and if you live in a major metropolitan area, you may find the array of such services offered bewilderingly large. Ask friends and acquaintances for recommendations. Look for reliability and quality of service, with price secondary. The best-designed list will not do well if the service is not reliable.

The same consideration applies to any service provider who may offer to handle your mailing list via his or her own server. Ask around, or if no one of your acquaintances knows of that provider, ask for references and check them. The provider who is unwilling to provide a few references is automatically one of doubtful reliability.

The key element in running a mailing list of your own for marketing purposes is your purpose, which should be very clear, since it will cost you something. You will have to pay someone for it, although it can be as little as $10 to $20 per month for a small list. Be sure that you know precisely what you expect to gain from it.

The general purpose of sponsoring a mailing list is to support the marketing of your consulting services, of course, but the specific objectives may be indirect ones, such as these: to increase your visibility, develop your professional image, gather marketing information, generate sales leads, announce and explain your products or services, and generally support your public relations program. Or you may have some specialized objective, such as explaining and publicizing some special service you offer. All these are valid marketing goals, but it is usually a mistake to target all: You are generally far more effective when you focus sharply on a single goal, rather than dilute your main message with a multitude of goals. Many marketers have done well by focusing on a free sample lesson, such as was offered by the Evelyn Wood speed-reading course, which offered free sample lessons in a series of free public seminars to illustrate what their system could do for the individual.

Make sure, too, that you have a clear idea of whom you want to attract as subscribers. It may be those who are themselves potential clients, or it may be those through whom you are likely to find potential clients—or both. Or it may be those who are sources of information that will help you in gaining new clients. Whatever the case, be sure that you know who you want as subscribers, and slant your coverage quite deliberately to achieve that goal.

A good idea, if you are not sure just what topics you want to focus on, is to begin with a general discussion of your area of interest or subject that is likely to attract the kinds of subscribers you want. For example, if you are a direct-mail consultant and you want to reach people who market by direct mail because they appear to be the primary candidates for your services, you may start with a mailing list that discusses direct mail in general. Eventually, as your experience guides you, you may find it most productive to steer the focus to some special area of direct mail, such as list selection or sales letters. You can use the mailing list as a powerful marketing research tool that costs you very little (unlike most marketing research).

It is possible that you may lose some control of your list and have the subscribers run off in another direction than the one on which you originally set your sights. In that case, you may want to make the list a moderated one, where you preview each message and decide which ones to forward to the list, or you may even make the list a private one and control who may subscribe. You may even charge for subscriptions, although it is probably in your best interest to keep it free, to maximize participation. In any case, you probably will do best to start with a public, unmoderated list, and see where that takes you before considering the many alternatives and refinements possible.

In terms of content, you must be the leader, inspire the discussions, and guide those inspired by others so as to keep them on track. One of the difficulties is keeping discussions on the subject of the list. There is always a strong tendency for the subscribers to get involved in interesting but irrelevant subjects. And one very common problem in unmoderated mailing lists is the tendency for individual subscribers to post personal messages to another subscriber via the list, so that all the others get a message that was intended for only one subscriber. Subscribers need often to be reminded to send personal messages to the other's individual e-mail address and not to the list.

Still another common problem is the tendency of some to get into arguments with other list participants, even to the extent of starting flame wars, in which increasingly bitter arguments and counterarguments develop. In many lists, a gadfly appears who seems to find it amusing to start such exchanges by deliberately picking quarrels.

Of course, there is also the individual who abuses the hospitality of your list by attempting to turn it into a blatant billboard for his or her own advertising aims—spamming, that is.

If you monitor carefully, you can usually control such abuses. If, for whatever reason, you find it difficult to maintain control, the alternative is to consider making the list a moderated one. However, most lists are not moderated, and it is usually possible to discourage the abuses by maintaining your own presence prominently and reacting promptly to provocation such as any of those listed.

USENET AND NEWSGROUPS

The Usenet (User's Network) is a separate network of discussion groups, referred to generally as *newsgroups*. Technically, the Usenet is not part of the Internet. Still, for all practical purposes, the Usenet and its discussion groups are in the Internet milieu, and access to it is normally included in Internet access.

Newsgroups are interactive forums: Subscribers post messages, original ideas, and responses to messages posted by others. They engage in extended discussions, ask questions, and exchange ideas. As a participant, you may post messages to the membership generally or you may send a personal message directly to an individual's e-mail address. You may indicate that you are responding to an earlier message by repeating a key section of that earlier message in both cases, but in the case of the newsgroup you have the option in responding of defining your message as a general posting or a follow-up.

In a mailing list, you decide what to do with the messages that have been posted and come to you; in the newsgroup, the messages remain posted semipermanently, until crowded off by newer messages. Messages in a mailing list are sent to you when you call for your mail; in a newsgroup you must invoke your newsgroup program and call up the groups to which you subscribe. In most news programs, current messages that you have not yet read are posted, but you can have older messages displayed, if you wish.

The variety of topics for newsgroups is almost unlimited. Many are suitable for serious use in marketing, but by far the majority are not. You will find, for example, that many newsgroups are static, having been inspired by some subject or individual of momentary prominence, flourished for a few weeks only, and are now as totally inactive as a dead volcano, although still listed. (Like a great many laws, they are inert and totally ignored, but still on the books.) You can search out newsgroups as you would mailing lists, via search engines on the Internet and by being alert for references you may encounter in other accesses you make to Internet locations.

As with mailing lists, you can use newsgroups to make contacts, do productive networking, plant seeds, and learn of opportunities. My activity in one newsgroup on consulting led me to profitable connections with several other consultants. Still, I find mailing lists a much more convenient means of doing these things because e-mail is (at least in my opinion) by far the easiest and most convenient element of the Internet to master and to use. Moreover, the exchanges and discussions in mailing lists always seem to me to have a great deal more immediacy than those based in any other Internet communications medium. (As one example, this morning I received a conventional letter from a reader of one of my books, and it was a letter that required a response. The writer included an e-mail address, so I was able to respond to him directly within minutes.)

Still, each system has its own advantages, as well as disadvantages. For example, your message posted to a newsgroup will remain on the board for some time, rather than vanishing after a single transmission to an individual subscriber. That persistence can be a decided advantage when posting messages to raise your visibility and professional image. Thus, although there are many functional similarities between mailing lists and newsgroups, there are a few significant differences, and those may be important enough to justify your spending time with both kinds of discussion groups.

As with e-mail and other Internet activity, you may be using any of a wide variety of software programs to access and use the Usenet. Most programs will permit you to sort the list of messages by date, subject, name of author, or perhaps other parameters. (I prefer to sort by date, beginning with the most recent message, but I can switch temporarily to another parameter when searching for an older message.) You may then respond to the group or to the individual author. Unabashed advertising messages on most newsgroups are a no-no, of course, as it is elsewhere than on Web sites or in a few newsgroups that permit flagrant advertising. However, you can do some discreet promotion in all newsgroups, if you are careful and include it subtly in messages that are basically in accord with the character of the newsgroup.

You can, of course, always respond directly and privately to individuals, offering your services. Inasmuch as many messages posted are requests for help or information—for example, "Would it help my image to incorporate?" "How do I get an Employer Identification number?" "What kind of rates can I charge?"—by implication, such responses are invited, and are often excellent sales leads.

YOUR OWN NEWSGROUP

As with mailing lists, it is possible to sponsor a newsgroup, but it is far more complex a problem to get a newsgroup going, and it is also much less manageable, unless you make it moderated and so keep close control over what appears in it.

To start a newsgroup, you go to a newsgroup named news.announce .newusers, where you present your proposal for a new newsgroup. The proposal should explain the concept and provide arguments for it, most important of which demonstrate the great numbers of people who will welcome the new newsgroup and support it with subscriptions and postings. Votes are called for, by *netiquette,* a voluntary moral/ethical code for the Internet, to approve or disapprove of the new newsgroup. The swiftly growing number of newsgroups suggests that this must not be a particularly difficult hurdle to leap.

Having started a new newsgroup, unless you moderate it, you soon are only another subscriber to the newsgroup and not especially identifiable with it. So it is probably less effective a marketing tool, in some respects, than is a mailing list you create and continue as its owner or sponsor. Still, its existence may be useful to you in attracting certain individuals and making your existence and the services you provide known to them. In any case, it is one of the proactive marketing measures you can use.

OTHER WEB SITES

As in the case of the Electronic Moneytree site (Chapter 5), many existing Web sites offer you opportunities to gain attention and develop sales leads by appearing on those sites with your own presentations. The Amazon Booksellers Web site, for example, offers an author the opportunity to have his or her autobiography added to a list of authors' bios, which it maintains. The site provides a form to fill out as a kind of canned interview, which is added to a file of authors' biographies made public there. There are many Web sites that offer free classified advertisements to writers and consultants or free listings, which amount to the same thing. None of these are highly productive of themselves, but in the aggregate, they add to your visibility.

There is another aspect to this, one from which you may infer that all approaches are beneficial and desirable to employ, even if some appear to be more effective than others. I was surprised not long ago when someone reported to me that my name is "all over the Internet," although I have taken advantage of only a few of these offers, and my own Web site has had only a moderate number of visitors. I subsequently checked on that by submitting my name to several of the major search services and discovered that all reported voluminously on my Web site and its contents, on many of the books I have written for traditional publication, and on the many articles I have written and published online. (I had no idea that the cataloging was this comprehensive and complete, with all the indexing, cross-indexing, and cross-referencing of material.) What this suggests to me is that the cumulative effect of all activities reflects a kind of synergy, a combination in which the whole is greater than the sum of its parts. It thus suggests that all the elements should be employed to achieve the maximum effect, even if some appear to be of relatively minor benefit. In any case, the idea seems to be well worth exploring.

There is another consideration: Serendipity is at work here, as elsewhere, but the probability of a beneficial serendipitous event showering a blessing on you is in some proportion to the number of opportunities you create for it. Obviously, the more active you are in making your presence and services widely known, the more often something beneficial to you will result. Recently, one of the many contacts I have made via my activities in several newsgroups resulted in an interesting proposition that I shall follow up. A successful consultant I have gotten to know rather well now invites my participation in a new venture: She proposes to launch a large Web site in which she will list and describe the credentials and services of other consultants in whom she places enough confidence and trust to endorse them. (I have benefited greatly from similar offers by others in the past.) She will broker the services of those she lists, taking a small percentage of all sales as a reasonable fee, so the listing will cost the subscriber nothing but the brokerage fee. It is thus a risk-free proposition for those consultants invited to participate and be listed.

NEWSLETTERS

Having your own newsletter on the Internet is a splendid way to market if you run it on a subscriber basis and can attract enough of the right kinds of subscribers. They should, of course, be individuals who qualify as prospective clients or who can somehow lead you to prospective clients and sales leads. As in the case of many other marketing approaches we have discussed here, a newsletter can be a proactive or reactive approach to marketing. If you run it as a feature of a Web site, rather than e-mailing it to a subscription list, it will be passive marketing because only those who opt to visit your site will see your newsletter. On the other hand, you can ask people to subscribe (and the subscription ought to be free, if the newsletter is to be maximally effective in reaching many readers) and fulfill each subscription via e-mail. I think of it as a kind of mailing list, with only one subscriber permitted to post on it. Of course, you can invite subscribers to contribute to the newsletter, run a letters-to-the-editor feature, or include a question-and-answer column. You may do just about anything you might do with a paper-and-ink newsletter, except use typography and graphics, unless your newsletter is a Web site presentation, which is another set of problems. Most online newsletters are distributed by e-mail, and the newsletter so distributed is restricted to what the e-mail format permits, which is very much a plain-vanilla form.

The downside of publishing a newsletter is the need to maintain the schedule and to come up with good material for each issue, so as to keep your subscribers. That's a good argument for inviting subscriber participation, as per the suggestions for features that involve information from subscribers. That lightens your burden as the writer/editor/publisher. And, of course, you need not worry about printing and mailing: You send the copies out electronically, as you would with a mailing list, using a support service, unless you can and want to do it all yourself.

Getting subscriptions to a newsletter is primarily a matter of publicizing its existence. Use whatever means you have—probably e-mail, primarily—to start passing the word to everyone you know. Make up an appropriate announcement and circulate it. You may also put some brief notice in your signature file, that file in your e-mail system that adds those lines you compose to appear at the end of every e-mail message you post. Or you may go to the direct-mail method—direct e-mail, that is. Send unsolicited copies to a large number of people, and invite them to continue receiving the newsletter, but offer to remove them from the list at once if they wish.

DISTRIBUTION

Typically, to send out the copies of a newsletter or the posts of a mailing list with a large number of subscribers, you use some kind of automatic device, a transponder or mailbot. Unless you are technically pretty much into the Internet and computers yourself, you generally turn to some service to do this for you at a small monthly cost, as I do with my own mailing list. However, if you are turning out some kind of newsletter or other material to a list of subscribers that is not too large (perhaps 50 to 100 names), it is possible to do the distribution yourself, using your own e-mail software system.

You can do this by collecting all the e-mail addresses of your list of subscribers or addresses into a single ASCII (plain text) file and using this file to send out copies in this manner: You take the first name off that list and use it as an e-mail address. You install the rest of the names in that file as copies, as shown in Exhibit 8-5. (The names in the figure are "dummy" names, of course, rather than the real ones, so don't attempt to send to

Exhibit 8-5
DISTRIBUTING TO A BRIEF LIST WITH E-MAIL

Return-Path: <srwatson@voltech.com>
Date: Fri, 14 Feb 1997 08:08:52 -0600
From: srwatson@voltech.com (S. Watson)
Reply-To: srwatson@voltech.com
Organization: Total Business Communications
To: bz@zz.com
CC: zat@z-mail.gs.com, Ann <watson@student.msu.edu>,
    75047.3333@compuserve.com, mhp@mail.net, scottb@sts.net,
    ryoun@voyage.net, books@rose.net,
    jo@intercom.net, tclare@mail.win.net,
    "Cozee (ZTI)" <COZEE@aol.com>, cspangury@aol.com,
    gundy@navigate.com, drag@ottawa.com,
    "Duff, Leo (PropGroup)" <PropGroup@lduff.com>,
    lng@zam.bs.com, fay@world.net, cfink@stin.com,
    char@netlin.net, wbkid@worl.net,
    "LouJ." <lpulou@spring.com>, wmanl@ix.netc.com,
    "Mern@adp.org>, ag75@dia.pip.com,
    smerce@wolfenet.com, DP@aol.com,
    "Prokus (ADP)" <bprokus@adp.org>,
    scribe-list@bell.com, southlady@nxs.com,

them.) Thus, your material, which follows the list of names, goes out to all but the first name as copies.

There is a drawback in this that the list of names may appear in the message received by each one on the list. However, in most e-mail software, it is possible to send both Cc: and Bcc: copies, and if the list appears after the Bcc: lead-in, the list should not appear in the copies.

I use this system to send out my monthly column to about 30 online publications and Web sites. I keep my list of e-mail addresses in a text file and copy it, after extracting the first name as the main addressee, to follow the Bcc: of my e-mail data form. Since I use Windows 95 and Eudora, I copy the list to the Clipboard and then paste it in place. With about 30 others distributing my column, presumably with each of those having several hundred addressees, my column manages to reach some thousands of readers, which is one way to change Internet statistics.

DIRECT E-MAIL

It was, of course, inevitable that some form of direct-mail advertising and promotion would appear on the Internet. Early on, it appeared in the newsgroups, as soon as it became known that an advertising message could be propagated electronically and in minutes to thousands of newsgroups. Mass distribution of advertising messages in this way was swiftly condemned as spamming and still is, with some exceptions. The exceptions are a relative few of the newsgroups where the spammers became so numerous that the other subscribers to those lists just gave up protesting and quit the groups. And since, the nickname has been applied to even a single advertising message posted in a single place.

In the paper-and-ink direct-mail world, there are a great many list brokers—organizations that will rent you mailing lists of just about any size you wish. The equivalent exists in the online world: There are suppliers of e-mail lists, lists of hundreds of thousands of e-mail addresses that can be addressed automatically by some sort of autoresponder. Hardly a week passes that I do not get e-mail solicitations offering me millions of e-mail addresses to which I can send advertising messages and sales solicitations.

For the independent consultant, online direct mail is no more effective than conventional direct mail, perhaps even less so, because it is an online version of commercial advertising, and commercial advertising has rarely worked well for the independent consultant.

That does not mean that direct mail has no utility for you. It can be useful to support your networking and other marketing efforts. Use it to raise your visibility as a consultant, to publicize and win subscribers for your newsletter or mailing list, and to expand your own grasp of all possible main and niche markets. If you run a Web site, use direct e-mail as one of the ways to promote your site.

Note here the many overlapping areas, in which one function or medium bears characteristics in common with or similar to another online. Probably not all the methods for using these facilities to market effectively have yet been invented, and certainly I have not covered all possible configurations. Use your own imagination and combine the best elements of various functions to invent the best methods for *you*.

CHAPTER 9

Special Resources and Opportunities for Independent Consultants

The Internet is rich with a diverse variety of resources related to independent consulting. A great many independent consultants and consulting organizations of all sizes and types—job shops, employment agencies, brokers, associations, and services of various kinds—maintain presences on the Internet and especially on the Web. Searches via any of the major search engines will produce a great number of responses by, about, and for consultants, with many of them also addressing clients and prospective clients for consulting services. Several have been mentioned in passing, in earlier pages. The Expert Marketplace, for example, was introduced and discussed in Chapter 3. It will appear here, too, along with several other entries, constituting just a sampling of what you can easily find for yourself on the Internet by searching independently or by using these listings as starters and following the many linkages that are offered.

Many individual consultants advertise on the Web, some with such simple presentations as their resumés and brief notes on the services they offer, others with far more ambitious and elaborate presentations.

Should you wish to offer an advertisement of your own via a Web site, you will have no difficulty finding models to emulate or inspire new ideas of your own.

BROKERS, TEMPORARY AGENCIES, AND REFERRAL SERVICES

There are organizations that are brokers for individual consultants. A great many simply supply consultant specialists on a temporary basis, usually at some hourly rate. Among those prominent of these are Volt Information Sciences and the Toner Corporation. These are among the largest such companies, but both of these and other such firms have many branch offices placing temporary technical and other specialized help every day. Most also permit you to register directly from your computer at their Web sites. (You will find a number of Web sites that offer you an opportunity to list yourself as an independent consultant, usually at no cost to you. Some services will charge a fee if the listing wins a contract for you or if they refer you to a prospect who becomes a client.)

Because many consultants are also writers and lecturers, not all are listed as consultants per se, but may be listed also as technical writers, technical specialists, public speakers, seminar presenters, and by various such titles and categories. Searching the Internet using any of these and sundry other search terms brings up the same of brokers, associations, temporary agencies, and other names found under the general category of consultants. Of course, as was noted earlier in these pages, many independent consultants offer a variety of services and even utilize an array of personal resumés and brochures representing themselves as specialists in various skills and services at which they are expert. Of course, the brokers and temporary placement organizations are familiar with this and, in seeking assignments, you may advise the recruiter for the organization of the several services in which you can specialize and discuss what areas are "hot" at the moment—that is, in what areas they have the greatest number of openings to fill.

Of course, not every independent consultant wishes to hire out as a temporary or may want to make that a last-ditch choice, to be turned to only when that is the only work available at the moment. But not all the listings here are of organizations that broker services by subcontracting with individual consultants or supply temporaries. There are also listings of consultants' associations and services of various kinds, and there are listings of organizations such as The Expert Marketplace whose main function is to assist prospective clients in finding suitable consultants, rather than serving the consultants. Even then, however, the organization is usually interested in adding your name to their registers of available consultants.

Some of the organizations charge fees to clients, some to the consultants. Some of those listed, however, are free, although in some cases they are membership associations and provide their free services to members only.

The listings appearing here are only a sample of those available on the Internet. They represent only a fraction of all that I surveyed. They were selected by using such terms as the following:

- Independent consultants
- Consultants' associations
- Consultants' services
- Technical temporaries
- Management consultants
- Professional placements
- Technical experts
- Specialist services
- Professional temporaries
- Consulting resources
- Independent contracting
- Technical communications

Many of the same organizations' names appeared again and again, regardless of the search term used, demonstrating the fluid nature of consulting, as well as the ease of searching. I used the Alta Vista search engine, a favorite of mine, but there are many others that would produce equal results, such as Yahoo!, Web Crawler, InfoSeek, and Lycos. However, each search engine has its own strengths, and one may prove to be better than others for some given search. A little experimenting with the leading search systems will soon reveal which works best for your purposes.

Because there is such a great multiplicity of specialties and services that are offered by those of us calling ourselves independent consultants, categorizing the lists of relevant URLs is necessarily more tentative than absolute. It reflects what appears to me to be the main activities or objectives of the organizations. I recommend that you take the time to look up any that appear interesting to you and judge for yourself. It will almost surely be time well invested. It is an education in itself and will make you feel much more comfortable using this capability of the Internet in doing your marketing research, as you become more acquainted with what it does and how it does it. Of course, you can easily do what I did and search out many names and offers independently. However, here is a short list I developed via searching on the Internet, and I offer it to you as a starter list:

> http://www.volt.com/
> Volt Information Sciences
> http://www.toner.com/register.htm
> Toner Corporation
> http://www.g-net.com/gjobs.htm
> Global Net Solutions Job Opportunities
> http://www.techtemps.com/ttihome.htm
> Tech Temps, Inc.
> http://www.laacn.org/firms/
> Los Angeles Area Consultants Network
> http://www.trans-tech.com/transtech/indep.html
> Transtech Independent Consulting
> http://interact.withus.com/oakwood/
> Oakwood International
> http://www.referrals.com/
> National Consultant Referrals, Inc.
> http://www.expert-market.com/seminar/
> The Expert Marketplace
> http://www.siemensrolm.com/about/consults/
> The Siemens Business Communications Consultant
> Resources Program
> http://www.consultapc.org/cameal.htm
> Association of Professional Consultants

http://www.pwgroup.com/ccorner/
  Consultants Corner
http://www.globalads.com/malla/wyatts/giving.html
  Wyatt Professional Contract Staffing Service Reply Form
http://www.techspec.com/techspec/working.html
  Tech Specialists
http://www.matrixres.com/pro_contract_ser.html
  Matrix
http://www.manpowertechnical.com/Professional.html
  Manpower Technical of Indiana
http://www.flash.net/~spartech/enterd4.htm
  SparTech Software
http://net-temps.com/
  Net-Temps
http://165.247.238.1/serv03.htm
  General Technology Corporation
http://www.cyberplex.com/ca/hotsites.html
  Computer Action IT Contracts
http://www.dldtech.com/dldcontr.htm
  BLD Technical Services, Inc.

MISCELLANEOUS OTHER RESOURCES

Among the many other items I encountered in my searching were the names of associations and organizations of various kinds, including publishers selling periodicals, books, training courses, legal information, white papers written by individuals on topics of interest to consultants, and even sample contracts. Again, as in the case of compiling the first list, I surveyed a great many more than the few I included here, again as a brief starter list:

http://www.ceweekly.wa.com/
  Contract Employment Weekly publication
http://www.fpd.finop.umn.edu/3/Sec7/Pol371/Contract
  University of Minnesota Contract for Professional Services

http://www.stcnet.com/arctic.html
    Society for Technical Communication
http://www.ntes.com/cefaq.html
    NTSA (National Technical Services Association) FAQ
    (Frequently Asked Questions)
http://www.smartbiz.com/sbs/arts/sbl2.htm
    Sample Employment Contract
http://stc.org/region8/svc/www/scon_ind.htm
    The Consulting Sig
http://www.sequelogic.com/ipa.htm
    Sequelogic Independent Advice for Contractors
http://www.expertcenter.com/ec/ecmember.html
    Expertise Center information

INFORMATION ON GOVERNMENT MARKETS

Until rather recently, the best and perhaps the only practical way to search out opportunities to submit bids and proposals to the thousands of federal, state, and local government agencies was to read print advertisements, usually headed "Bids & Proposals," in the newspapers, magazines, and the federal government's publication, the *Commerce Business Daily* (CBD). Trying to cover more than a local segment of the state and local government markets was nearly impossible, of course, since you would have had to read hundreds of publications every day. Even the specialized publications, such as those published daily to announce bid and proposal opportunities in construction, could not cover the complete market.

That has changed quite substantially with the Internet. Today, you can find long listings of bid and proposal opportunities announced every day on the Internet. Simply listing the search term "Bids & Proposals" in one of the Internet search engines will bring up long lists every day. It is indicative of a trend in government purchasing: Electronic online methods of procurement activities are coming into vogue more and more and soon will be dominant in every phase and aspect of procurement, from initial announcement to contract award and even delivery of contracted-for services, in many cases, where that is a practical possibility.

Searching the Bids & Proposals category will produce mostly announcements of state and local government agencies, but many of the announcements are those of Mexican and Canadian government agencies, too, and even some announcements of federal agencies appear there. In addition to that, there are also some announcements of anticipated future needs and procurement programs planned for the future.

It is also useful to study contracts awarded, since many major contractors award numerous subcontracts to support their efforts. Thus notices of contract awards may be most important marketing intelligence and should be part of your research.

With the procurement activities gravitating to online facilities, there has been a sharp growth in information sources and numerous services available to help you master the intricacies of winning government contracts or even doing much of the work for you. Announcements of such offers also are abundantly in evidence as you search the files, which you may reach under that general term or by searching out a few other locations. Following is a starter list of those other relevant locations on the Web, which I reached by using such search terms as *procurement, purchasing, bids,* and *proposals.*

> http://www.govcon.com/public/CBD/current/
> GOVCON access to CBD
> http://www.fedmarket.com/statejump.html
> Government procurement information
> http://www.govsolutions.com/
> Proposal information
> http://www.lightworld.com/govl.htm
> Federal government procurement links
> http://www.pinn.net/~rhudson/links.html
> Links to procurement activities
> http://www.state.nm.us/spd/spd_how.html
> New Mexico Purchasing Guide
> http://governor.state.co.us/gov_dir/gss/pur/
> Colorado Purchasing Guide
> http://www.pr.doe.gov/prsolit.html
> Department of Energy Bidders Mailing List

http://just4u.com/webconsultants/listinfo.htm
    Web Consultants Mailing List
http://www.experts.ca/medmalmail.html
    Medical Litigation Consultants Mailing Lists
http://www.marrak.com/distlst.html
    Short Runs, newsletter for magazine consultants,
    others in short-run publishing

GLOSSARY

AN ABRIDGED GLOSSARY OF INTERNET TERMS AND RELATED JARGON

Unless you are already quite familiar with computers, and especially the Internet, the glossary promised early in these pages will be a great convenience, for in its relatively brief life, the Internet has developed an extensive jargon of acronyms, contractions, nicknames, and other code words. The glossary offered here is by no means a complete list of all such terms, for there are many that are more esoteric and more highly technical than those included here. These, however, are probably most of those you are likely to encounter, unless you are a computer specialist or enthusiastic "netizen," as some refer to those who spend a great deal of time and enthusiasm exploring and otherwise using the Internet.

Address   code for e-mail to find you: *your name@host name*—e.g., *holtz@paltech.com*. *Your name* is whatever name you have chosen to be and registered as your e-mail name.

Alias   An e-mail address using a name other than your own—e.g., a code name, chosen by some for concealment, by others for brevity.

Alt   Identifier for unofficial newsgroup, such as *alt.biz, alt.aliens.*

AOL   America Online, a leading commercial online service widely used for access to the Internet.

Application   The term used in Windows for a program.

Applet   Term used in Windows for small programs that come with and/or are developed for use with Windows 95.

Archie   One of the several electronic search assistants to help you find files and programs on ftp servers.

Archive   A storage of files compressed for efficiency of transmission and storage, of which PKZIP is the most popular and best known for DOS, and WinZip for Windows.

ARPANET   Forerunner of the Internet, a network used by the Advanced Research Projects Agency, from which it derived its name.

ASCII   Pronounced ASS-key or ASS-see, it stands for "American Standard Code for Information Exchange" and identifies a simple font for storing and transmitting documents that can be read by virtually all editors and word processors, such as those used for e-mail.

Automatic mailing list (also **Mailing list**)   Mailing list maintained automatically by a program, such as the well-known Listserv and Majordomo.

Autoresponder   A system wherein an e-mail message to the address of the autoresponder will bring back a file transmitted automatically to the sender of the e-mail request.

Bandwidth   Refers to how much information may be transmitted over a communications link such as a mailing list; also and/or how much of that capacity is being used in a transmission.

Baud (see also **bps**)   Old telegrapher's term for transmission speed, used now to rate speed of modems.

BBS   Stands for "Bulletin Board System" and is a computer with a bulletin board program that permits subscribers to call, read files, leave messages communicating with others, and otherwise participate in activities. BBSs are operated by individuals and organizations of all kinds.

Binary file   File containing data other than text (although it may include text), such as executable files presenting information, graphics, video, audio, and documents of various kinds and formats.

Bit Abbreviation of "binary digit," the smallest unit of data; a single electrical pulse or space between pulses.

Bitmap All the little dots that make up an illustration on the screen or provide the data for a printout of an illustration.

bps (see also **baud**) Stands for "bits per second," a measure of transmission speed of data.

Bios Stands for "Basic Input/Output System," codes stored in the computer that define basic operations and are needed to tell programs how to do things.

Boolean A special strategy for searching, defining, or describing, using the operators "and," "or," "not and (nand)," and "not or (nor)" as the basis for including and excluding variables. Also Boolean algebra, the system and set of rules for using such operators.

Browser A program for navigating about the Net and Web, and for viewing sites, including Mosaic, Cello, Netscape, and Explorer.

BTW Frequently used shorthand in messages, meaning "by the way."

Byte A set of eight bits, used to measure computer storage and other computer characteristics. Various combinations of the eight bits (255 such combinations are possible) are used to represent alphabetical characters and numbers—each character transmitted is a byte.

Case sensitive Term for software that distinguishes uppercase letters from lowercase letters, especially in commands and addresses.

CD-ROM Stands for "compact disk read only memory." Computer equivalent of music CD. Holds huge amounts of data, hundreds of megabytes, and requires a special drive.

Cello See **Browser.**

CERN Physics laboratory in Geneva, where the World Wide Web was created in 1991.

Chat (see also **IRC**) Spontaneous online discussion (via keyboard) with others on the Internet.

CIS Abbreviation for "CompuServe Information Service," a leading commercial online service that provides access to the Internet, among other services.

Client A computer or program that uses files provided by another machine or application called a *server.*

Click Press and release mouse button.

Clipboard Windows program that holds data clipped from one file and permits it to be pasted in another file.

Conference A chat session on any online system.

Config.sys A program the computer refers to when booting up to determine how the system is to be configured with various programs and priorities.

Cross-posting Broadcasting a message to several groups.

Cyberspace All but indefinable mythical kingdom of communication used primarily to refer to online communications carried on as best exemplified by the Internet.

Cursor That bright line, block, or other on-screen indicator, which may be blinking, that tells you where whatever you type will now appear or make its effect felt.

Desktop The opening area on a Windows 95 screen, with all the icons ready for command.

Dial-up connection Any connection made to an online service via dialing a number.

DLL Stands for "Dynamic Link Library." It appears as the suffix of files containing information a program needs to function properly.

Domain The network identification appearing as a suffix—e.g., *edu* for educational institution, *gov* for government agency, *com* for commercial organization, *org* for organization, *mil* for military, and *net* for network.

Domain name The name by which messages are routed correctly— e.g., "paltech.com" and "okstate.edu."

DOS Stands for "disk operating system" and is the universal system for just about all pcs except the Macintosh variety.

Download Verb and noun for copying a file from another computer; opposite of *upload*.

EDI Stands for "Electronic Data Interchange," a system for conducting business online without paper—with electronic documentation.

Elm E-mail software program favored by some.

E-mail Electronic mail, transmitted via telephone lines and appearing on the screen of the addressee.

Emoticon Any combination of standard keyboard symbols that can be used to represent a facial expression, such as ":(" or ":)" for frowns and smiles (presented sideways).

Eudora   E-mail program, probably the most popular and most widely used.

FAQ   Stands for "Frequently Asked Questions," a document that exists for many newsgroups and other discussion groups to help newcomers learn quickly what it's all about.

Fax   Short for "facsimile" and represents both the device that sends and receives fax messages and the message itself.

Fax modem   A circuit card that may be installed in a computer (included in most computers sold today) to transmit e-mail and fax messages.

Finger   A UNIX program to search for a single user on the system by name.

Firewall   A method for protecting your transmissions on the Internet from being intercepted or overheard by unauthorized others.

Flame   Angry response or attack on another via online messages and exchanges, such as e-mail; angry and bitter can escalate into a "flame war," often with several others drawn into the angry and bitter exchanges.

Folder (directory)   Newer Windows name for what was formerly called a "directory."

Format   Organization of a document or a disk. Disks need to be formatted, having their tracks and related elements organized to receive and store data so that it can be found and retrieved later. Your computer has programs to format the disks you buy, but more and more disks are sold already formatted.

Forum   A fixed central location where participants with a common interest—e.g., computer technology, foreign affairs, or stamp collecting—post messages as a means of holding discussions.

Freenet   A facility in a community providing at least e-mail access to the Internet without cost, usually from some public service facility, such as a library.

Freeware   Software that the author permits everyone to use without charge, but usually claims copyright and imposes certain requirements for its use without charge.

ftp   Stands for "File Transfer Protocol," a program to move files to you from some remote source.

Gateway   A connection from the Internet to a given network.

GIF   Stands for "Graphics Interchange Format," used to identify a popular type of graphics.

Gigabyte   One billion bytes or 1,000 megabytes.

Gopher   A software program for searching the system.

GUI   Stands for "Graphical User Interface," the system of icons, scroll bars, toolbars, and other nonverbal devices to help users maneuver and navigate.

Header   The top portion or "head data" of any e-mail or other such message.

Hit   A term used as a unit to detect and count the number of times a Web site is accessed by someone.

Home page   The base page of an individual's or organization's Web site presentation, on which links are offered.

Host computer   A computer connected directly to the Internet that others may call in to and use as a source of data or connection device.

HTML   Stands for "Hypertext Markup Language," the source code for writing Web site presentations in hypertext.

http   Stands for "Hypertext Transfer Protocol," used to find information presented on the World Wide Web.

Hypertext   A method for referencing data through links, used in Web sites to jump to other sites.

Hypertext link   A reference word, phrase, sentence, or illustration that can be used to reference another site/other information.

IANAL   Stands for "I am not a lawyer," a shorthand expression in online discussions for someone offering an opinion on the law but making it clear that it is a lay opinion.

Icon   Graphic symbol that represents an action, program, or other larger item.

Ini   Abbreviation of "initialization." Found as suffix of files defining system settings.

Internaut   Expression to designate a regular Internet user.

IP address   Internet Protocol address identifying each machine on the Internet with a unique four-part series of numbers, such as 123.456.78.9.

IRC   Internet Relay Chat is software that permits group discussion on the Internet, a party line that several individuals can log on to and conduct discussion spontaneously.

ISDN   Stands for "Integrated Services Digital Network." Requires special telephone connections, but then provides high-speed data transfer.

ISP   Stands for "Internet Service Provider," that organization that connects you to the Internet. (Sometimes IAP for "Internet Access Provider".)

Java   A Sun Microsystems computer language for adding animation and moving games to Web sites.

Kill   Usually means to erase a file.

Kilobyte   Nominally, 1,000 bytes; actually, 1,024 bytes, a unit of measure for programs, disks, and other devices handling or storing data. Now, with larger and larger capacities, *megabyte* is becoming more widely used.

LAN   Stands for "local area network," a network of computers within a small area, such as a single office or set of offices.

Link   Basically, a connection. In relation to the Internet, it is used most often to refer to a line (a URL or line representing a URL) in a Web site presentation that can be clicked to transport the browser to another Web site. In many systems now, a URL in an e-mail message can also be used as a link, clicked to access and log on to the Web site described directly from the e-mail message.

Listserv   A family of mailing lists; also one of the programs that manages mailing lists; those programs that behave very much as forums or newsgroups, but use e-mail to do so.

Log off/on   Opening communications with an online system, usually furnishing a name and a password to do so.

Lurking   Reading the messages of a forum or similar group, but not participating in the discussions.

Lynx   A browser that can be used under DOS. (Other browsers require Windows.)

Mailbot   A program that automatically processes e-mail, as an autoresponder that adds or deletes your name as a subscriber to a mailing list.

Mailing list   A program that sends a copy of each letter submitted by a subscriber to the list to everyone on the list.

Majordomo   Another family of mailing lists, with the management software.

Maximize   Increase the size of a window so that it fills the screen.

Megabyte (MB)   One million bytes or 1,000 kilobytes.

Memory   Temporary housing of data and programs you are working on; the areas into which you load them when you summon them from a disk. Not the same as *storage,* which refers generally to fixed storage on disks and tapes.

MIME   Stands for "Multipurpose Internet Mail Extensions," a program that permits you to attach files to e-mail messages.

Minimize   The opposite of maximize: to shrink the window so that it occupies only part of a window or becomes only an icon.

Modem   The device (stand-alone or card in your computer) that enables your computer to communicate with other computers for e-mail and all the other Internet and Web presentations.

Moderated mailing list (also **Moderated newsgroup**)   List or group messages controlled by a moderator who will filter out inappropriate messages.

Netiquette   Name applied to generally accepted standards for behavior on the Internet, intended to preserve decorum and use resources efficiently.

Netizen   Name used by some to identify a regular visitor to/user of the Internet.

Newsgroup   Internet bulletin board system or discussion group, usually dedicated to some single subject.

Newsreader   The program that permits you to read and participate in newsgroups and their activities.

Pine   Another e-mail program.

PKZIP   A popular compression file used to condense files for economy of storage and transmission time.

PMFJI   Stands for "pardon me for jumping in," a term used in discussion groups when one wishes to offer some observation or comment in re a discussion in progress between or among others.

Port   Refers usually to the serial and parallel input-output connections of your computer, usually accessed via a plug or jack on the back of your computer.

Protocol   System or set of rules for exchanges among/between computers, such as a file transfer protocol.

Public domain software   Software that is free to everyone who wants to use it.

RAM   Stands for "random access memory," the basic memory system of the computer.

ROTFL   Stands for "rolling on the floor laughing," another shorthand term used in discussion groups.

Search engine   Systems and services for searching documents and sites on the Internet and Web, such as Yahoo!, Alta Vista, and Magellan.

Server   A computer providing a service or facility for other computers to use, such as a mail server.

Shareware   Software that you may use freely on a trial basis, but are expected to pay for on the honor system if you continue to use it after a trial.

Shell account   A service in which you use your access provider's computer and software to navigate the Internet, via a dial-up connection.

Signature   A message of three to six lines (usually) that you can arrange to have attached automatically to every e-mail you send, bearing your name and whatever else you wish to add. Many use this message for promotional purposes.

Signature file   The file contained in your e-mail software system, bearing the signature message you choose to run.

SLIP   Abbreviation for "Serial Line Internet Protocol," another Internet transmission protocol.

SMTP   Stands for "Simple Mail Transfer Protocol," a system for transferring e-mail between/among computers and systems.

Snail mail   Mocking reference to conventional surface mail.

Socket   A software "port" for connecting your computer to another program on another computer.

Spam   A derisive term for posting advertising messages indiscriminately to a large group of receivers, such as newsgroups, mailing lists, or e-mail lists in general.

Surf   Browsing the Internet casually, as one does the TV channels.

TCP/IP   Transmission Control Protocol/Internet Protocol, a set of rules which permits communication among computers on different networks. The adoption of TCP/IP enabled the Internet to come into existence.

Telnet   An Internet protocol enabling one computer to act as a terminal of another computer at some other location, permitting the terminal computer to send commands to the other (host) computer.

Transponder   See **Autoresponder** or **Mailbot.**

Upload   To send copies of data to another computer; opposite of *download.*

URL   Stands for "Uniform Resource Locator," an address for identifying the location of a given Web site so that it can be located.

Usenet   User's Network; the system of newsgroups.

Virtual   A modern, computer-inspired term used to describe or refer to realistic simulations, as in "virtual memory," to describe disk-storage space borrowed by the computer to simulate additional memory.

Wallpaper   The background for the desktop. Windows offers several choices, and you can find others that you can import

WWW   Stands for "World Wide Web," that area that presents all the graphics and other multimedia (sound and motion) presentations in hypertext formats, a place for home pages and other promotional sites.

Zip file   A file that has been compressed with the PKZIP program (which see) and can be decompressed with that program.

INDEX